AESTHETIC DEVIATIONS

A Critical View of American Shot-on-Video Horror, 1984–1994

by Vincent A. Albarano

HEADPRESS

A HEADPRESS BOOK
First published by Headpress in 2023, Oxford, United Kingdom
headoffice@headpress.com

AESTHETIC DEVIATIONS
A Critical View of American Shot-on-Video Horror, 1984–1994

Cover design: MARK CRITCHELL mark.critchell@gmail.com
Layout: GANYMEDE FOLEY & MARK CRITCHELL
The Publisher thanks Gareth Wilson

10 9 8 7 6 5 4 3 2 1

A CIP catalogue record for this book is available from the British Library

ISBN 978-1-915316-23-3 paperback
ISBN 978-1-915316-24-0 ebook
ISBN NO-ISBN hardback

HEADPRESS. POP AND UNPOP CULTURE.

CONTENTS

INTRODUCTION

THIS BOOK, IN its present form, began as my master's thesis at The Ohio State University. Somewhere near the end of that process I became aware that I had overshot the length requirement by a good deal. I had a book on my hands. As much as I wanted to blow open the doors of academia with this strand of trash filmmaking, that isn't where my real interest rests. In reality, it goes back several years prior, as I immersed myself in shot-on-video (SOV) horror films through the latter half of my undergrad years. I was well-rounded in my appreciation of genre films by that point, so it seemed a good time to move onto the next realm of cinematic refuse. Long averse to the peculiar pugnacity of analog video, this was largely uncharted territory. But something clicked for me; I was finally able to appreciate the unique look of video, and the alternately ugly and average images captured on magnetic tape. The last decade or so has been one of continued discovery and immersion in the video netherworld, one whose encouraging discoveries and more frequent displeasures don't look to let up. So my own journey with SOV horror films has largely mirrored my time in and out of academia, for better or worse. Every new idea or theory I was exposed to, every course, regardless of subject matter or focus, I've found myself trying to apply those concepts to the world of video horror. More often than not, I've found that they fit in fairly well, despite their wholly un-scholastic origins and ambitions.

What was it about these terrible, hideous-looking movies that captivated me so much? Why did the images in **Black Devil Doll from Hell** stick with me and so many others longer than more competent celluloid obscurities from the same year? Plenty of people love and appreciate SOV horror, and there's no shortage of passionate work on the films. But I always found the commentary to be lacking, like nobody was quite willing to take them as seriously as I thought they deserved. The enthusiasm is there, but not always the articulation, and if I was going to overthink these throwaway movies, then I may as well get my thoughts down on paper. Much as I have a distaste for the formal

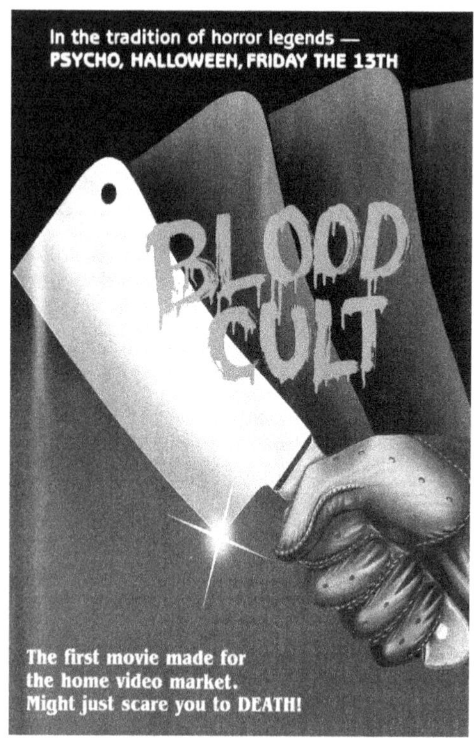

restrictions of film theory and find it often inaccessible, I can't deny that there's some ineffable quality to a lot of SOV films that merits a more thorough analysis. Over the years, I've convinced myself that I'm taking these movies too seriously, but time and again, I find some details there to remind myself that they really are as strange and thought-provoking as I'd always believed.

In a lot of ways, SOV horror seems like a parallel universe to mainstream horror, the dark sibling to the celebrated independent horror wave of the 1980s that saw films like **Re-Animator**, **The Evil Dead**, and **Street Trash** celebrated in every corner of the genre press. SOV horror titles shared the same video shelves as those films, but they weren't of the same world in any realistic sense. These films aren't underground in the sense of the 1960s experimental film scene, or even the Cinema of Transgression and its various offshoots. As an alternative to the more visible independents of the 1980s and 1990s horror film scene, however, they stand out as a decidedly subterranean sort of film culture, even when they received "wide" release, as in the case of **Video Violence** or **Blood Cult**.

Many of the films discussed in the following pages are among the most popular, visible, and talked about SOV horror films around. I could go on endlessly about the various obscure offshoots and aberrations of this film cycle, and do at some points as asides, but the fact remains that the most notable titles are popular for a reason. They offer the most to work with, and there's more material available to study their histories. Even where the critical approaches I take may be unfamiliar, the films themselves will likely strike a chord. I also largely stuck with films that I know best, have seen the most and am comfortable with elaborating on. As much as I'd love to perform a theoretical deep dive on Matthew Samuel Smith's **Blood Summer**, I just don't think it holds up the same as the Polonia brothers' **Splatter Farm** as an example of SOV slasher style. That's a project for another day. I wouldn't be writing this if I weren't a fan foremost, regardless of whatever academic experience I've had, and one thing that I found strange in the small bit of academic material addressing SOV horror was the outsider's perspective taken to the films themselves.

This isn't the definitive history of SOV horror, nor the direct-to-video era of genre filmmaking. This is one obsessive fan's notes on what ticks beneath the surface of a handful of exemplary features. There's still a lot of work to be done with SOV horror, and even plenty of obscurities deserve to have their day. Hopefully this is one step in the right direction for SOV horror to generate some serious discussion.

01

AMATEUR CINEMA AND THE DAWN OF SHOT-ON-VIDEO HORROR

AMATEUR CINEMATIC EXPRESSION dates to nearly the beginning of filmmaking technology itself. As outlined by Patricia Zimmermann, amateur cinema has always been differentiated and removed from industrial practice as "marginalized, yet integrated, production wedged within the private sphere."[1] This prioritizing of subjectivity was also championed by avant-garde auteur Stan Brakhage, one of the most notable proponents of small-gauge filmmaking as a means of independent expression. Despite the intellectual rigor associated with his work, Brakhage was open in his writing about the vital "'clumsiness' of continual discovery" demonstrated in amateur works.[2] While Brakhage worked extensively with 8mm and Super 8 film throughout the 1960s and 1970s, these projects were later ensconced within the walls of academia and the accepted avant-garde underground, achieving notable respect for their innovations. The distribution of narrative works utilizing the format, however, was rarer until the 1980s, when a new generation of fan filmmakers honed their craft and began to pursue their visions of independent cinema with more serious dedication.

Discussions of amateur art are often woven with commentary on fan cultures, particularly pertaining to genre and expression regarding film. Horror fandom has long been one of the most inspired and interactive subcultures in the United States, and it's logical that horror cinema saw one of the most distinctive and fertile outgrowths of amateur filmmaking in the late twentieth century. The availability of consumer-friendly mediums set the stage for a previously unparalleled explosion

1 Zimmerman, p.5.
2 Brakhage, p.145.

of untrained film production. This isn't to say that other genre fans themselves embraced this development, however. Bill Landis' **Sleazoid Express**, the first and most important modern trash cinema fanzine, savaged Sam Raimi's classic 1981 debut **The Evil Dead** (one of the foundational inspirations for later amateur horror cinema), attacking the film with the headline "Exploitation Cancer" and bemoaning its "stamp collector mentality." This early example of the underground horror community's aversion to amateur productions distinctively affixes an outsider status to works of this caliber.

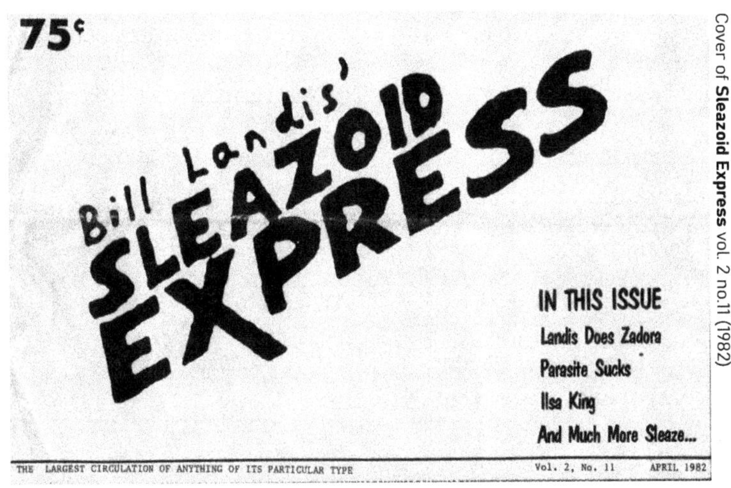

Cover of **Sleazoid Express** vol. 2 no.11 (1982)

Long Island filmmaker Nathan Schiff perhaps best exemplifies the amateur-fan tendency in 1980s horror cinema. Beginning at age seventeen and working between 1979-1991, Schiff produced four feature-length Super 8 gore films around his Long Island neighborhood. Inspired by George Romero, and especially groundbreaking gore auteur Herschel Gordon Lewis, and cast with friends and family members, Schiff's films were amateurish in every sense of the word. Reveling in cheap but extensive butcher shop gore effects, teenaged non-actors portraying scientists, cannibals and police detectives, and unsupervised use of power tools, Schiff's gore epics redefined small-grade cinematic carnage for the gorehounds of the 1980s. Working in obscurity, Schiff's profile was elevated by notice in popular zines of the day, including Chas. Balun's **Deep Red** and Rick Sullivan's **The Gore Gazette**, the latter of which organized screenings of the films in Manhattan.

The G.G. Film Series sucessfully continues into 1986 every Wednesday night at The Dive, 257 W. 29th St. (at 8th Ave) in Manhattan. The program for the month of January is as follows:
1/8: THE LONG ISLAND CANNIBAL MASSACRE- Because you demanded it, Nathan Schiff's grisly tale of leprosy, carnage and bad acting is back!
1/15: BLACK FRANKENSTEIN- Celebrate Martin Luther King's Birthday with this blaxploitation rarity about an Afro monster who only kills white women!
1/22: EL TOPO- A rare screening of Alejandro Jodoworski's lobster bloodbath featuring real amputees and Spanish mutants!
1/29: FLESH FEAST- A bloated, alcoholic Veronica Lake, flesh-eating maggots and Adolph Hitler! Who could ask for more? This 1971 rarity is a NY premiere!

All shows start promptly at 8:00 and feature the famous G.G. Trailer Reels. See you there!

Gore Gazette film series featuring Nathan Schiff's **Long Island Cannibal Massacre** (#80, 1986)

Contemporaneous to Schiff's work was the most productive development of underground horror cinema, sharing many of the same concerns and aesthetics as his creations but effecting a utilitarian appropriation of the video format. While scores of amateur horror filmmakers in the 1980s experimented with Super 8 and 16mm film, analog video revolutionized the course of independent moviemaking, allowing them to realize their visions and build followings among fellow horror fans. At no previous point in history had there been such an egalitarian economic process of film production and distribution, and amateurs would benefit from this revolution first and foremost. Shot-on-video (SOV) horror has gained much traction with fans and cult audiences in recent years but has yet to attract much serious attention from critics and academics. This despite the fact that works produced on analog video and made for direct release are inextricably linked to the technological advent of home video technology, long a scholarly area of focus.

While magnetic videotape has a history dating back to the 1930s, the first significant development bearing on video horror is the 1976 introduction of the VHS format. Initially prohibitively priced and rivaled in popularity by Betamax, VHS quickly gained traction as a luxury media format.[1] VHS technology, especially the VCR player, was at the center of much controversy and legal wrangling in its earliest years, a result of major studios' fear of the potential for Japanese-produced goods to subvert their intellectual property via time-shifting (recording programs for later viewing) and piracy or duplication. This concern, exemplified via the groundbreaking **Sony v. Universal** suit, marks a distinct line between corporate and industrial interests in consumer desires. Video technology was immediately cast as a benefit to the consumer population, something inherently subversive (yet commodified) before Hollywood harnessed it as another profit-making device.

VHS was slow to infiltrate beyond the upper-middle class, with only twenty-five percent penetration into U.S. households by 1985. By 1987, however, as the technology became more available and affordable, over fifty percent of American households owned VCR equipment.[2] This growth was also reflected by the proliferation of independent video stores throughout the country. In their initial resistance to video technology, major studios miscalculated, allowing independent outfits to promote their B-grade exploitation product in the growing free market of mom-and-pop video stores.[3] This, as well as its ever-present status as popular entertainment, bolstered especially by the lucrative slasher and creature film subgenres of the period, partly explains why returns on horror videocassettes were so substantial throughout the 1980s. It also offers an answer for why so many would-be filmmakers took influence and inspiration from previously

1 Hilderbrand, p.247.
2 Hilderbrand, p.248.
3 Walker, **Blood Cults**, p.224.

limited run features with garish titles and low production values. VCR technology promoted a second life for obscure genre works, while planting a seed for the next generation to begin their quiet revolution of democratic cinema.

Camcorder technology developed more slowly than did the VCR following the release of the first single-system device in 1983.[1] Previously, video equipment was available only as dual-system Betamax and VHS, cumbersome devices with separate mechanisms for recording audio and video. Ultimately, VHS won the format war over Betamax due to its cost and content efficiency relative to Betamax cassettes.[2] Lucas Hilderbrand connects this development, much like the burst of successful pre-recorded tapes, to pornography's embrace of the video medium.[3] Homemade pornographic films were the initial amateur output of the video era, an important point given that horror and pornography have long been equated by critics for their supposed lack of redeeming social function. Many studies on genre filmmaking and the home video era fail to consider the fully realized potential of these devices to promote and foster an alternative cinematic lexicon. In fact, very few scholarly texts, even concerning the subject of home video technology, acknowledge shot-on-video features as a legitimate form of amateur expression. Serious consideration of SOV horror has lagged much in the way that video technology did in its first decade, leaving the appraisal of these films largely to fans, collectors, and hobbyists.

Stan Brakhage was a film loyalist, so his conceptions of amateur cinema never extended to analog video, even as he worked throughout the medium's rise to prominence. In her 1995 survey of camcorder technology and prime time television, Laurie Oullette omits the role of video in giving a voice to amateur filmmakers without economic resources or industrial connections. William Brown's survey of "noncinema" points toward a larger acceptance of amateur works utilizing digital video technology while resisting the conventions and expectations of traditional "good" filmmaking. His focus is limited to the twenty-first century, emphasizing the political elements of

1 Young, p.91.
2 Young, p.89-91.
3 Hilderbrand, p.66.

the technology around the world. Hilderbrand's work restricts its focus on video production to amateur pornography and bootlegging. These texts constitute a wealth of work on the emergence of VCR/VHS technology and the importance of the camcorder's operation by untrained artists. Only recent works by Daniel Herbert and Johnny Walker have mentioned SOV horror as a legitimate outgrowth of video as cinema, but they too are concerned with the economic aspects of recent re-releases of VHS-lensed features and the financially-motivated works of United Entertainment International, respectively. None of this writing considers the homegrown cinematic world developed by a network of enterprising amateur filmmakers using little more than their family camcorder and their passion for genre features past. That these films made a significant economic impact, saw nationwide release, and quite literally laid the groundwork for the current manifestation of underground horror cinema today is reason enough to merit a deeper look at their contents.

First, the technical specifics: Video is immediate, and unlike film there is no need for processing or development; once filmed, a tape is ready for review instantly. This also reflects the ease of shooting procedures themselves, as video requires a fraction of the light needed to shoot even high ISO Super 8 film, enhancing the portability and utility of the camcorder device itself. Still, camcorder technology did indeed lag as noted above, with even the earliest SOV features relying on Betacam technology, commonly known as broadcast standard video, before being transferred to film for post-production.[1] The full infiltration of camcorder-shot features was delayed, with a handful of direct-to-video examples appearing sporadically throughout the early 1980s, each significant in some way.

Video experimentation within celluloid filmmaking was not a new phenomenon by the dawn of the 1980s. Fernando Arrabal's **Viva La Muerte** (1971) utilized Betacam technology to film several surreal dream sequences for its narrative, later transferring the video inserts to film to impart a jarring visual discontinuity. Ken Russell's **Altered States** (1980) likewise used video to capture its protagonist's startling hallucinations in more experimental sequences throughout

1 Mogg, p.3.

its runtime. These integrations demonstrate an awareness of the raw appearance of video itself and its potential for serious creation, but also suggest a hesitance at embracing it in a fuller capacity.

On the other side of the production world, avant-garde artists and filmmakers took video far more seriously as a medium from the 1960s forward. Rather than simply capture high-concept and highbrow happenings, however, a portion of the established cinematic avant-garde turned to the format for its honesty and versatility, with George Kuchar in particular documenting his life through an endless series of video diaries throughout the 1980s-2000s. These covered everything from his storm-hunting Oklahoma vacations to his daily bowel movements and romantic partners. From its earliest usage, video was split between the virtues of easy expression, immediacy, and the high/low divide in subject matter.

Arguably the first SOV horror feature is 1982's **The Toxic Slime Creature**, which was hopelessly obscure until at least 2017, when it was uploaded to YouTube.[1] It's worth mentioning only as a precursor to the most well-known of the early SOV horror features, though it does display many of the charming missteps which have come to define SOV films as a broad category. Occurring in a single office park location and rarely offering a glimpse at its monster, the film instead centers on the meandering efforts of the building's staff to survive. More important to its footnote status, however, is the fact that even the earliest-known SOV horror film existed in absolute obscurity for thirty-five years. The subgenre remains overlooked and neglected—not to mention obscure by its very nature—so that even a notable milestone in technical advancement is without any notoriety due to its marginality.

Boardinghouse (1982) was the first major SOV film with a demonstrable impact on the genre film world. Shot on Betacam and later transferred to film by director John Wintergate, and intended as a low-budget horror comedy, the film is a bizarre mess of banal group scenes in the titular abode, grotesque scares, and confusing Eastern mysticism. **Boardinghouse** is also notable as the only SOV horror feature to see national theatrical release, playing on the exploitation

1 Cobb, #5, p.17.

circuit of inner-city grindhouses and rural drive-in theaters in 1983.[1] Bill Landis reviewed the film after it played New York's 42nd Street, noting that it defied all expectations of being "another fanzine movie" in the mold of **The Evil Dead**, and even recalled Arrabal's debut in its bizarre video-to-film look.[2] Noting its strange production history and the realistic depiction of its unknown cast's motivations, he claims that the "movie defines the narcissist fantasies of fringe mindfuckers."[3]

Discussing **Boardinghouse** nearly twenty years later, Landis zeroes in on the bizarre qualities that make it stand out despite its many failings, capturing as it does a "microcosm of tacky early-1980s Americana."[4] Due to the singular personalities of Wintergate and partner/star Kalassu, **Boardinghouse** harnesses formal experimentation, cinematic naivete, and uncontrolled strangeness to offer a portrait of personal amateur expression in defiance of all prior conceptions of acceptable genre cinema. While no film to follow matches Wintergate's surreal romp for outright strangeness, its approach and clear demonstration that format and budget are not limitations to successful productions proved inspirational to fans looking to create their own films.

Boardinghouse set the stage for feature-length genre films to be produced on video equipment, galvanizing independent filmmakers. In 1983 came David A. Prior's **Sledgehammer** (the film was not released until 1984), a bizarre, static slasher film set in a single vacation house location. **Sledgehammer** is most notable today as "the first horror film made and distributed on videotape," despite later claims by Oklahoma-based United Entertainment International regarding their own **Blood Cult**.[5] Several minor producers and distributors followed suit quickly, with obscurities **Copperhead**, **Blonde Death** (directed by author James Robert Baker), and even the British possession feature **Suffer Little Children** appearing for rental and purchase later that year.

In 1984 came Chester N. Turner's **Black Devil Doll from Hell**, which quickly became one of the standard-bearers for SOV horror's negative

1 Mogg, p.12.
2 "Psychedelic Fortune Cookie," p.12
3 Ibid.
4 Landis & Clifford, p.142.
5 Mogg, p.14.

reputation. The film's lasting infamy, as well as its status as an independent production overseen by an entirely African American cast and crew, make it a notable early SOV feature. Even more than **Boardinghouse** and **Sledgehammer**, **Black Devil Doll from Hell** marks the point where amateurs and fans appropriated available video technology to realize their own filmmaking ambitions. Turner filmed entirely on the South Side of Chicago, using his own apartment as protagonist Helen's home and several local businesses and a church to provide authentic locations. The titular dummy alternates between unskilled onscreen ventriloquism and several shots where an identically-dressed child is subbed in to depict motion. An extended sexual assault scene represents an early nadir in video filmmaking, with the puppet repeatedly insulting Helen and forcing itself on her until she comes to enjoy its wooden charms. The camerawork is incredibly rudimentary, as is Turner's Casio keyboard soundtrack and its six-minute credit sequence. Nothing about the production suggests anything resembling competence or good taste, and as off-putting as these qualities may be for mainstream audiences, its impact is undeniable on the SOV works to follow. Whether they were aware of one another's work or not, Wintergate, Prior, and Turner's features are important examples of video technology being employed by first-time directors to make films, a utilitarian approach that initiated the SOV cycle.

Despite their notoriety among collectors and fans today, none of the above films made much of a significant impact in either the genre press or the home video market. While these four features and other early efforts successfully utilized video technology to produce and distribute finished works, they were still aberrations within the realm of independent horror cinema. If one were to select a point where SOV horror was crystallized into a distinctive cycle of production, 1985 would be the defining year. Seeing the success of independent titles on the home video market, including their own second-string exploitation titles, United Entertainment International (UEI), a subsidiary of successful distributors VCI Video, set about producing a shot-on-video feature expressly for the home video market which was simultaneously informed by classic exploitation promotional tactics.[1] Budgeted at $27,000 and with a promotional budget of between

1 Walker, **Blood Cults**, p.225-226.

$75,000-$100,000, that year's release of **Blood Cult** (dir. Christopher Lewis) was a massive event in exploitation promotion and marked the true arrival of SOV horror to the unwilling masses.

Full-page United ad for **Blood Cult** from the back cover of **Fangoria** #49 (1985)

Produced by a professional crew and demonstrating greater polish and finesse, **Blood Cult** stands out from the amateur productions which preceded it but also fits more concisely into the larger fabric of 1980s horror cinema. Lewis' film is a straightforward slasher concerning cannibalistic murders occurring on a college campus (with several direct nods and lifts from H.G. Lewis' pioneering 1963 gore film, **Blood Feast**) and an elderly detective's attempts to solve the crimes. Despite its technical competency, **Blood Cult** demonstrates several questionable deficiencies, from overaged actors playing college students, ponderous stretches of characters chatting and eating in between grisly murders, and a total lack of terror and suspense. **Blood Cult** fails as a slasher and has nothing truly innovative to contribute, save proving that cheaply made SOV features could be genuinely successful and generate industry buzz. As a contemporary review from **BLEEDING SKULL!** notes, "[e]very trend needs a defining trendsetter. In the case of SOV trash...It was **Blood Cult**...Professionally shot and edited, it feels like a studio-backed slasher that just happens to be SOV."[1]

What set **Blood Cult** apart and truly put the SOV cycle into motion, however, was its incredible promotional campaign, which saw full-color ads on the back cover of mainstream genre magazine **Fangoria** and notices placed in industry trades like **Variety.** Perhaps most notable is the campaign's claim that the film was "the first movie made for the home video market." While this was demonstrably false given the existence of Prior and Turner's earlier works, for consumers confronted with the bold magazine ads and greater number of videocassettes available, it may as well have been true. As a result, the video release was an instant success, proving that marketing savvy and financial resources were enough to move 25,000 copies of **Blood Cult** and generate more than half-a-million dollars in profits.[2]

Unfortunately for their legacies, no SOV works to follow had the resources UEI did, meaning that such sales were not to be replicated. **Blood Cult** was SOV's first true economic success, particularly as a calculated effort to exploit the fertile home video market in search of significant profits. Aesthetically speaking, however, it worked

1 Ziemba, **1980s**, p.15-16.

2 Walker, **Blood Cults**, p.228.

toward defining the category's negative reception and low cinematic standards. The lack of success for UEI's follow-up films also reflects a growing displeasure among audiences with the conventions of SOV horror which would plague films from the cycle for decades. Teenage horror fans anticipating a new gory slasher were met with cheap, rubber effects and a languidly paced mystery that saw normal-looking people doing banal things. Ironically, SOV horror became something of a dirty word because of its greatest financial success.

These four features (excluding **The Toxic Slime Creature**) were among the first and most visible SOV titles on the home video market for years to come and laid the foundation for nearly every film to follow. They set the pace for promotion and distribution in the SOV era, which for my purposes will be confined to 1984-1994. Knowing that consumers could hardly afford to purchase copies of tapes for their homes (VHS releases cost as much as $99.99 per tape throughout the 1980s) and would rely on rentals instead, distributors often provided eye-catching box art with lurid images that rarely appeared in the films themselves. Moreover, they never directly called attention to the fact that the film within was shot-on-video, further duping the consumer into renting what would most often be a disappointing title given the high expectations set by their promotional materials.

Regarding the films themselves, several important points need to be addressed. Most significantly, there has long been an aversion to feature films shot on analog (and in recent years, even digital) video. On the most basic level this reflects the dominance of celluloid for much of the twentieth century, with audiences worldwide having grown accustomed to the specific appearance of film itself. At the same time, video was never intended as a serious medium for expression, but as a recording and duplication device[1], explicit in its loss of audiovisual fidelity from the celluloid standard. Much as features shot on film *look* like film to spectators, anything shot on tape resembles a home movie to the same audience accustomed to viewing video in this context. This

1 Hilderbrand refers to several early advertisements for Betamax and VCR technology that emphasized the devices' ability for timeshifting as "the first publicized use of home video." This practice, recording televised programs for later viewing, "presented new modes of televisual temporality, existing both over time (as timeshifting, preservation, or decay) and in time (as duration or manipulated playback speed)" (9-12).

condition is worsened by the fact that most SOV features relied upon low-budget technology within a non-industry that could not replicate standards of cinematic production. Thus, the inherent technical deficiencies of analog video as compared to film stock, as well as audience acculturation to the latter, instantly put the newer technology at a disadvantage. Coupled with this is the fact that amateur-lensed video efforts bear the inherent marks of unprofessional craftsmanship, furthering audience displeasure with the finished product. While they are by no means uniform, many SOV horror features display the same hallmarks: blurry visuals with smearing and poor exposure (particularly when non-professional reproduction of tapes comes into play), dialog muffled by nondiegetic soundtracks and inadequate in-camera microphones, and cheap-looking credit sequences. Beyond the properties of videotape itself, works by amateur SOV directors are often bereft of distinctive technique, relying on static camera work, excruciating long takes broken only by nonsensical editing, and prolonged stretches of interminable boredom due to unprofessional scripts. Performances are almost uniformly terrible and unconvincing, as are the gore and special effects, and sets are rarely more elaborate than actual living rooms and local businesses. Editing typically fails to comply with classical conventions, with shot/reverse shot frequently forfeited in favor of single characters speaking or wide shots of entire rooms. Montage and linear editing feature only when essential, as in showing a victim receiving their wounds in gory close-ups, and suspenseful intercutting is typically absent.

These aesthetic deficiencies alone put off even seasoned horror fans, but the genre found a great deal of homegrown success, due in no small part to the large demand for genre productions during the 1980s. Before Blockbuster Video's monopoly on home video rentals in the 1990s, independent video stores thrived around the United States, working to satiate the needs of consumers and rapidly looking to expand the available product on their shelves. As previously mentioned, a handful of distributors such as Camp Video, Donna Michelle Productions, and other more obscure outfits took full advantage of the gulf between film and video in consumers' minds and offered packages that promised more than the features themselves could deliver.

Until recent years, SOV horror has been typically regarded as the nadir of genre filmmaking, a backlash that began even as the cycle was ongoing. Richard Mogg notes in an overview of the period that renters began to complain about the low quality of the films, and SOV works were "overwhelmingly frowned upon and regarded as bottom of the barrel crap."[1] Likewise, countless zines and books on horror cinema regularly denigrate any video features as below consideration. SOV horror has no distinctive style or approach, save its medium, and films in this category take on all manner of subject matter and content. There are, however, numerous shared qualities that impacted their negative reception as well as their singularity as a cycle. Because the films themselves are typically so idiosyncratic, I feel it important to outline some of their finer details to give a better understanding of the form.

Definitions and Qualities

FOR MY PURPOSES, SOV horror will be largely referred to as a category or cycle, rather than a style, in an attempt at flattening the huge number of releases into a manageable range. There are many stylistic and technical similarities between the films to be discussed, but to refer to SOV as a style is disingenuous and does a disservice to the individual features themselves, not to mention the artists responsible for their creation. The term category is also useful over the concept of genre or subgenre, for while every film to be analyzed fits within the horror genre as a whole, there are SOV films within every horror subgenre: slashers, ghost stories, vampire and werewolf films, anthologies, and even science fiction horror. Regarding the question of genre specifically, director Todd Sheets argues "what's the type of movie you can sell...horror. Everyone starts with horror because it's safe, because there is always a crowd for it."[2] SOV horror was the most dominant form of video production from this period, with the number of SOV comedies, action films, and even straightforward dramas paling in comparison to the deluge of horror titles released between 1984 and 1994.

1 Mogg, p.16.
2 Gallagher, #17, p.30.

Ad for J.R. Bookwalter's **Ozone** from **Film Threat Video Guide #10** (1994)

Recalling Sheets' comment, filmmaker J.R. Bookwalter discusses his preteen years as a fan of science fiction films before being exposed to gory stills from horror films in **Fangoria** magazine, noting that "[s]eeing all this blood and gore triggered something deep inside me...no more sci-fi and fantasy for me!".[1] A large part of the appeal for likeminded fans were genre films' engagements with all manner of bloodletting and graphic terror, awakening as with Bookwalter the impulse to replicate such spectacles in backyards and basements with the help of friends. Testimonials such as these go some way to explaining the appeal of these elements as inspirations, but there is also a long-standing tradition of genre films capturing the attention spans of young audiences at home.

Low-budget, utilitarian exploitation filmmaking in the United States dates back to the earliest days of the art form. These films were in regular syndication around the country, playing television on late night Creature Features often featuring regional horror hosts, exposing a new generation to the pleasures of fantastic cinema. Prior to its emergence as a professional magazine, Michael

1 **B-Movies, p.22-23.**

Weldon's **Psychotronic** existed as a newsletter detailing worthwhile exploitation and genre films airing on television in the New York area. As the 1980s progressed and video technology became more accessible for average Americans, VHS tape rentals became the predominant means of exposure to films, and the horror genre had a particular appeal to consumers. Caetlin Benson-Allott connects this trend toward horror on video to the emergence of even more ruthless splatter films during the decade, noting that "**Friday the 13th** was the result of a new era in filmmaking: it was too bloody and sexually explicit for TV, yet it addressed itself to a home viewer."[1] Even prior to **Blood Cult's** aesthetic disappointments, gory slasher films drew unprecedented attention from fans with little parental supervision and access to the exciting home video technology slowly infiltrating middle class American households. This generation of fans enthralled by the vivid spreads in **Fangoria** could now access the films they had read about for so long.

Every film to be discussed was shot and distributed on analog video, which entails early Betacam technology (also known as broadcast video), Hi8, Super VHS (S-VHS) and various other formats. Specific technological details aren't of much importance, as unlike the relatively few choices of film stock available for use in celluloid production, there is often little information on what was used to record particular films. While none of the works were made using Super 8 (except for a brief segment in Carl Sukenick's **Alien Beasts**), they will largely be referred to as *films*. This term has become a de facto referent for motion pictures themselves, regardless of their format. Likewise, modern amateur and independent horror films have largely been filmed using affordable digital video (DV) technology. In fact, the celluloid standard has largely fallen out of practice even in studio filmmaking, with recent blockbusters and mainstream productions shifting toward high end DV technology. The analog format of actual magnetic video tape is the baseline for works produced during the SOV era, separating them from earlier amateur experiments such as Schiff's as well as the more recent digital video underground scene.

Analog SOV horror has a distinctive visual quality, which is by no

1 Benson-Allott, p.3.

means uniform, but consistently bears the unmistakable imprints of amateur cinematography and consumer technology. Accustomed to the celluloid tradition of film production, consumers renting the earliest SOV releases in the 1980s were appalled by the gritty, smeared visuals of films lensed on magnetic tape. Richard Mogg draws connections to the distinctive looks of both pornography and home movies in recalling his first exposure to SOV horror via a rental of **Boardinghouse**.[1] Contributing to this is the fact that video screens at 29.97 frames per second in contrast to film's standard twenty-four frames. This gives video images a flatter appearance, with the extra frames adding to the visual disorientation of the picture quality itself. Nearly a century of celluloid production has acclimated audiences worldwide to the look of film playing at twenty-four frames per second, despite there being nothing inherently realistic about the projected speed of film. Video's faster frame rate more closely resembles the unbroken motion of everyday life, with the playback's proximity to realism largely responsible for the "home movie" tag commonly thrown at SOV works.

Of the early SOV features, **Boardinghouse**, **Sledgehammer,** and **Blood Cult** were shot with Betacam technology, giving them a more polished and cleaner appearance. **Black Devil Doll from Hell**, however, utilized a single-system camcorder, resulting in a rougher and grittier picture, with the film's audio elements suffering as a result of the in-camera microphone and post-production dubbing of its musical soundtrack. While the availability of consumer-grade video technology enabled Turner to shoot his debut film, it was also an early indicator of how amateur video efforts were to suffer for their lack of more professional equipment. By the 1990s, as video had developed and refined its technology, SOVs began to look better, with clean picture quality in later titles such as J.R. Bookwalter's **Ozone** (1994), made using higher-end S-VHS-C technology.[2] At the same time, however, Texan Todd Cook was still working with the more standard consumer VHS-C format, meaning his 1994 release **Frightmares** is visually comparable to the earlier SOVs of the 1980s and early-1990s in its raw audiovisual quality.[3] Many

1 Mogg, p.2, p.26.
2 B-Movies, p.205.
3 "Horrorscope," p.8.

amateurs had only consumer-grade equipment, often repurposed family camcorders, at their disposal, meaning that first-time directors and even seasoned independents worked with technology never intended for commercial use. Clarity and sharpness are sacrificed, and distinctive visual styles are lost in the wash of video's harsh colors.

Video offers none of the grain or feel of actual celluloid, and the pixelated images are stark and uncompromising. This is often worsened by the technical components of video itself, which still looks better when properly lit for filming despite its accessibility and low-skill operation. Thus, more professional SOV outings like **Blood Cult** and **Video Violence** (1987) benefit from their production quality and proper usage of cinematic lighting. Still, underlit, grubby video images are what come to mind when SOV is invoked for many. Despite the inherent unpleasantness of video's appearance, the format itself is not destined to look bad. Instead, amateurs tend to create unprofessional visuals that further undermine the contents of the narrative itself. The immediacy of the preserved image often recalls the hasty inspiration which occasioned it, and as such this lack of technical quality does not necessarily suggest a lack of value in the finished work itself. This is filmmaking as impulse, the sort of deterministic devotion displayed by Brakhage, and the roughness of the feature is as interesting and essential as any other attribute.

Sound is another area where many SOVs fall short compared with lower-budget celluloid genre efforts. As with picture quality, the reasons are multifold: with the advent of single-system camcorder technology, many first-time directors and amateurs were forced to rely on in-camera microphones to record dialog, ambient tracks, and most special sound effects all at the same time. Not only could this be a problem for long shots where actors were placed at distances too great to capture their voices, but exterior scenes were left to the mercy of environmental conditions. Chester Turner's **Black Devil Doll from Hell** features an incessant Casio keyboard score that does not simply add ambient texture to various scenes, but often fully overpowers entire exchanges of dialog between characters. Lack of access to proper post-production facilities, not to mention ignorance of mixing techniques, ultimately hinder the audio components of many SOV features, but do impart a distinctive quality at the cost of legibility.

Original music is also a unique concern in many SOV works.

Todd Cook scored his earliest features using his own original heavy metal compositions, with the theme song to his 1992 debut **Evil Night** consisting only of himself on guitar and wife/actor Lisa singing. As his works became increasingly popular, however, he was able to attract the attention of underground heavy metal musicians and labels, culminating in 1995's crossover feature **Death Metal Zombies** featuring a soundtrack by various Relapse Records artists. Likewise, Missouri native Todd Sheets scored every one of his 1990s productions through his heavy metal recording project, Enochian Key, going so far as to feature himself performing with a full band in 1992's **Dominion.** This intermingling of fringe subcultures recalls the shared lineage of shockumentary true death tapes and extreme death metal music, as outlined by Johnny Walker.[1] Similarly, Charles Pinion's debut feature, **Twisted Issues** (1988), features local bands from the Gainesville, Florida punk scene, including his own Psychic Violents. His follow-ups, **Red Spirit Lake** (1993) and **We Await** (1996) are scored by relatively well-known noise rock and industrial musicians such as Cop Shoot Cop, Neurosis, and Unsane.

These developments suggest a number of things. First, that SOV horror and the underground music scene were treading the same ground both thematically as well as economically. Second, the insular nature of niche interests such as low-budget horror and extreme music were often better suited to complement one another than traditional film scores, particularly when the pre-existing music was more accomplished and appealing than untrained keyboard soundtracks could prove to be. Third, in the case of Pinion's first film, as well as Cook's and Sheets' early soundtracks, there was a documentary function in utilizing acquaintances and friends to create reliable soundtracks. In this sense, it seems perfectly logical that amateur-produced videos would be scored by amateur, or at least obscure, musicians whose lack of formality suits the visual proceedings with equally unpolished aural accompaniment.

As with the directors themselves, the majority of performances in SOV horror films were delivered by unschooled and first-time actors. Portrayals were considered valuable less for the conviction of the actors themselves and more for the convenience of the people

1 Walker, Traces, p.148-149.

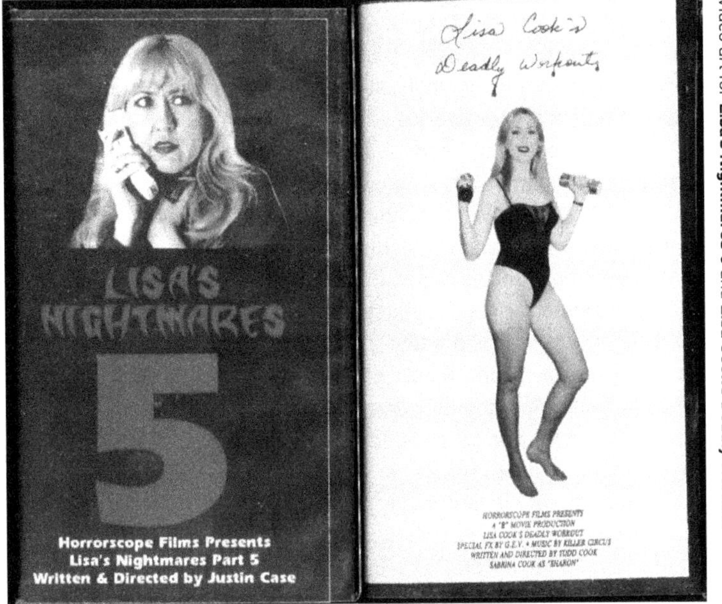

Video art for **Lisa's Nightmares 5** and **Lisa Cook's Deadly Workout**

employed. Credits are littered with friends, acquaintances, neighbors, and scores of relatives who were called upon to act for their sheer availability rather than their talents. Mark and John Polonia's **Splatter Farm** (1987) has a cast of eight, primarily comprised of the brothers and their friends and family. Similarly, Todd Cook cast himself and his then-wife, Lisa, as primary characters in every film he made during the early and mid-1990s. Despite the massive response to a casting call for 1992's **Evil Night**, Cook often worked with small casts, with 1993's **Demon Dolls** reflecting a legitimate intent to make a scaled-down film with a cast of six performers in total.[1] The ease of working with fewer people, as well as the greater amount of authorial control no doubt impacted these decisions, but it also suggests a more personal approach to filmmaking.

Professionally speaking, these performances are terrible: unconvincing, unpolished, and without any sort of effort beyond reading

1 "Horrorscope," p.8.

lines straight and reacting to onscreen actions. The filmmakers, however, embrace their cast's limitations, proceeding with their shaky performances unquestioningly, suggesting their personal connections to every aspect of their work.

Regional accents and various speech affectations are commonplace in many SOVs, imparting a unique veracity and offering a refreshing alternative to the clean and dialect-free speech patterns commonplace in mainstream films. Brian Albright recognizes this as a key component of regional horror film production, noting that "[once] you watch enough of these movies...you also start to recognize the distinct local flavor present in each one."[1] This also applies to the variety of in-jokes and local references utilized by SOV directors, which are often intentionally impenetrable to viewers removed from their own social circles and locations. Todd Cook slips references to his own earlier works in his 1990s productions, including one segment in his anthology **Horrorscope** (1994) where Cook's character rents all of his previous films from a video store. The self-aware intertextuality and effacing humor work with the lackluster performances to undermine the effectiveness of the horror elements. At the same time, however, they stand as innovative recognitions of technical/budgetary/performative limitations, knowing that the films themselves cannot compete with more visible horror films and must rely on clever asides and knowledge of the genre to subvert audience disappointment. Where some might be inclined to dismiss SOV horror broadly for its assumed interchangeability, closer and more open-minded viewing reveals unique elements that allow the independent artists and their works to stand out.

The other major peculiarity-turned-strength of SOV horror filmmaking worth discussing is *mise en scène*, which often extends into special effects. Operating as a truly utilitarian film art—or just severely lacking in means—SOV horror largely (though not exclusively) employs common locations as primary settings. **Boardinghouse** and **Sledgehammer** use a rental property and vacation home, respectively, as their only locations. Every one of Todd Cook's six features from the 1990s (that number not including his five-part custom tape series,

1 Albright, p.3.

Lisa's Nightmares or the self-explanatory **Lisa Cook's Deadly Workout**) uses his Texas home as its primary, and occasionally sole, setting. As the SOV cycle grew into relative maturity, coinciding with its economic decline in rental outlets, so too did the filmmakers themselves turn inward with their creativity, the locations of their films reflecting the insularity of their community.

Video art for Todd Cook's **Special Techniques of Low/No Budget Movies**

As a result of such common places taking prominent roles, the settings are often the height of realism, deviating from the staginess of most films. Todd Cook's home has various details reflecting his and Lisa's life there, including unscrubbed shower tiles, unexplainable collected tchotchkes, and even an entire room dedicated to his collection of horror film posters, memorabilia, and video tapes. This again taps into the topic of home movie realism, as the director acknowledges his desire to preserve and memorialize his home through his films, making it a famous horror location to his fans. The films following this model enact a sort of *vérité* effect that captures real people and places in their elements at the time of production.

As horror films above all, SOV features are concerned with every sort of fantastic and supernatural occurrence, not to mention more realistic slasher bloodletting. Their special effects, central to the success of any genre film, are often as mundane, or even outright embarrassing, as the other production elements outlined above. For example, the ventriloquist dummy in Turner's **Black Devil Doll from**

Hell is a Charlie McCarthy doll, painted and given a braided wig to appear African American. Any fear provoked by the dummy is a result of the uncanny effect of dolls alone, and its stuffed limbs and familiar face lack any sort of threat in the scenes where it is not controlled by an obvious puppeteer. This is not to say that all SOV, or even all amateur SOV, productions bear the marks of poor craftsmanship with their special effects. There is quite often a definable lack of resources and execution that makes these elements suffer by all standard expectations. The question is not a matter of skill or talent, or even familiarity with cinematic production. Eric Stanze's **Savage Harvest** (1994) is an SOV production with excellent, convincing effects and legitimate scares, and was the director's second feature film, produced before filmmaking had become his full-time career. But in the former case, there is something both endearing and puzzling in the sheer badness of many SOV horror films' effects that speaks to the stripped-down production techniques as well as the need for graphic content to hook potential viewers.

Strategies and Approaches

FILMS THAT DIVERGE so severely from conventional cinematic experiences and expectations require distinctive and unorthodox critical perspectives. B-movies and exploitation cinema have long been the site of re-evaluations regarding their artistic merit, though very little of this early work took place within academia. Instead, this critical revision originated from the underground itself, propagated through fanzines, genre prozines, and a handful of books. RE/Search's 1986 **Incredibly Strange Films** was a landmark appraisal of non-avant-garde underground and genre films which were long deemed beyond the legitimate pleasures of film viewing experience. The book's contributors make serious, unironic cases for the cinematic legacies of long-dismissed figures such as Ted V. Mikels, Ray Dennis Steckler, and Doris Wishman. This amounts to an approach that insists trash films are capable of being serious art, wherein the perspective of the viewer or critic is responsible for their renewed status. Ultimately the long-standing issues in their perception at large were the result of mainstream taste politics. In his introduction, V. Vale asserts that the individuality of low-budget filmmaking is a means of liberation, that "the films are eccentric—even *extreme*—presentations by individuals *freely expressing their imaginations*, who throughout the filmmaking process improvise creative solutions to problems posed either by circumstance or by budget."[1] Elaborating on the appeal of trash cinema, he notes that many of the films profiled in the text exist as challenges to all standards of decency, offering "*pure enjoyment and delight*, despite improbable plots, 'bad' acting or ragged film technique."[2]

While the majority of the films covered are 1960s and 1970s exploitation, gore, and sexploitation features all shot on celluloid, the book offers a groundbreaking reappraisal of cinematic refuse. My own focus on SOV horror diverges from Vale's approach, as does my lack of insistence on the "enjoyment and delight" that he celebrates. Countless SOV films are interminable messes, so unappealing and amateurish in their executions that their obscurity seems wholly deserved. Additionally, many titles are so deranged and offensive that they seem designed to actively negate any form of pleasure from the outset. As much as it may be a part of the same generic lineage, it is important to highlight the differences that mark SOV horror as distinct from celluloid exploitation cinema.

Despite the collaborative nature of many SOV films, my readings of SOV horror follow the appropriated auteur theory proffered in **Incredibly Strange Films**. Directors of video horror features may employ regular casts and crews of friends, family, and acquaintances, but their names alone are often responsible for the notoriety of their output. As much as this approach may recall auteurist arguments within Film Studies proper and Vale's assertion of individuality, it also has roots in the subject of amateur cinema as a broadly-defined category. Particularly, this notion recalls Stan Brakhage's assertion of the filmmaker working "in *no* collaboration with others...alone and at home, on films of seemingly *no* commercial value", which is most often cited as a detriment.[3] For Brakhage, this definitive characteristic of amateur cinematic production is valuable, something to be encouraged: "I suggest the conscious cultivation of an *honest* pride in

1 Vale, pp.4-5.
2 Ibid, p.4.
3 Brakhage, p.142.

all 'neurotics'...*and* in the 'neurotic' medium of 'home-movie' making...I would like to see 'fat' films carry their own weight of meaning and stuttery montages reflect the meaningfullness (sic) of repetition, the acts of mis-take as integral steps in motion picture taking."[1] The conception of film as a neurotic medium relates to Brakhage's own personal concerns in filmmaking, the capture of everyday insecurities and happenings too marginal for widespread acceptance yet endemic to the experiences of the artists themselves as well as all audiences, willing spectators or not. While Brakhage's application of these ideals may not have appealed to popular audiences and been resisted by less scholarly cult film viewers, his position is compatible with common preconceptions of SOV features.

The so-called failure that inspired such widespread derision toward SOV horror within the genre press is consistent with earlier backlashes against exploitation cinema of the past. Budgetary lack, low technical competence, excessive self-indulgence, and poor performances were nothing new to the world of marginal cinema. These deficiencies in fact reflect the SOV cycle's continuation from regional exploitation cinema of the 1970s and 1980s, including films outside of the date range examined in **Incredibly Strange Films**. Several notable celluloid exploitation directors of the 1970s and onward are responsible for numerous "badfilms"[2] which bear strong stylistic connections to SOV horror in their haphazardness. Nick Millard's **Criminally Insane** (1975) features a single home setting, wooden performances, and extended moments of tedium as protagonist Ethel seems to spend half of her scenes eating incredible amounts of food in between murders.

1 Ibid, p.146.

2 Badfilm as a conceptualization of film failures is included in Jeffrey Sconce's "Trashing the Academy" as one example of a paracinematic category (372). The term predates this reference, and is employed frequently in fanzines of the 1980s to define particularly challenging works of ineptitude. Greg Goodsell clearly defines the term in reference not to overly campy 1980s horror comedies, but inept sci-fi horror films of the 1950s and 1960s, such as the notorious works of Ed Wood (33). A use of the term in Cecil Doyle's **Sub-Human** employs badfilm in reference to the gore films of H.G. Lewis and Andy Milligan, suggesting the term's mutation to include all nature of technically unsound genre films (12). Returning to the concept in 2019, Sconce notes that badfilm was "generally issued from the margins (and marginalized) of the industry at mid-century," and continues through later cult and exploitation styles ("Canonical" 1).

A decade later, Millard was one of several established exploitation directors who moved from film to video production in the 1980s.

In his mammoth **Nightmare USA: The Untold Story of the Exploitation Independents**, Stephen Thrower tracks dozens of these 1970s and 1980s exploitation films, taking a revisionist critical approach similar to Vale's: "These are films so *damaged*, so wonky and graceless and brilliant, that you feel a need for an anti-semiosis, where movies gain points for being *beyond* bad, for being truly incoherent."[1] This rejection of signifiers valorizes a filmic impulse toward poverty rather than depth and complexity, arguing for the merits of surface-level conceptions which remove subtext from the equation. While many SOV and underground horror features ultimately can be read along more substantial semiotic lines with dedicated application, Thrower's point advocates meeting the works on the terms of the filmmakers themselves rather than the doctrines of academia proper. Poor technical and aesthetic qualities may not be solely confined to SOV horror, but they are certainly what have defined it for audiences since the earliest titles appeared in video shops. Throughout the 1980s, reception of SOV horror was minimal, with little coverage existing in the fanzines and magazines of the day save for the occasional review. Craig Ledbetter of the **European Trash Cinema** zine exemplifies many fans' attitudes when denigrating the bulk of "shot-on-video atrocities.[2]" Charles Kilgore takes a more understanding approach in his **Ecco** zine, commenting "the video medium at least provides the means for independent filmmakers to affordably realize their ambitions...[resulting]in the availability of homemade productions that are immune to the stilted demands of Hollywood."[3] At the same time, none of the video features reviewed are given much of a warm reception, despite Kilgore's willingness to meet the medium on its own terms as it made its place in the genre market.

Regular coverage was much less common throughout the 1980s, only appearing in the following decade once video had become the default format of independent filmmakers with few resources. Of the publications that took more favorable views of SOV horror, the majority were

1 Thrower, p.43.

2 Ledbetter, vol.2, p.3.

3 Kilgore, p.3.

Snarky **Film Threat** subscription ad from **Film Threat Video Guide #1** (1990)

more industrially-oriented zines that dealt as much in the promotion and sales of underground films as they did straightforward coverage. Two notable outlets fostered the growth of SOV horror in the 1990s in both print and via mail order businesses. The first was **Film Threat Video Guide**, a sibling publication to **Film Threat** created to focus on the world of underground film following the flagship magazine's sale to Flynt Publications. Packed with reviews of seemingly every tape submitted for screening, interviews with underground luminaries like Survival Research Laboratories' Mark Pauline, filmmakers such as Richard Kern and Nick Zedd, as well as ramblings from notorious fringe figures like Randall Phillip, **Film Threat Video Guide** was a catch-all of beyond-independent visual culture. It also served as the house publication for the **Film Threat Video** label, with the last twenty or so pages of any issue given to advertisements for their distributed titles, including SOV features like Charles Pinion's **Twisted Issues**. The other was **Alternative Cinema**, itself an outgrowth of **The B's Nest**, the promotional newsletter for J.R. Bookwalter's Tempe Video and Video Outlaw labels. Early issues alternated between standard interviews and profiles of horror filmmakers unlikely to see coverage in mainstream magazines, as well as promotional materials for Tempe and Video Outlaw releases and a wide-ranging reviews section, including for titles yet to find distribution.

Alternative Cinema subscription page, **Alternative Cinema #1** (1994)

Michael Weldon's pivotal and long-running **Psychotronic Video** and Steve Puchalski's **Shock Cinema** regularly reviewed scores of obscure SOV productions, seemingly in an effort to catalog every bit of marginal genre filmmaking available. Hugh Gallagher's **Draculina** featured regular coverage of SOV directors and reviews of more obscure titles than many similarly visible publications. Gallagher also directed a trilogy of SOV horror titles—**Gorgasm** (1990), **Gorotica** (1993), and **Gore Whore** (1994)—which he promoted through the magazine alongside other distributed features. **Draculina** existed for a time as a publishing empire centering on independent horror films, with other titles such as **Scan**, **Oriental Cinema**, and the one-off **Playgore** (a making-of for Gallagher's video trilogy, its title reflecting the softcore scream queen nudity that regularly appeared in **Draculina** itself) appearing throughout the 1990s. The comparably obscure **Independent Video** was unique in covering regional Super 8 and SOV projects and providing a platform for the filmmakers themselves to detail their productions and promote their work in their own words. While the emphasis was still on the sale and distribution of SOV films in this context, the focus shifts from careerism and industrial aspirations as evidenced in **FTVG** and **Alternative Cinema**, to a purer amateurism recalling Brakhage's insistence on the love of the creative process itself.

DRACULINA #13:

Interview with S.F. BROWNRIGG (DON'T LOOK IN THE BASEMENT)! The making of EVEN HITLER HAD A GIRLFRIEND! CINEMA OF TRANSGRESSION! Interview witf underground film maker RICHARD BAYLOR! No-budget distribution with JAMES TUCKER! A look at TERI WEIGEL, BOBBIE BRESEE & MATHILDA MAY! ROCK N' SHOCK! A NEW DRACULINA MODEL! Video reviews and more! Only $3.75!

Still available: DRACULINA FEAR BOOK with interviews with: BOBBIE BRESEE, HERSCHELL GORDON LEWIS, TIMOTHY BECKLEY. Plus PLAYMATES OF TERROR, MEMORIES OF MISHKIN, NECROPHILIA IN THE MOVIES with tons of photo's! Only $4.00!

DRACULINA #12: DAVID FRIEDMAN, KITTEN NATIVIDAD, NICK ZEDD, Making of BACK STREET JANE and much more! Only $4.00!

SPECIAL: Get all three for only $11.00! (Includes 1st class postage!)

Send to: DRACULINA - PO BOX 969 - CENTRALIA, IL - 62801

Draculina ad from **Film Threat Video Guide #6** (1992)

Only in recent years have attitudes toward SOV horror begun to turn toward more serious appraisal and endearment. Many of the modern publications have been borne out of collectors' nostalgic sensibilities. My own work does not approach works shot-on-video from this angle, though one must be a collector of some sort to write about these films, given the obscurity of some titles involved. Many contemporary reviews of SOV films are often comical, poking lighthearted fun at the poor decisions on display while also not excusing the moments in especially poor taste and the resulting discomfort they inspire. At the same time, there is a willingness to recognize the serious contributions made by SOV horror to underground film culture and vernacular filmmaking, offering the seeds of a more nuanced approach.

If in-depth coverage of SOV features in fanzines and popular genre-oriented texts is sporadic at best, it is rarer still within academia. Daniel Herbert's "Nostalgia Merchants: VHS Distribution in the Era of Digital Delivery" examines the recent (2009-present) revitalization of VHS releases of cult and horror films, both contemporary and archival. Beginning with MPI's 2009 release of Ti West's **The House of the Devil**, Herbert identifies the significance of Severin Films' subsequent VHS re-release of **Sledgehammer** in a limited run as a significant moment in the retrospective appraisal of SOV horror by modern audiences.[1] The trend of VHS re-releases continues through labels such as Lunchmeat (with its attendant fanzine dedicated to VHS culture), Horror Boobs (also responsible for the VHS-themed zine **Blood Video**), Massacre Video, and VHShitfest (yet again responsible for a modern zine, **Tape Mold**), as well as numerous others. These efforts and re-releases (several of which have made my own research possible) "unearthed the shot-on-video horror movie as a new frontier at the bottom of American media culture."[2] Herbert confines his focus to the releases themselves and their economic and subcultural status as objects and artifacts. Paramount to his analysis is the capitalistic underpinnings of this system, with "VHS distributors [valorizing] personal, private ownership as much as the Hollywood studios."[3] SOV horror and other obscure films re-released to the market, albeit in limited editions, are a product of nostalgia culture, with the format of videotape itself the signifier of this impulse in fans, collectors, and producers themselves.

THE NEXT ISSUE OF
INDEPENDENT VIDEO
THE JOURNAL FOR MOVIE MAKERS SPECIALIZING IN THE MACABRE
IS TO BE PUBLISHED NOVEMBER 1ST, 1992

SEND IN YOUR WRITE-UPS, PHOTOS, TIPS, COMMENTS, LETTERS TO THE EDITOR AND ADVERTISEMENTS AS SOON AS POSSIBLE, SO THAT YOU CAN BE PART OF ISSUE #4

CUT OFF DATE FOR SUBMISSION OF ITEMS FOR PUBLICATION IN ISSUE #4 IS OCTOBER 1ST

Publication information from **Independent Video #3** (1992)

In his contribution to **The Routledge Companion to Cult Cinema**, "Blood Cults: Historicizing the North American 'Shot-on-Video' Horror Movie," Johnny Walker examines the birth of the SOV category through its early economic successes, particularly **Blood Cult**. For Walker, SOV horror films, "pieces of garbage or otherwise—are *worth* preserving after all," though he makes no concerted effort to analyze the films themselves beyond the general opinions offered in contemporaneous zines and more recent collector-oriented documentaries such as **Adjust Your Tracking: The Untold Story of the VHS Collector** (2013)

1 Herbert, p.6.
2 Ibid, p.9.
3 Ibid, p.13.

and **Rewind This!** (2013).[1] This point emphasizes the divide between modern retrospective appreciation and the original derision inspired by SOV. The final portion of the essay highlights the need for more considered coverage of this category within academia—or at least the importance of looking carefully at these works by scholars of contemporary media culture.

Brian Albright gives broad attention to SOV horror in his **Regional Horror Films, 1958-1990: A State-by-State Guide with Interviews**, but the wide scope of his focus and catalog format prevents SOV from receiving much detailed discussion on a film-by-film basis. Albright does, however, highlight video's operations as a continuation of regional genre film production outlined earlier by Vale and Thrower. Their connections to and engagements with earlier independent exploitation productions is undeniable, despite their lack of quality. Perhaps most importantly, Albright notes the imitative qualities inherent to many SOV horror (and exploitation cinema in general), arguing that they were "made by a new generation of DIY filmmakers who had been inspired by watching either George Romero or Sam Raimi films."[2] Bill Landis' premonition about the negative potential of Raimi's **The Evil Dead** had come true.

Beyond these three texts, there is scant mention of SOV horror in any academic publication, let alone any detailed analysis of the films themselves. SOV horror, by virtue of being the ultimate acquired taste, or at the least its slowly diminishing obscurity, still falls outside of the realm of serious film studies. In-depth analysis of SOV horror on a film-by-film basis is still undeveloped terrain, a major omission and oversight given the richness of the cycle and the increasing visibility of the works themselves.

Jeffrey Sconce's concept of paracinema does not address SOV horror directly, but does provide some indications as to how this work could be undertaken. His 1995 essay "Trashing the Academy," works with a range of genre cinema long deemed inessential and aesthetically worthless, which demonstrate a "counter-aesthetic" in the aims of valorizing a particular form of "cinematic 'trash'".[3] I

1 Walker, **Blood Cults**, p.230.

2 Albright, p.10.

3 Sconce, "Trashing," p.372.

will not be taking a strictly paracinematic approach to SOV horror, largely disregarding the ironic approach that defines the sensibility in "Trashing the Academy." This would be disingenuous given my genuine affection for many of the films included, and the lack of irony in the readings I will undertake; I have no aims to challenge the academic cinematic canon.

Because of their threadbare production styles, uninformed aesthetic and technical decisions, and especially due to their overwhelmingly negative reputations among many fans and scholars, SOV horror features are often not thought of as "real" movies at all. In 1978, Jean-François Lyotard delineated the concept of "acinema," addressing moments known by the critical spectator to have been removed from the finished, polished feature film. Dominant cinema removes flaws during post-production (or corrects them during production) because of "incongruity, and in order to protect the order of the whole (shot and/or sequence and/or film) while banning the intensity it carries."[1] This loses the realism and honesty of the filmmaking process itself, ultimately presenting a sterile work which reinforces the capitalist interests of traditional film practices and robs the finished work of a certain vitality. By their nature, many SOV horror films include all manner of mistakes and errors, whether by ignorance, neglect, or financial/temporal restrictions, and these flaws not only define many of the works to be discussed but are both a large part of their honest charm as well as their outside derision.

William Brown directly cites Lyotard's discussion of acinema in his 2018 book **Non-Cinema: Global Digital Film-Making and the Multitude**, while also speaking to the uncinematic medium of digital video. Taking a global approach to his topic, Brown discusses numerous works of various cultural origins sharing the common component of the digital video format and the resultant exclusion from dominant cinematic practice as his concept's unifying principle. Non-cinema, then, is "an attempt to challenge the limits of cinema and, by extension, the limits of what is constituted as real in our world of cinema-capital."[2] Cinematic exclusion is a practice by which certain films—and especially certain

1 Lyotard, p.53.
2 Brown, p.2.

types of films—are barred from inclusion in academia, popular reception, and even the marketplace by their failure to conform to the expected standards of the filmic, whether these failures be aesthetic, technical, ideological, or economic. SOV horror is a body of motion pictures that has been long neglected by all but the most devoted of cult fans, which are excluded from any cinematic canon for reasons shared with the films in Brown's text.

The lack of in-depth scholarship on SOV films of any nature, and horror films specifically, is just as important to evaluating SOV horror as the wealth of material provided by underground and popular publications. I contend that SOV horror films, particularly those produced by amateurs, are valid and legitimate works of cinematic art that perform a number of important functions despite their exclusion from serious criticism. In fact, the reasons for their exclusion are often the very qualities which make them valuable to the study of genre cinema at large. These features display a great deal of honesty, invention, and economic independence, and dispense with the pretenses of so-called serious cinema to deliver a populist art that is no less challenging in its appeal than many avant-garde works of higher critical regard. Their dismissal and exclusion have not been significant enough to hinder their production, nor did they prevent them from gaining a loyal audience. They succeed because, following Sconce, they are beyond the boundaries of acceptable cinematic material, and following Brown because they are not cinematic by any traditional standards. These films leave in mistakes and interstitial moments, be they excessive or merely uninteresting, that remain part of the complete filmic experience and essential to their value. Ultimately, they thrive via cult networks, having never been afforded traditional screening spaces or widespread audiences. SOV horror films are not strictly paracinema nor are they necessarily acinema, or non-cinema. They are unique, distinctive products of independent American cinematic production, unconstrained by acceptability and demonstrating ingenious engagements with several manners of established film theories and practices.

I do not hold the assumption that the SOV features discussed here are "so-bad-they're-good" or any other sort of ironic appraisals. I do not attempt to defend my own tastes as a viewer or those of the growing number of SOV horror fans. These distinctions of high and low culture, as well as good and bad taste, touched on by Sconce

Burglar From Hell ad from **Draculina #19** (1994)

in "Trashing the Academy," are valid and relevant to this material, but to undertake such discussion would steer me away from close analysis of the features themselves, which is where my concern lies. Whether good or bad, defensible or inflammatory, many of these films operate in ways that are distinct from other forms of cinema, even the exploitation works that immediately presaged and influenced them.

In many cases, the works I examine speak for themselves in terms of their noncinematic merit. Their titles are as lurid and off-putting as their contents: **Zombie Bloodbath, Cannibal Campout, Burglar from Hell**. In several cases, they betray no surprises save the sheer lack of visible competence or entertainment for most viewers, not to mention their explicit contents, almost always handled with little subtlety or finesse. Despite its off-putting subjects and fanbase, shot-on-video horror cinema constitutes a distinctive brand of American independent filmmaking that has been woefully under-studied to this point in time. Throughout its ranks are dozens, if not hundreds, of talented men and women of all economic and racial backgrounds who seized the opportunity afforded by the advent of video to break free from Hollywood's control of genre cinema—or simply to imitate it—and execute their myriad personal visions. Whether they succeeded on aesthetic terms is irrelevant, as the sheer wealth of material yet to be studied proves that this is an essential strain of uncompromising movie making.

Methodology and Contents

BLOGS, INTERNET POSTS, fanzines, and an increasing number of print books are uncovering the lost video horrors of the 1980s and 1990s, according them their due as integral parts of American genre cinema. The prices of original tapes continue to soar, and more formerly obscure and neglected titles are seeing legitimate reissue each year. Still, these celebrations and re-evaluations rarely approach the films themselves with any sort of rigor or seriousness beyond appraisals of technical peculiarities and logical failings. While most of these films are as resistant to critical perspectives as their titles would imply—no theoretical investigation could truly salvage the contents of **Las Vegas Bloodbath** for deeper insights—there are countless examples that do unlock richer understandings when viewed through scholarly approaches. The most exemplary SOV works demonstrate an ineffable quality; they stick with the viewer despite their every wrong move. As a fan of these films, I've been puzzled by their very existence as much as I'm transfixed by their unique operations. Informed by early fanzine writing as much as crucial works of Film Studies as a discipline, my own project has enriched my understanding and appreciation of these cinematic undesirables.

Early writings on cinematic realism bear a distinct relationship with the presentation of SOV horror's preoccupation with everyday mundanity. For my own purposes, Chester N. Turner's **Tales from the Quadead Zone** (1987) and Todd Cook's **Demon Dolls** (1993) are the strongest examples of the relationship between realist film theory and SOV horror aesthetics. Their reliance on consumer camcorder technology, as well as the employment of friends and family members as actors and actual home spaces as sets, essentially mirrors the function of home movies themselves. By adding full narratives and fantastic content to their features, however, Turner and Cook ultimately approximate realism far more capably, if unintentionally, than they have previously been given credit for. Analyzing the films' performances and technical approaches with the lenses provided by Siegfried Kracauer and André Bazin outlines their legitimate claims to a unique form of film art deemed desirable by the earliest cinephiles.

In highlighting video-lensed films exclusively, the medium

specificity of analog video itself seems an important idea to investigate. Using the 1989-1993 works of Kansas City director Todd Sheets as a case study, I believe that feature films made on the VHS format have an inherent videobility that is far more vital than it has previously been credited with. Excepting **Boardinghouse**, no SOV horror film was given widespread theatrical release, confining the movement to direct-to-video status which mirrors its method of production. Sheets produced and released a dozen SOV features during this four-year window, gaining a strong following and notice in the alternative fanzines of the period. Because of his exclusive reliance on analog video, Sheets represents the egalitarian potential of the format as well as the opportunities available to independent horror directors at that time. Through his tireless production and promotion of his features, Sheets grew and developed into a legitimate filmmaker, removed from the mainstream model of industrial production, yet no longer an amateur. Similarly, a handful of established genre directors moved from celluloid to video production as a means of extending their careers and taking advantage of the new opportunities afforded by the technology.

Many recent commentators on SOV horror note the cycle's proximity to avant-garde cinema, typically as a result of their logical fallacies and seemingly inhuman constructions. Another important area of overlap is the presentation of subjective concerns in unrestrained formal contexts. P. Adams Sitney's classification of Lyrical and Trance Films bears remarkably well on Charles Pinion's **Twisted Issues** (1988) and Carl J. Sukenick's **Alien Beasts** (1991). Pinion's surrealist punk rock splatter film uses several metacinematic devices which effectively evoke the Trance Film style of Maya Deren's **Meshes of the Afternoon**, while Sukenick's amateur sci-fi/horror epic emphasizes the personal concerns of the filmmaker in a manner that recalls Stan Brakhage's mid-period Lyrical works. These films demonstrate how the innovations of avant-garde cinema can be unlocked from academia proper and appropriated by amateurs to create works of stunning invention and creativity. The limitations of analog video, as well as the means and skills of the filmmakers themselves, become oppositional tools of personal expression that not only recall forebears in experimental filmmaking, but point to the acceptance of video works as a unique experimental cinema all their own.

Where any and every permutation of genre and subgenre are represented throughout the annals of SOV filmmaking, the most pronounced and popular is the cycle's engagement with the slasher film. While there are numerous SOV slashers that follow the formula laid out by Carol Clover, a handful of films do much more with these generic constraints, and both mutate and pervert the style. Mark and John Polonia's **Splatter Farm** (1987), one of the most notorious SOV features removes the gendered paradigm of the traditional slasher film, focusing its shocking sexual violence on male characters, with the brothers themselves receiving some of the most heinous torture depicted onscreen at the time. In its original, rough edit release, **Splatter Farm's** cruelty exists as a point where industrial ambition and reckless creativity produced a work which is still shocking, but ultimately rewrites the rules of the limited genre it operates within.

The proliferation of generic excess and transgressive content of **Splatter Farm** and other SOV horror films is a common point that bears closer analysis as well. So many films in this category demonstrate no redeeming qualities, are defined by excess and outrageous content for their own sake. Arthur C. Danto's concept of disturbation in art is a helpful tool in examining works by Joe Christ, and Chester N. Turner's 1984 debut **Black Devil Doll from Hell.** These films go to greater lengths of excess and bad taste than most celluloid exploitation films, and their reputations are founded upon these disturbing representations. They exist to disturb and provoke and, met on their own terms, accomplish these unpleasant goals very capably.

I would be remiss to ignore the current popularity of SOV horror films, especially given that this newer audience mirrors the original insular network of fans that supported the movement in its heyday. Following the initial video store boom and the underground era of the 1990s, the primary force driving the lasting impact of these features is a younger audience loyal to the VHS format and the peculiar charms of SOV horror. SOV operates entirely outside of academia, but reflects a devotion and active labor which mirrors the earlier input of filmmakers and writers working during the 1984-1994 period. Fandom and critical reappraisal are active efforts and should be recognized for their lasting impact on the resuscitation of this cinematic oddity.

SOV horror can be as simplistic, challenging, or offensive as any audience perceives it to be. It can also be enlightening, terrifying, and revealing both regarding cultural mores during the time of production as well as the minds of the filmmakers themselves. These are films that compare to no others in existence, and for that reason alone it's long past time to accord them some measure of serious consideration. I'm aware that I might be overthinking several works to follow; that speaks to the incredible impact these amateur productions can make on even a jaded fan of genre cinema. Then again, fans wouldn't continue to pay four figures for certain original VHS releases if they didn't take the films seriously in some manner. Much like the contents of **Incredibly Strange Films** and "Trashing the Academy" have had their day in both popular and critical consensus, SOV horror itself will not disappear and is bound to increase in regard. This is one step toward that embrace.

02

DEMON DOLLS AND QUADEAD ZONES: AMATEUR CINEPHILIA AND THE ALTERNATIVE FUNCTION OF REALISM[1]

On Badfilm, Exclusions, and the Nature of Filmic Reality

THE STANDARD RESPONSE to amateur filmmaking is typically derision, dismissal, and utter disregard for the process and work involved. This attitude, which supposes a theoretical sanctity for the standards of "good" or "professional" filmmaking techniques, often targets works of lesser quality as objects of ridicule, rightfully excluded from the accepted cinematic canon. Much of the sensibility surrounding "badfilm," or works deemed "so-bad-they're-good," centers around low-budget genre features produced on the margins of the Hollywood industry by idiosyncratic laborers-turned-visionaries. Covering a broad swathe of works, from 1950s creature features to 1980s splatter films, the academic approach to this sensibility was largely influenced by Sconce's concept of "paracinema," defined by the author as "a particular reading protocol, a counter-aesthetic turned subcultural sensibility devoted to all manner of cultural detritus."[2] Since the 1995 publication of Sconce's work, a number of responses to paracinema have emerged which bring all manner of lowbrow films into greater critical focus. Connecting many films in amateur and paracinematic categories is their reliance on elements of the fantastic and unreal. Surrealist writer and director Jacques Brunius discussed this quality, noting that "cinema can reign supreme in that enlargement of reality

1 This chapter first appeared in an altered version in **The Journal of the Fantastic in the Arts.**

2 Sconce, "Trashing," p.372.

which is the marvelous."[1] From the earliest days of cinematic theory, the medium's ability to mutate the real into something more fantastic was central to discourses on motion pictures. The SOV horror cycle, however, presents a handful of cinematic outliers which read in a more straightforward manner than the ironic strategies suggested by Sconce.

Filmed with consumer-grade camcorders and other analog video formats, amateur SOV efforts are generally regarded as the lowest-common-denominator of genre films by fans and scholars of paracinema, if acknowledged at all. These attitudes are largely a result of their technical ineptitude and narrative incoherence, as well as the inherently undesirable and unprofessional look of analog video. Daniel Herbert succinctly states that "shot-on-video horror films manifest their poverty in their content and 'pro-filmic' production values, as well as in the visual deficiencies rendered by the technology used to capture the images in the first place."[2] While not all SOV horror features were unschooled, the works of amateurs are the most insightful, as in almost every sense of the word they are complete cinematic failures, neither compelling or plausibly frightening, and long regarded with little retrospective cult appreciation beyond collectors and hardcore fans in search of untapped avenues of entertainment. These amateur efforts are models of economic independence and unfettered creative autonomy, just as they demonstrate oppositional and near-avant-garde technical and formal experimentation, often by sheer luck or accident. Writing over two decades after his pioneering work, Sconce notes that features produced by "amateurs, almost by definition, display a naïveté that cannot fail."[3]

Chester N. Turner's 1987 anthology **Tales from the Quadead Zone** and Todd Cook's 1993 narrative **Demon Dolls** are striking examples of amateur SOV's uncanniness. While many of the hundreds of SOV features produced during this period likewise fit the bill, these two films exemplify the qualities that make SOV horror so unique and challenging. Filmed with negligible budgets by skeleton crews and with casts comprised of friends and family members, they lack any

1 Brunius, p.102.

2 Herbert, p.8.

3 Sconce, "Canonical," p.6.

recognizable finesse or technique. Although they are commonly regarded as artless trash, they reveal surprising richness and depth, often unintentionally, which hold up to serious analysis. Their honest failures at being frightening or even logically sound in construction are the very reasons they are worth investigating. Their unconventional approaches to both the mundane and the fantastic are remarkable for offering a genuine sense of unease at odds with their presentations. Private moments play out before the camera, recast as entertainment for public consumption; ordinary events are tempered with traces of the supernatural with little shift in tone, ultimately proving more illuminating, exposing the workings of alternative cinematic function. André Breton wrote that what fascinated surrealists about cinema "to the point of taking no interest in anything else, was its *power to disorient*."[1] Ordinary happenings captured on film or video produce an undeniable distancing effect, an estrangement due to the sheer uncanniness of the familiar being rendered onscreen. As much as they engage cinematic realism, these SOV works also approach the fantastic in a manner that transforms their presentation of both into a disorienting unreality.

Cinematic realism was one of the foundational concerns of early film theory, connected to the form's very artistic legitimacy. Equipped to capture motion and temporal change unlike still photography, early filmmaking demonstrated a preoccupation with the everyday, no doubt a manifestation of the novelty of the device itself. For critics and theorists, this preoccupation with normal occurrences was the very duty of the technology itself, with Siegfried Kracauer delineating the medium's obligation to extend beyond mere recordings of staged events such as ballets or opera.[2] Instead, Kracauer believed that the true measure of film's aesthetic significance was in its reproduction of actual events, attending to the otherwise imperceptible exchanges and details endemic to life itself, which were lost to any form of still reproduction or representation in other arts. Mundane events comprise the physical reality in which we live, and are thus the subjects with which cinema concerns itself. For André Bazin, these

1 Breton, p,73.
2 Kracauer, p.29.

cinematic captures themselves become the realistic artefacts via the "transference of reality from the thing to its reproduction."[1] While physical reality in its everyday execution was the receptor of the cinematic device for Kracauer, Bazin believed that "the photographic image is the object itself, the object freed from the conditions of time and space that govern it...it *is* the model."[2]

Recalling Sconce, failings as a result of naïveté are detrimental only to established viewing practices, while they represent a sort of oppositional success in the insular world of sub-cult fandom and the filmmakers' own aspirations. In presenting such blunt captures of mundane existence, albeit within the context of fantastic narratives, these amateur works exist as vital, unique counterpoints to the dominant film lexicon, rewriting and updating the concept of cinematic realism in a uniquely unskilled manner. Budgetary lack and aesthetic failure do not produce illegibility, but rather a sort of art-in-negative (to borrow Stephen Thrower's term) which privileges their visual honesty and alternative critical functions.[3] Modern life is not so much put under a microscope as it is laid bare in the simplest of terms, with montage itself often eliminated, leaving little else beside the interstitial moments, small gestures, and peculiarities of individuals and places. One can't simply dismiss their failings outright or ironically elevate them to high art status, but instead should explore their commonalities with the realist theories of early film studies as a way of grasping their unique affective qualities.

A key component to Sconce's conception of his term is the ironic sensibility it entails, which ultimately "seeks to promote an alternative vision of cinematic 'art,' aggressively attacking the established canon of 'quality' cinema."[4] Many paracinematic readings appropriate the innovations of avant-garde cinema when discussing lowbrow works in order to invest them with a degree of reputability. I believe that the most fascinating operations of these films occur entirely onscreen, located in the diegesis of the film experience itself, which also entails production being brought before the camera. Perhaps the most

1 Bazin, "Ontology," p.14.
2 Ibid.
3 Thrower, p.43.
4 Sconce, "Trashing," p.374.

notable feature of many reviews of SOV horror films (beyond mentions of their badness) is the insistence on their home-movie quality. This is a result of the analog video medium and its commonplace usage for such purposes, but also the fact that the nonexistent budgets of amateur works necessitated a utilitarian approach to settings, props, and effects. Turner and Cook's features exemplify this: both prominently feature the artists' own homes as primary settings, with their real decorations and furnishings left untouched for the cameras. Likewise, their reliance on friends and family members as production staff and performers results in unconvincing performances that suggest average people reading lines for the camera rather than convincing portrayals of roles. In effect, what is depicted onscreen is then the very definition of reality, with the bare minimum of artifice and supernatural content remaining to remind the viewer that this is indeed a fictional work. This emphasizes how the supposed worst film failures effectively "foreground, often embarrassingly, the entire imaginary that brought forth these fantasies in the first place."[1] This uncanny representation of reality follows the concepts outlined by Kracauer and Bazin in their writings, just as it perverts these theories through the decidedly acinematic operations of SOV filmmaking.

My interest in cinematic realism is primarily informed by André Bazin and Siegfried Kracauer, who contend that the basic tenet of the realist approach is the most artistically successful and therefore the most valid works are those which present reality in the most honest fashion. Kracauer argued that cinema itself "is uniquely equipped to record and reveal physical reality and, hence, gravitates toward it," which suggests the technological aspect of the medium has as much to do with the matter as human agency in developing it.[2] For Kracauer, physical reality is "the transitory world we live in," thus film's duty to realism is its genuine capture, actuality rendered honest via representation.[3] Recording, rather than outright replication, presents audiences with cinema's capability to capture motion "[acquainting] us with normally imperceptible or otherwise induplicable movements."[4]

1 Sconce, "Canonical," p.2.
2 Kracauer, p.28.
3 Ibid.
4 Ibid.

Emphasizing this quality in the works of Louis Lumière, Kracauer argues that the "bulk of his films recorded the world about us for no other purpose than to present it."[1] Thus the realist tendency of film was concerned with the everyday and commonplace, presented in a manner that was valued for its unobtrusive power of revelation.

Bazin, on the other hand, distanced his theories from human input and forwarded his belief that cinema was valid because it offered "an image of the world...formed automatically, without the creative intervention of man."[2] This impulse is famously connected to the concept of preservation or embalming, emphasizing Bazin's concerns with the temporal elements of the real world itself.[3] The benefit of cinema's objective representations, then, is making the image "the object itself, the object freed from the conditions of time and space that govern it."[4] Unlike Lumière's works as assessed by Kracauer, the event captured itself is not of principal importance, but instead its rendering on celluloid as the vessel through which reality is transferred. Cinema's unique value is in its "power to lay bare the realities" of events, suggesting honest captures are those that can reveal universal truths in even constructed narratives.[5]

While both men were preoccupied with the same goal of physical reality in the cinema, the means by which this could be achieved varied greatly. Turner and Cook's films may be uncanny and impart elements of the fantastic but are also populated with events so banal and mundane as to create near-documentary portraits of middle class American life. There's a tension that is never adequately resolved between the realism and awkward supernatural elements that creates the disorientation cherished by Breton. Their honesty emerges from the unpolished *vérité* presentation, while their realism often serves to reveal the entire creative impulse that occasioned the films themselves, recalling Sconce's claim about filmic failure. In this way, there is a subversive quality, almost certainly accidental, in these films that makes them all the more valuable in the subcultural realm of disposable motion pictures. Jacques Brunius

1 Ibid, p.31.
2 Bazin, "Ontology," p.13.
3 Ibid, p.9.
4 Ibid, p.14.
5 Ibid, p.15.

discussed this tension between the enactment of everyday life and its capture by the camera, arguing "the work of the artist in no way differs from the work of reconstructing external reality as faithfully as possible. For the filmmaker, reality itself does not entirely imitate nature."[1] By this logic, even the mishandled fantastic elements are truer to the realities of the artists themselves as genre fans than if they were freed from their generic trappings. Kracauer also discusses this tension with regard to the realist works of Lumière and the formalist tendency exemplified by Georges Méliès' staged fantastic narratives. In his view, this tension and intermingling between tendencies is valuable when "[benefitting], in some way or other, the medium's substantive concern with our visible world."[2] Elements of fiction and the fantastic can be legitimized as cinematic art so long as they serve the purposes of physical reality as the true aim of filmmaking.

Both Turner and Cook's features meet at the point where Kracauer's insistence on cinema's duty to physical reality and Bazin's dismissal of excessive technique converge. This approach provides a theoretical entry point, a way of making some sense of their contents, as the films' failures as dominant cinema often makes them incomprehensible in any traditional sense. What remains, then, is the filmmakers' presentation of their particular worlds and lives, dressed in the trappings of genre filmmaking to offer viewers not so much a sense of familiarity or comfort, but of the purest cinematic pleasures outlined by Bazin as the medium's Basic Concept.

While amateur films fail by all conventional measures, approaching them as valuable aesthetic properties enables a new film language to emerge, allowing technical ineptitude, budgetary failing and aesthetic shortcomings to be read as unique sites of identification rather than outright flaws or weaknesses, a "parallel universe" to the more familiar film world.[3] These awkward moments are striking contributions to the concept of unintentional realism. Their tenuous grasp on both genre conventions as well as filmmaking savvy magnify the moments of cinematic excess to the point of exaggeration. Only the identification of mistakes, errors and unprofessional touches remains to root the

1 Brunius, p.100.
2 Kracauer, p.39.
3 Thrower, p.43.

viewer in any sort of plausible filmic experience, which heightens their realistic effects. Because of these idiosyncrasies, we are forced to complicate our understanding of suspension of disbelief—or to disregard it entirely—in order to comprehend the films in any meaningful manner.

Further echoing Kracauer's theories, amateur horror cinema is uniquely equipped to represent the peculiarities of its cast and creators' physical realities due to what some would term the deficiencies of its construction. Both intensely personal in the specific manifestations of their content, as well as applicable to wider critical perspectives, Turner and Cook's films may not be considered high art, but they do offer alternatives to standard understandings of filmic realism. While so many films are singled out for their successful construction of gritty realism, the unaffected and undisciplined actuality of these two features stands out as a fascinating deviation from cinematic expectations. Born of their creators' cinephilia, the pleasures in these films are found through an awareness of the filmmakers' processes and the ability to look beyond what is being presented onscreen via the narrative alone. The rudimentary construction of the films is often so evident that this knowledge becomes part of the films' diegeses. This works to further destabilize viewer expectations and genre conventions, with even the rules of narrative filmmaking becoming sites of unease and unpredictability. Even if they were never intended to be taken seriously, neither were the earlier trash films that Sconce detailed in his influential essay. Beyond mere questions of good or bad filmmaking, let alone cinematic respectability, Turner and Cook's video horrors are films excluded from every canon that remain fascinating and valuable.

Writing several decades before the category's advent, Kracauer essentially defined the workings of SOV horror:

Imagine a film which, in keeping with the basic properties, records interesting aspects of physical reality but does so in a technically imperfect manner; perhaps the lighting is awkward or the editing uninspired. Nevertheless such a film is more specifically a film than one which utilizes brilliantly all the cinematic devices and tricks to produce a statement disregarding camera reality.[1]

1 Kracauer, p.30.

Following this guideline, amateur works such as Turner and Cook's are legitimized artistically precisely because of the failures which mark them as unsuccessful and undesirable to standard reception strategies. Their ineptitude and miscommunications create moments of brilliant and unintentional film realism, subverting notions of authorial control and success on aesthetic terms in order to offer a more personal and singular vision of independent filmmaking. Read as unironic examples of realist films, Turner and Cook's works open a space for understanding the broader range of SOV horror as a truly independent filmmaking practice, distanced from industrial convention and separated from discourses on taste politics. These two features are honest and valuable expressions of personal and subjective art delivered on the filmmakers' own terms to provide the most basic thrills which define film as a distinctive art form.

Tales from the Quadead Zone and Performative Failure

CHESTER TURNER PRESENTS an incredibly compelling case: one of an unfortunately small number of African American horror directors, he produced and self-distributed two independent works in the 1980s, disappeared for thirty years and was presumed dead before ultimately being rediscovered and having his films re-released by Massacre Video in 2013. Despite the mystery surrounding his life, as well as the relative obscurity of his works compared to most of the era's independent horror films, Turner's 1984 debut, **Black Devil Doll from Hell**, is one of SOV's most notorious features, with early reviews decrying the misogyny of its narrative as well as its unpolished style and slow pace. Herb Schrader's **Video Drive-In** zine notes the "great sleaze script goes awry in the hands of CHESTER NOVELL TURNER'S vain direction...[and] inept shortcomings: hissy, unintelligible soundtrack; bad reproduction, and overzealous camera work" [sic].[1] Steve Puchalski took a more outspoken stance in **Shock Cinema**: "this repulsive, unprofessional, piece of shit is so

1 Schrader, p.2.

crude and vile-headed it's like some deviant's chromosome-damaged home movies...without a shred of good taste or technical savvy. It revels unashamedly in its own misogynistic mindset and utter incomprehensibility."[1] Everything from its attitude and format to its stunted film language is ridiculed.

Cover of **Video Drive-In #8**, featuring **Black Devil Doll from Hell**

That being said, there remains something in Turner's work that stands out as unique, an ineffable quality recognized by Greg Goodsell, who notes that, despite the film's gender politics and lack of taste, it is "so kitchen sink banal it's a work of primitive genius."[2] The video is discussed as an example of the so-called "Unwatchables," cult films that negate even the base spectatorial pleasure found in other such lowbrow works. As a result of this categorization, as well as Puchalski's efforts at exclusion, Turner's debut is separated even from the alternative canon of cult horror cinema. However, Goodsell's noting its "primitive genius" and kitchen sink approach touches on the unconventional success of its budget approach to filmmaking, casting it not only in the category of the avant-garde, but more specifically a gritty, realistic brand of alternative film art. Dropping the misogyny of his first film, Turner's follow-up anthology, **Tales from the Quadead Zone** further explores the concept of unintended realism, though it unfortunately remains the more obscure of his two works.

Concerning the strange tales read by a mother to the ghost of her

1 Puchalski, #3, p.16.
2 Goodsell, p.34.

dead son, the film is completely transparent from its first moments. The primary setting is a semi-rural house, decorated and laid out exactly as it must have been lived in. Gone are any elements of staging or set design, with only the actual possessions and furnishings of real people providing the sequence with any context. Joseph Ziemba notes the appeal of this particular effect, arguing that a large part of SOV horror's novelty is its "regional-*vérité* qualities; real people making movies on their own terms and having fun."[1] This specific aspect touches on the counter-aesthetic offered in amateur works, with their unfettered settings and performances adjacent to documentary realism. The second half of Ziemba's statement also alludes to the audience's awareness of the film's constructed nature, an element that runs counter to traditional viewing habits in emphasizing the performers' input as creators rather than characters.

Narrative films are meant to inspire entertainment via the suspension of disbelief, so that for the duration of the feature's runtime, the audience is able to disregard the construction of the film. When the seams show, as they do throughout **Quadead**, the work is dismissed as a failure and the question of unironic entertainment reduced from the equation. Because of their oppositional techniques and outsider status, SOV films by nature reject this common reception strategy. In many ways, they can't be read successfully except on their own terms, reflecting the insularity of their creation. Even genre conventions and clichés fail in their application here, further demarcating a line between films which "work" and those which do not. Turner's conviction to his material, if not his consideration of its construction, evidenced by his willingness to not bog his narrative down with unnecessary exposition, is one of his greatest strengths. While not convincing against Hollywood production values, the insularity of Turner's production, signified by its stripped-down presentation, taps into a version of the fantastic that unnerves precisely because it does not successfully frighten his audience. The combination of low-budget effects, authentic settings, and unschooled performances bridges elements of the fantastic and the realistic to heighten their effect into a uniquely unsettling tension. To unlock any sort of meaningful

1 Ziemba, **1980s**, p.192.

interaction or exchange with the film requires looking beyond its miscalculated delivery and engaging with the veracity of the events themselves. Ignoring the standard implementation of suspension of disbelief and setting aside critical expectations allows for an appreciation of Turner's anthology that centers its alternative and innovative nature.

The most obvious scene of the film's failure, and certainly its centerpiece, is the seven-minute monologue delivered by Keefe Turner (the director's brother) during the second story, "The Brothers." The entire sequence is a clear example of the film's breakdown as successful filmmaking, both regarding its aesthetic intentions as a horror film as well as its plausibility as a fictional work of art. After paying off two friends to steal the body of his recently deceased brother, Keefe's character, Ted, berates the blanket-covered corpse, recounting every past wrong he has suffered, from being the least favorite of their father's sons and losing out on his inheritance, to his brother's affair with his wife. Perhaps his brother's gravest offense, however, was dying before Keefe had a chance to poison him, a plot he details in full while shouting at the shrouded figure. After his monologue, the living brother cackles unconvincingly for several minutes, dresses the corpse in a clown suit with make-up, and plans to bury him in the basement. Even before touching on the credibility of Keefe's performance, there is nothing believable about the over-the-top delivery of such a long-winded speech to a corpse. This ridiculous scenario, however, is more revealing than would be assumed when given a closer look.

The menacing tone of the scene is undermined from the start, as Keefe enters the room containing his brother's corpse while holding a mug in the shape of a woman's breast. Even more puzzling is the moment when Keefe mimics throwing its contents on the body while the cup is clearly empty. Shown earlier as he toasts his friends following their robbery, there is no justifiable explanation for its inclusion, save being a novelty item owned by one of the Turners. The fact that such a comically absurd prop finds its way into a crucial, serious scene in the film exemplifies the lack of consideration put into the feature. Why should the crew bother tailoring to their production's needs when plenty of compatible materials were already on-hand at no additional cost? Much like a failed jump-scare in the earlier grave-robbing scene, where the moment meant to startle is unseeable due to poor lighting, the mug emphasizes the film's inability to generate anything approximating a realistically frightening atmosphere. What remains, then, is the filmmaking process itself, laid bare for those willing to look beyond the initial disappointment the scene provokes.

It's clear why Keefe's performance is unsuccessful: he is an amateur actor, likely performing here for the first time, and can do nothing to make himself convincing. His speech is rigid, with few contractions and an odd sense of formality, despite his supposed anger and disrespect for his brother. The entire convoluted monologue relies on any number of clichés, from adultery and familial disharmony, to questions of proper burial and the reclamation of personal honor. It all serves as verbal exposition, telling rather than showing perhaps via flashback what inspired Keefe's hatred in order to justify his act of vengeance. As unconvincing as his atonal delivery may be, the entire scenario fails to connect as anything remotely believable in its construction. That said, just because his performance is so awkward and impossible to read literally, it is no less commendable. This would be a demanding scene for many actors, given the high emotional affect of the scripted event and the bizarre nature of its realization. Keefe is not a career performer, but an amateur just like his brother directing him, and the amount of labor he invested in the role is still evident, even if it does not deliver the intended effect. We may not believe the brother's quest for revenge, but we do believe Keefe Turner the performer as he gives his all to the project. His bad acting may fail to convince the audience, but it does not fail to connect as a fascinating indicator of methodology.

In addition to shaping the film's visual impact, Turner's direction and editing is also responsible for a great deal of its semiotic disconnect. The scene features a handful of camera angles and positions repeated arbitrarily, despite taking place within a single small room and bearing no notable details or revelations outside of the dialogue. Despite this, the scene is edited frenetically and completely at random, as frontal close-ups of Keefe's face cut to over-the-shoulder shots of him during the same line of dialogue, and long takes alternate with choppy jump cuts. There is a complete absence of continuity in the editing style, with the axis of action violated with no purpose. Theoretically speaking, the action could have been impressively rendered via a single long take, or even through calculated use of close-ups. Discussing the relationship of realist cinema to editing, Bazin asserts that excessive montage is manipulative and deceiving, undermining the miraculous objectivity of the camera apparatus through excessive tampering with the film itself following production. While it is tempting to conflate Turner's poor grasp of proper editing technique with this idea of distraction from reality, his overly-affected techniques call attention again to the veracity of his staged scenario, emphasizing his subjective vision over the camera's objectivity. In breaking all standard rules of presentation and rupturing the logical core of his film, Turner's random edits ultimately make the viewer aware of the constructed nature of filmic conventions themselves. This again echoes Sconce's insistence on badfilm failures foregrounding their very extrafilmic inspirations.[1] Physical reality and perception in the real world do not follow the mandates of accepted film grammar, just as Turner's structural decisions defy these standards. In his failure to conform to expectations of cinematic art, the director accidentally frees himself from the confines of dominant film logic and approximates realistic perception. Rather than undermining his work's believability, this unintended effect allows for a new appreciation of cinematic failure or badness as enlightening and valuable.

The film's lack of logic and explanation opens a conflict between realism and the fantastic, with the frame narrative of the anthology itself suggesting unreality from the start of the film. Kracauer discusses the clash between the realist and formalist tendencies, and Turner exemplifies the theorist's description of a filmmaker "bent on creating an imaginary universe from freely staged material [who] also feels under an obligation to draw on camera reality."[2] While the film's fantastic (or formalist) components distract from the realistic elements of its physical reality, the mundane elements ultimately win out, proving far more graspable and corporeal than the fleeting moments of the supernatural. Discussing realism in cinema and audience familiarity with its conventions, Jacques Brunius notes that film is "the *least realistic of the arts*, the art in which the mechanism of formation of the images gives them as concrete a character as

1 Sconce, "Canonical," p.2.

2 Kracauer, p.36.

possible, but in which the disposition of these elements is as distinct from temporal and spatial reality as it is possible to be."[1] Turner's film not only defies the expectations that allow audiences to "carry the fiction on the screen over into reality", but literalizes the clash between concrete, represented reality (Keefe's performance, the ordinary props and setting) and the fantastic material through its traditional shortcomings.[2] Because **Tales from the Quadead Zone** is so rooted in mundane reality and captures it authentically, it is even more unsettling as a horror film that fails to horrify. The seeming incompatibility of the representational strategies results not in terror, but a surreal uneasiness that is not explained away by knowledge of its amateur production.

It isn't just that Turner himself failed at making a film, but rather that everyone involved in his production is so horribly inept by all established expectations. More than this, it never occurred to Turner to look to any larger or more established wells of talent, resulting in what Puchalski calls "one-man, one-take filmmaking at its worst."[3] He insisted on using his friends and family, working every technical element himself, and because of this strong-headed independence, his films are at a disadvantage to entertain. Speaking in critical terms, he failed on all counts at making a commercial horror film; what he did succeed in making, however, is a distinctive statement of outsider cinema, independent both economically and aesthetically. Within paracinema especially there is a tendency to elevate the oppositional filmmaker as auteur in order to give more credence to claims of legitimacy and authenticity.[4] In many ways, through the sheer volume of his missteps and the uniformity of his errors (soundtrack music overpowering important dialogue, threadbare special effects, lack of continuity editing), Turner reads as something of an anti-auteur, the negation of unified vision via technical mastery. From this negative space, however, **Tales from the Quadead Zone** offers an intriguing vision of personal filmmaking that is surprisingly and remarkably unsettling. The film's implausibility and awkwardness do not ultimately

1 Brunius, p.101.

2 Ibid.

3 Puchalski, #9, p.23.

4 Sconce, "Trashing," p.382.

deter the *unintended* effect it inspires in viewers. The eeriness of "The Brothers" results from its mishandled effects: the dead brother's garbled, unintelligible speech, his words secondary to their unnatural impact as uttered sounds from beyond the grave. The underlit, dirty cellar becomes a place of uncertainty that works precisely because of its familiar origin, an unpleasant yet recognizable stage for the narrative of otherworldly vengeance. Not so much the result of an attention to detail, but an inattention to effective production and staging techniques, between the lines of Turner's directorial vision exists an axis of alternative critical inquiry which can unlock other films in its mold. Freed from the confines of tradition and convention, Turner's realist feature demonstrates the vitality of SOV cinema as a challenging yet rewarding field of art in line with early theory's embrace of medium-specific potential.

Demon Dolls: Re-Staging Reality

EVEN AMONG THE marginal mail order SOVs of the 1990s, Todd Cook's **Demon Dolls** brings a distinctive domestic insularity that can seem impenetrably dull, featuring only six actors, one setting, and a decidedly un-horrific depiction of the banality of married life. André Breton praises cinema's ability to "make concrete the forces of love" so lacking in all other art forms.[1] Following this, Cook's factual presentation of his marriage is one that is honest if not necessarily attractive in its lack of romantic convention, depicting realistic details such as dirty dishes and unscrubbed shower tiles alongside inarticulate expressions of affection. Arriving some five years after Turner's retirement from filmmaking, Cook ran his own production and distribution company, Cemetery Cinema (later Horrorscope and then Screamtime Films), exemplifying the further need for fans-turned filmmakers in the 1990s to work under the radar of all established cinematic operations. Entirely self-distributed, Cook's output appeared at the point when commercial viability was confined to direct mail order sales and promotion via fanzines and convention

1 Breton, p.74.

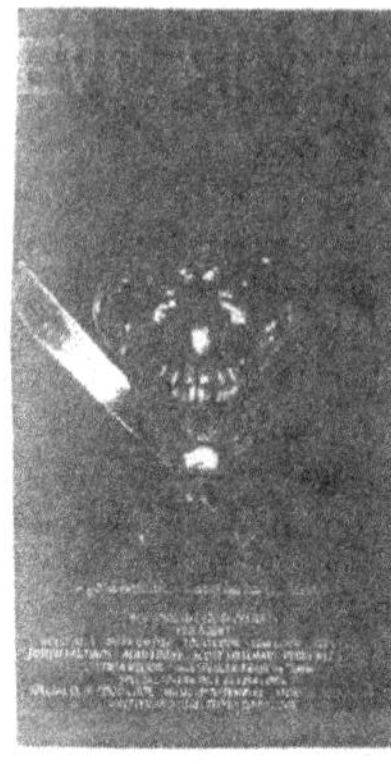

THE BONEYARD
4034 GREENBRIAR
MISSOURI CITY TX 77459

BRAND NEW VIDEOS!!! ALL OF THESE ARE HARD TO FIND RARE TAPES!
ALL VIDEOS ARE VHS FACTORY SEALED TAPES IN ORIGINAL COLOR BOXES
THE BEING (1981)-CREATURE CREATED FROM NUCLEAR PLANT TERRORIZES! $20.00
THE BURNING (1981)-EXCELLENT SLASHER FILM! TOM SAVINI FX!!! GORY! $20.00
A DAY OF JUDGMENT (1981)-SLASHER WITH A SCYTHE KILLS! $20.00
DEADLY INTRUDER (1984) COOL SLASHER FILM WITH GORE!!! $20.00
GIRLS NITE OUT (1981)-EXCELLENT SLASHER FILM WITH ORIGINAL KILLS! $20.00
HEAVY METAL (1981)-VERY RARE ANIMATED R-RATED CLASSIC! 5 STORIES! $30.00
HORROR HOUSE ON HIGHWAY 5 (1985) ROCK/HORROR MOVIE CLASSIC!!! $20.00
HOUSE OF 7 CORPSES (1974) CAST/CREW OF HORROR MOVIE ARE KILLED! $20.00
THE INITIATION (1981)-EXCELLENT SORORITY GIRL SLASHER FILM! GORY! $20.00
MADMAN (1981)-SCARY, EERIE, GORY SLASHER FILM!!! EXCELLENT!!! $20.00
MARTIN (1977)-GEORGE ROMERO'S CLASSIC GORY VAMPIRE FLICK!!! $20.00
ONE DARK NIGHT (1981)-SORORITY GIRLS DIE IN A MORTUARY!!! GREAT! $20.00
WATCH ME WHEN I KILL (1981)-GREAT ITALIAN SLASHER/SUSPENSE FILM! $20.00
XTRO (1983)-GORY FILM! WOMAN GIVES BIRTH TO A FULL GROWN MAN! $20.00

BRAND NEW EXCLUSIVE RELEASES-ONLY AVAILABLE THROUGH THE BONEYARD!
DEMON DOLLS (1993) AN EVIL DOLL POSSESSES AND MURDERS! COOL FX! $20.00
DEMON DOLLS-THE BASEMENT TAPES (1994) SEE THE ORIGINAL AMATEUR $20.00
MOVIES THAT WERE COMBINED TO CREATE THE FINAL VERSION! BLOOPERS!
EVIL NIGHT (1994) SEE MURDERS NEVER BEFORE DEPICTED IN A B MOVIE! $20.00
HORRORSCOPE (1994) 3 VERY FREAKY STORIES!!! AWESOME MOVIE!!! $20.00
SPECIAL TECHNIQUES OF LOW/NO BUDGET MOVIES (1994) MOVIE DIRECTOR $20.00
TODD COOK SHOWS YOU HOW TO MAKE HOME MOVIES BECOME PROFESSIONAL!
VERY HELPFUL AND INCITEFUL FOR AMATEURS AND INDEPENDENTS!!!
BUY ANY TITLE ABOVE AND GET ONE FREE!!! INCLUDES NEW TITLES!

THE BONEYARD
4034 GREENBRIAR
MISSOURI CITY TX 77459

Ad for Todd Cook's mail order distro, The Boneyard, **Independent Video #9** (1993)

spaces, with unabashed cinephilia and unschooled enthusiasm inspiring creativity rather than industrial aspirations. Examining any one of Cook's dozens of classified ads in **Fangoria** makes this position clear. Forced to take matters of promotion, much like production and all creative aspects, into his own hands, Cook was left to draw attention to himself via paid advertisements, the sort of marginalia read only by the most devoted genre fans. Cook's "NEW B MOVIES!" for sale were destined from the start to obscurity.[1] As such, some of the only other contemporaneous notice Cook drew was in the more underground publication **Alternative Cinema**, which covered the home video market for independent horror features. Featuring **Demon Dolls** under the column "Up for Adoption: b-movies currently seeking distribution," the notice emphasizes Cook's eminently outsider status in the genre market.[2]

DEATH METAL ZOMBIES, BLOODY ANNIVERSARY, & more! New B movies! For complete catalog, send $3 to Cemetery Cinema, 2601 Cartwright Rd, Box 118, Missouri City, TX 77459.

Todd Cook classified ad in **Fangoria #145** (1995)

While Turner's film itself is transparent, Todd Cook himself has always been clear about his intentions and motivations. In every available interview, he mentions his love of the **Friday the 13th** film series, noting that his "career literally started one week after [seeing] the original...in 1980."[3] As a result, his filmmaking aspirations were rooted in having a chance to make his own installment, something he realized on one level through various amateur production attempts which remain unreleased.[4] Matt Hills responds to Jeffrey Sconce's delineation of paracinema by discussing the **Friday the 13th** series as examples of outliers, "languishing outside the sanctuary of legitimate film culture as well as outside the trash-as-art revaluations of paracinema."[5] Because of its commercial transparency, lack of clear authorial voice combined with workmanlike technical proficiency, and the disposability of sequels, Hills terms the series "para-paracinema." As an avowed member of this sub-sub-cult, Cook's own feature films are imitations of para-paracinema, the ultimate undesirables

1 Anon., p.84.
2 Griffith, #2, p.54.
3 Kinem, "Chairman," p.17.
4 Mogg, p.313-314.
5 Hills, p.232.

and works wholly unqualified as legitimate art. Despite this, his filmography, and specifically **Demon Dolls**, benefit from deeper critical discourse, particularly by analyzing his honesty and cinephilic motivations, which make the film such a bizarre, effective piece of SOV realism.

Telling the simple story of a man who uses an ancient curse to bring a doll to life for his wife's birthday, **Demon Dolls** defies no expectations and attempts no narrative innovations. Little remarkable action occurs during the first forty-five minutes of the film, and while its climax stands as a minor marvel of nightmarish low-budget insularity, the pure mundanity of the earliest sections is its most remarkable feature. Casting himself, his wife Lisa, and a handful of friends as exaggerated versions of themselves, Cook (as Scott) offers little in the way of escapism or even remaking himself—instead, he generally presents his life and home as they were at the time of filming. After animating the doll, Scott returns to his daily routine, undermining the terror intended in the scenario, and eats breakfast with Stacey (played by Lisa). Nothing significant occurs, no major developments emerge, and instead the scene presents a reconstruction of the couple's everyday existence. Following this, Cook retreats to his room, which is featured so prominently throughout the rest of the film that its importance cannot be overlooked.

Decked from floor-to-ceiling with all manner of posters, stills and lobby cards, as well as various shelves containing books, magazines and video tapes, Cook's room is actually the storage/display space for his collection of horror memorabilia. In fact, so much attention is paid to these possessions that much of the film's middle section seems to be showing off Cook's own personal holdings and, thus, his capital as a fan of horror cinema. Throughout the feature, a premium is placed on the consumption of horror films and the attendant fan culture, so much so that the only defining characteristics of Scott's character are his fandom and passion for horror culture. At this level, and because of the use of Cook's own home as a setting and his possessions as the film's only props, there is little reason to separate Cook himself from his character. With few exceptions, there is no ego-stroking or attempt on his part to exaggerate his world. The markers of Cook's subcultural status, along with his domestic life form the core of the entire film, rendering the supernatural possessed-doll narrative secondary in appeal. Picking up on the essence of the film, Ziemba calls it "an exploration of mundane occurrences that happen in and around the filmmaker's house."[1] The film functions, despite itself and against all traditional notions of success, as the truly unexceptional brought to life onscreen. The spectacle of its supernatural narrative may be the driving force of the work as a whole, but the most lasting and fascinating aspects are its capture of a real place and time, complete with the presence of more-or-less real people.

Fan reactions to SOV horror films often invoke surrealism in discussing the films' logical fallacies without reference to or apparent awareness of any specific theories. Looking to the Surrealists themselves, a compatibility with their theories emerges, albeit one rooted in familiarity and presentation of the real world more than the usually cited elements of the bizarre. Writing on the concept of décor in film, surrealist poet Louis Aragon states that film was the first art form to "use the false harmony of machines and the obsessive beauty of commercial inscriptions, posters, evocative lettering, really common objects, everything that celebrates *our* life, not some artificial convention that excludes corned beef and tins of polish."[2] In this view, common and vulgar objects such as Cook's various pop cultural ephemera, are not only artistically valid, but also speak much more to the honesty of modern life than any sort of constructed *mise en scène* could hope to do. Kracauer also discusses the cinematic use of objects, arguing that in bringing "the inanimate to the fore and mak[ing] it a carrier of action, film only protests its peculiar requirement to explore all of physical existence, human or nonhuman."[3]

Not only does **Demon Dolls** emphasize this aesthetic via its continued attention to Cook's actual possessions, it also taps into the immanent realism that fuels his personal vision. Even as the narrative's various convoluted turns make little sense as a successful horror plot, effectively defamiliarizing the viewer as they baffle, there is a logic to the honest presentation of the filmmaker's reality. Only in identifying with Cook's sensibility and understanding his motivations is there a chance of finding pleasure in his film. Much like the breast-shaped mug

1 Ziemba, 2013.
2 Aragon, p.50.
3 Kracauer, p.45.

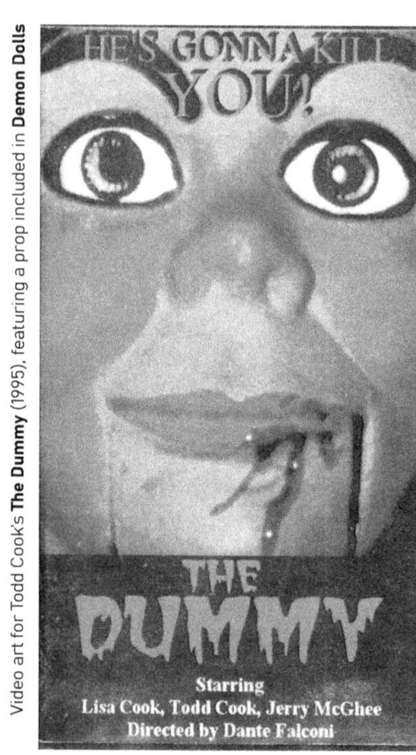

Video art for Todd Cook's **The Dummy** (1995), featuring a prop included in **Demon Dolls**

in **Quadead**, the availability of the objects in Cook's possession makes them suitable as props for his artistic vision. The variety of the inanimate dolls in Cook's home—no doubt common possessions given their recurrence in several other of Cook's features from the 1990s—is rendered threatening despite their normalcy. These props may appear odd or distracting, but convey a sense of the everyday, existing as mere possessions, ordinary items transformed into things both fantastic and menacing.

The film's rudimentary techniques and raw performances barely even merit the sort of close analysis **Quadead** warrants; there is nothing sublime or transcendent about their badness. Speaking again on the generally unremarkable nature of the film, Joseph Ziemba notes that "Cook celebrates the mundane. But he doesn't mutate it...He's not Chester Turner."[1] Directly invoking Turner's ability to sublimate his limitations and arrive at a bizarre form of subversive realism, Ziemba contrasts Cook's more mundane approach to his art. This can be read as a deficiency on the latter director's part, but this banality is also one of Cook's greatest strengths. André Bazin discusses the silent film and the minimal techniques of editing employed by Erich von Stroheim as the most desirable of approaches, rejecting the devices

1 Ziemba, 2013.

of expressionism and montage by allowing reality to lay "itself bare" before the unblinking eye of the camera.[1] Speaking to this sensibility, then, he argues that this is indeed a deviation from most theorizations: "a language the semantic and syntactical unit of which is in no sense the Shot; in which the image is evaluated not according to what it adds to reality but what it reveals of it."[2] Cook's failure to produce any exceptional qualities via his film's presentation of real life may not add to any discourse, but it offers a distinctive and appealing capture of reality specific to both the director and Bazin's own sensibilities. Not even an outright failure in these terms, **Demon Dolls** instead evokes the vital essence of cinema that so captivated early theorists, despite its exclusion from any sort of canon. The techniques do not call our attention to the artifice of the film viewing experience and its divergence from physical reality as Turner's do, but instead, this lack of flair and excess ground Cook's film in a plainer, more streamlined version of the real.

Even more than Turner, Cook offers his audience the type of film one would expect a horror fan to make, even if this expectation is itself loaded with possible meanings. A premium is placed by the director on not only the celebration of horror film fandom, but also on the very act of viewing the films themselves, a metatextual touch that speaks to the self-reflexivity in the SOV category during this period. Just as important as Cook's poster and memorabilia collection is his library of films on video, to which he and his friends-turned-actors return throughout the feature's runtime. When threatened with murder by the doll, Scott invites his friend Danny to stay over and watch horror movies as a means of relieving tension. The pair, along with Stacey, do this again in the following scene (watching Cook's own 1992 feature **Evil Night** to add another layer of self-reflexivity) and discuss the movie and its gore effects, plot points, and the nature of horror film sequels. Their inarticulate expressions of pleasure and disappointment with the video, constructed though they may be, read as honest captures of real fans interacting, no doubt inspired by actual antecedents in Cook's own life. Later, David and Amy, two other friends, come over

1 Bazin, "Evolution," p.28.
2 Ibid.

to watch horror movies with Scott as well, and while this session is interrupted, Cook still manages to insert knowing dialogue and convincingly authentic, if technically stilted, exchanges into the scene.

While Turner's realism reveals his film's artificiality and that of all creative labor, Cook's instead highlights the insular experience of spectatorship and fandom, regardless of its appeal (or lack thereof) to non-niche audiences. **Demon Dolls** achieves the sort of realism that appealed to Bazin and Kracauer, making it and similarly-conceived SOV works honest recreations of daily life through the subjective lens of fans harnessing the potential of consumer video technology. Kracauer, discussing staging and constructed sets, notes that a "film maker is often obliged to stage not only the action but the surroundings as well...The important thing is that studio-built settings convey the impression of actuality."[1] Cook's reliance on his own home and possessions frees his work from the constructed replication of reality, bringing actual settings and objects into focus and reinforcing his preoccupation with the rendering of his physical reality. The film's true finale reveals Scott at his computer, writing the script for **Demon Dolls** itself, pulling back from the nightmare of the narrative and casting the entire work as a creation of everyday life. Everything shown previously has been a bizarre device conceived by Scott in his normal hours, reframing the film as something wholly innocuous, yet no less bizarre for the turns his imagination has taken previously. The entire film is an exercise in making his existence as a filmmaker uncanny, something that estranges his reality as much as it relies upon it. Kracauer concludes his discussion of the tension between formalist and realist tendencies by arguing that a balance emerges only when "the latter does not try to overwhelm the former but eventually follows its lead."[2] At the conclusion of **Demon Dolls**, Cook reveals how the Fantastic itself is often a product of the real, resolving the conflict of his work's approach more successfully than he has been given credit for.

1 Kracauer, p.34.
2 Ibid, p.39.

Conclusions

TALES FROM THE Quadead Zone and **Demon Dolls** challenge established sensibilities: they lack technical competence, narrative coherence, budgetary plausibility, and even spectatorial investment. For films so surface-level simplistic, they are surprisingly challenging for many viewers. They exist as such outliers and bastardized takes on filmmaking as a whole that they work best when speaking for themselves. There's little doubt that both directors intended to deliver serious features, despite the limitations of their budgets and technology, not to mention their respective lack of skill. Certainly, Cook allowed parody and self-reflexive humor to slip into **Demon Dolls**, but there is no indication that he wanted his work to be relegated to sub-subcultural (or para-paracinematic) status in its reception and appreciation. Even as it was made for a niche horror audience, there is a clear ambition in his marketing of the film that was limited only by his distance from industrial practices and the exclusionary efforts of even the underground press. Both men display a great deal of ambition throughout their films, and regardless of the temptation to react to them with irony or ridicule, the fact remains that they self-financed and distributed several completed works.

There's an interesting paradox in discussing cinematic realism: one of the most derided aspects of SOV films is their audiovisual pugnacity and tonal misdelivery, the very things which root their representations in physical reality as experienced by spectators. However, this sort of realism has been deemed desirable by early film theorists and critics, even though they likely could not have predicted this trend at the time of their writings. Reconciling these two perspectives requires a more complex negotiation of taste politics than I'm interested in pursuing here, but it remains a pertinent question. Perhaps the challenge in appreciating amateur SOV films, beyond their obvious limitations, is that their inherently personal and insular nature makes them unknowable in some way to those not responsible for their creation. This may render my analysis speculative, but it does speak to Guy Barefoot's belief that, generally speaking, trash films "may be more revealing, in the sense that they are unguarded but also closer to the world in which we live. Trash cinema has a particular documentary value."[1] This sentiment echoes Kracauer's observations on Lumière and his ability to capture life's "least controllable and most unconscious moments", but also Aragon's discussion of décor in its concern with the real world and the viewer's own access to it via art.[2] Also evident here is the reminder that while they may be excluded from cinematic criticism, amateur SOV productions are indeed part of the larger discourse on non-normative cinematic practices.

There are qualities in Turner and Cook's films that remain unshakeable, unique, and impossible to define by any established film language. Of all the surrealists, Antonin Artaud comes closest to detailing the disorienting approach that makes amateur SOV horror so effectively unsettling. Writing on cinema in general, he notes that "any image, even the slightest and most banal, is transfigured on the screen. The smallest detail and the most insignificant object take on the meaning and the life that pertains to each of them."[3] The breast-shaped mug, Scott's video collection and dolls, and the various personal effects-turned-props in each film become crucial details in the worlds presented onscreen. Even the familiar and commonplace, and especially the unremarkable, are cast as bizarre, otherworldly artifacts, their everyday functions essentially erased by the demands of the fantastic narratives. This also echoes Bazin's comment on the surrealist appeal of photography, which "produces an image that is a reality of nature, namely, an hallucination that is also a fact."[4] These fleeting moments of the supernatural inhabiting the common world are rooted in the diegesis of everyday existence, but bear distinct imprints of the otherworldly.

Joseph Ziemba's comment about the appeal of "regional-*vérité* qualities" of SOV horror hits closest to the strange qualities that render these two films so memorable. On the surface, these are simple works—technically, narratively, and even affectively—which is a large reason for their dismissal by all but the most devoted cult film spectators. Any number of amateur works, such as Mark and John Polonia's **Splatter Farm** (1987) and Carl J. Sukenick's **Alien Beasts**

1 Barefoot, p.9.
2 Kracauer, p.31.
3 Artaud, p.103.
4 Bazin, "Ontology," p.16.

(1991), are similarly rooted in the banality of the filmmakers' real lives. Because of the peculiar affectations of amateur moviemaking, they also reveal striking contributions to the canon of cinematic realism as well as the fantastic. Their valid, if unknowing, commitment to realism as consequences of their threadbare production methods and unschooled approaches are successful due to the filmmakers' naivete and lack of means to properly realize their expressions. They offer the intrusive discomforts of real life, awkward interstitial moments, and the defamiliarization of the commonplace. Their fantastic contents defy expectations of not just traditional film, but amateur and home movie conventions, unnerving in their confrontationally unpolished aesthetics. Turner and Cook provide reminders that crude art can still shock and stun with its bluntness and distracted nature. As much as they capture the banality of everyday life, they also show how strange, unpleasant, and even uninteresting it can be at turns. These qualities are considered undesirable but are arguably more valuable due to their disrepute and absence from dominant cinema. In including these moments, whether intentionally or not, Turner and Cook use the framework of horror cinema to unseat all expectations of how or why films work, delivering not the expected entertainments but the discomfort of the familiar stripped of all control.

03

TODD SHEETS AND SOV MEDIUM SPECIFICITY

THIS IS THE modern exploitation cinema. Pulp Video is where the narrative limits for sex, violence and depravity can be expanded and transcended. The makers need answer to no one but themselves. Gruesome and prurient surface narratives combined with affordable reproduction techniques make pulp video "the bastard amalgam of the Hollywood B-Picture and the Xerox machine" (Tonya Chthonic).

Before the modern world's waking rem sleep (at thirty frames per second) reading was an activity much treasured. Fine books are still a beautiful aesthetic experience: acid-free archival papers made of rag, marbled end papers, and hand-tooled leather covers. Content: writing of the masters. Ponder and snort while drinking your port. Meanwhile, people have always loved junk: the dime novels and horror magazines, their brown and crumbly pages (made of wood pulp) turning your fingers a shiny black. The kind of popular-culture detritus that painter Robert Williams referred to as "the garbage... the good stuff!!"

The cigar-chomping moguls of the past, coming from an environment of adversity (Eastern Europe), shot from the hip and went with their gut. As the expense of making a Hollywood film has grown more bloated and obscene, these latter-day risk-taking mensch have been replaced by corporate-style CEOs with the collective heart, aesthetic, and eye for figures of an accountancy firm..."

How long will our nascent police state tolerate these obnoxious examples of creative autonomy?

—Excerpted from A Pulp Video Manifesto, by Tonya Cthonic (1994)

This statement, published pseudonymously by SOV filmmaker Charles Pinion, represents one of the few articulated writings by an underground director in favor of the video medium. Intended as a call to arms as much as a tongue-in-cheek defense of limited-means filmmaking, the manifesto (no fuller version exists beyond this excerpt) is a notable if marginal moment in the SOV cycle. Even if the intended revolution never occurred within the underground, it did signify the desire and potential for video to be taken seriously by artists and fans alike. Also explicit in Pinion's words is the ability of video to exist as a legitimate alternative to normative film industry practices, although his particular emphasis is on works of exploitation cinema, given the insistence on lurid content repeated throughout. Writing over a decade after his initial statement, Pinion commented on the massive changes in the filmmaking industry since his original missive appeared, lamenting that:

Granted, there was a naive faith here in video's subversive potential. I was shooting in VHS, 8mm and Hi-8 video, unaware that digital video was coming down the pipeline to change everything. The "video feature" became less an obnoxious post-punk art statement and more of "the way things are." As a filmmaker, today, I couldn't be happier. As a rebellious shit-stirrer, I am somewhat subdued by it.

- Charles Pinion, 4.12.06

As much as non-theatrical filmmaking and distribution has come to prominence in recent years, the very emergence of video editions of feature films inspired debate among scholars and fans alike. In 1991, Charles Tashiro introduced the concept of "videobility" to refer to the material and technical qualities of films re-released on commercial home video formats. For Tashiro, the increasing output of motion pictures onto video resulted in "little attention to the technical issues raised by the movement of a text from one medium to another or to the consequences of film evaluation based on video copies."[1] Originating from the celluloid-theatrical standard of film exhibition and appreciation, Tashiro's essay works to accord a greater deal of credibility to home video releases. He does, however, demonstrate an apparent displeasure with VHS, which may provide fast-forwarding and rewinding capabilities, but lacks the speed, clarity, and freeze-frame functions of laserdisc. Much of the resistance to video was inspired by the concept of shifting celluloid features—primarily mainstream, large budget 35mm productions—to

1 Tashiro, p.7.

smaller grade formats. There is an intrinsic dissonance with the intended exhibition of the work itself, the public and dominant form rendered private and minor, not to mention a downgrading involved in the transfer between mediums. For Tashiro, the matter is of the "translation" of film to video, with the minimization of the differences in format being the ultimate goal of "conscientious" transfers.[1]

Building on the question of acceptable transference of audiovisual information, he suggests that we "call the ease of translating a particular film to video its 'videobility,' a concept defined by both technical and experiential components."[2] The visual information imparted by film's technical attributes cannot be adequately recreated on a television screen or videocassette/disc. Likewise, the home viewing experience cannot compare to that of a theatrical screening, lacking proper stereo sound and the possibility of immersion into the screening environment. Nearly a decade after the arrival of SOV horror filmmaking, and well into the market dominance of VCR technology, the celluloid theatrical experience reigned as the definitive judge of a film's character for many critics (it would be interesting to speculate what Tashiro would make of **Boardinghouse**'s reversed video-to-film transfer process).

It could be argued that because they do not originate on film and are rarely transferred to celluloid, Tashiro's term cannot be applied to works shot-on-video. However, by concentrating the entire production and exhibition process on analog tape, SOV features have an intrinsic videobility by their very nature. There is no concern with fine detail on an SOV filmmaker's part because they understand the limitations of analog tape, meaning translation is rarely a factor. SOV films bear a distinct videobility from the moment the camera captures the action being staged. The only loss of visual information in filming with video is a result of magnetic tape's inability to produce anything but a poorer reproduction of the original image. Regarding the deficiencies of video as a transfer format, Tashiro discusses the flattening of depth, noting that the "video image is acceptable within the limitations of the medium but unsatisfactory as a reproduction of the film image."[3] While video is not the ideal format for the presentation of materials, it

1 Ibid, p.8.
2 Ibid.
3 Ibid, p.9.

also represents a divergence from the standard means of production, doing away with the very concerns expressed in Tashiro's article by rendering them obsolete. Tashiro never engages with the possibility of works filmed using video, even when noting that video and disc transfers are just "hints of the original."[1] SOV horror—and by extension all video-lensed features—*are* the original in and of themselves, the only version of the text that has existed, a fact which continues through reproduction for distribution.

The 1980s and 1990s saw a proliferation of direct-to-video (DTV) films, produced on both celluloid and tape, no longer requiring one to "wait for it" on video as Tashiro suggests. The DTV market handily provided consumers with titles they could screen immediately on release, offering independent and low-budget productions on the same shelves as mainstream blockbusters. Caetlin Benson-Allott notes that since 1988, "US audiences have watched the majority of their movies on a video platform...movies are now primarily videos for both their makers and their viewers."[2] Even before Tashiro's writing, the home video market had redefined the relationship between audiences and motion pictures, not to mention the nature of movies themselves being considered "films." Nowhere was this revolution of format more apparent than in the underground world of SOV horror at the turn of the 1990s. By this point, video stores had caught onto the false promises of crafty distributors and production houses, no doubt rebuffed by customers who complained that Jon McBride's **Cannibal Campout** (1988) in no way lived up to its gruesome box art. This backlash and the reduction of sales to rental outlets forced filmmakers and distributors to rely on more DIY tactics, meaning magazines such as **Alternative Cinema**, **Independent Video**, **Draculina**, and **Film Threat Video Guide**, as well as conventions and direct mail order, became the chief means of disseminating SOV horror. The audience may have shrunk, but those who sought out these projects were dedicated fans who knew what to expect from low-budget videos and were converts to their bizarre charms.

Discussing the idea of subcinema, Ramon Lobato argues that one of the category's key principals is that it is "noncinematic—in

1 Ibid, p.10.

2 Benson-Allott, p.1.

P.O. Box 6573
Akron, OH. 44312-0573
Phone: (216) 628-1950
FAX: (216) 628-4316

TEMPE VIDEO is your B-video outlet for today's unrated horror films! In addition to our own line of horror features, we also carry nearly one thousand other videos from all genres at prices from $10 and up! Call or write today for your **FREE** sample issue of our newsletter The B's Nest, which includes interviews, feature stories and reviews of today's hottest horror flicks!

ALL TITLES NEW, FACTORY-SEALED, SP SPEED VHS NTSC VIDEOTAPES!
NO ILLEGAL DUBS!

CALL TODAY! ORDER $100.00 OR MORE & GET *FREE* UPS C.O.D. SHIPPING!

Send a check or money order for fast service. UPS Ground $3.50 for the first tape and $5.00 for two or more tapes. C.O.D. orders add $5. No credit card orders. Overseas $15.00 for the first tape and $20.00 for two or more tapes in U.S. funds only. OH. residents add 5.75% sales tax. Please list alternates, some titles are in limited supply. Sign that you are 18 years of age or older & please include your phone.

COMING SOON:
"My Sweet Satan/Roadkill" "Ozone" · "The Scare Game" "Shreck" · "The Witching" "Sorority Babes in the Dance-a-thon of Death" · "Dominion" "John Russo's Filmmaking Seminar" "Night of the Living Dead" 25th Anniversary Documentary
and more!

THE DEAD NEXT DOOR
84 mins. · Cat. No. 8984 · $20.00

The Dead Next Door is a zombie lover's dream come true! An inventive scientist has created the ultimate virus: it takes over and replaces a corpse's cells, using it as a slave to keep supplying its favorite dish ...humans! When the virus goes awry, the government fights back by creating a crack team of soldiers called The Zombie Squad. Their mission: save the humans, and seek out and destroy the dead! From the streets of Washington, D.C. to the fields of Virginia and on to the suburbs of Akron, Ohio, our heroes fight a non-stop struggle for life and death, along the way stumbling onto an insane religious cult bent on keeping the dead alive and well until the day comes for their ultimate mission ...to replace the living as the Earth's inhabitants! It's non-stop terror and violence when your neighbors become... *The Dead Next Door!*

WINTERBEAST
77 Mins. · Cat. No. 8985 · $30.00

Something **strange** is going on up in the mountains of a tiny winter resort community. Every time you turn around, innocent townsfolk are disappearing in increasing numbers. But this isn't just **any** mountain... this is the Indian burial ground of the Chakura tribe! Worse yet, the sleepy town's hills are infested with living totem poles, creatures of all shapes and sizes and the legend of the *Winterbeast!* Fearless park ranger Sgt. Bill Whitmanand his bumbling right-hand man Stillman are hot on the trail when one of their rangers returns from a scuffle with an unknown entity. Along the way they come upon Sheldon, the owner of the nearby Wild Goose Lodge and a permanent fixture in the town's history. Unbeknownst to them, Sheldon hides a dark secret that could lead to the destruction of the entire village ...and the world! It's *The Evil Dead meets Northern Exposure!*

HEARTSTOPPER
96 Mins. · Cat. No. 8986 · $30.00

In colonial Pittsburgh, Benjamin Latham, a progressive Tory physician wrongfully accused of vampirism, is hung. To prevent his return from the grave, he is staked through the heart and buried at a crossroad. Now, two hundred years later, the burial site is unearthed by a construction crew and the young doctor emerges from the grave... alive. In his quest for answers, Benjamin falls in love with Lenora Clayton, a photojournalist researching colonial Pittsburgh, and through her locates his descendant, Matthew Latham, an antique dealer obsessed with his unusual family history. To feed his special needs, Benjamin compulsively continues to kill but disciplines himself by limiting his prey to evil members of society. The resulting death spreebecomes the obsession of policeman Ron Vargo, who is determined to put an end to the horror.

MIDNIGHT 2: SEX, DEATH AND VIDEOTAPE
70 Mins. · Cat. No. 8987 · $30.00

Abraham, the last surviving member of the crazed family in *Midnight*, has taken up residence in the suburbs of Pittsburgh. Armed with a video camera and his various implements of death, he stalks the streets of the city to satisfy his bloodlust ...searching the psyches of his victims for his perfect mate. Enter Rebecca, a beautiful young bank teller who has unwittingly come under Abraham's deadly camera lens. With the help of a hard-boiled police detective, she may be able to solve the murder of her best friend ...or become the ultimate sacrifice in a deadly game of cat-and-mouse. From director John A. Russo comes a suspense-filled, nightmarish voyage through the mind of a serial killer ...a voyage that leads straight into the heart of *Midnight 2: Sex, Death and Videotape!*

THE MAJORETTES
93 Mins. · Cat. No. 8988 · $30.00

Someone's killing the beautiful young majorettes at the local high school. Could it be Harry, the voyeuristic janitor? Tommy, the nerdy photographer for the high school yearbook? Mace Jackson, the sleazy local drug pusher? Jeff Halloway, the star quarterback for the high school football team, whose rugged good looks could possibly be hiding a dark and terrible secret? Or could the identity of the killer be just one of the many incredibly shocking twists you'll discover as you watch *The Majorettes*? From the first gruesome murder to an ending that literally explodes with violence, you will descend into a high school nightmare, where greed, lust, and murderous revenge pass for school spirit, where every locker could be hiding a dead body, where the price for being beautiful is paid in blood ...and where everyone's favorite subject is the art of survival!

DEAD IS DEAD
75 Mins. · Cat. No. 1029 · $20.00

A man named Eric is out to avenge his brother's death at the hands of drug dealers. Along the way, Eric is attacked and partially dismembered by a mutant creature and left for dead. A beautiful young woman named Laura finds him and uses an experimental drug on him known as Doxital. The drug grows back Eric's severed limb within a twenty-four hour period. And if administered soon enough, Doxital can also revive the dead! Eric uses his supply of the drug to pay off a large debt to his brother's killers, but unknown to him, the Doxital he gives away is a bad batch... a batch that can turn those who use it into the walking dead! Eric's search for the spoiled Doxital leads him to New York City, where he discovers that the drug is hidden in an abandoned school mere miles from his home. Can he get it back in time... before it falls into the wrong hands?

THE ZOMBIE ARMY
80 Mins. · Cat. No. 1030 · $20.00

Army Sergeant Eileen Saddow has a problem. The Pentagon brass bought a former insane asylum to use as a base for the elite experimental female unit The Lethal Ladies. The problem is that they didn't check the asylum fallout shelter for leftover inmates! Two were left behind when the nuthouse was abandoned. Jim is a deranged psychotic who thinks that he's a psychiatrist. He likes to experiment with shock therapy equipment. Mary, a looney nymphomaniac, helps. And she really likes soldiers! The two freaks wreak havoc on the Army by capturing soldiers and turning them into mindless zombies. Trapped in the tunnels under the old asylum, The Lethal Ladies must invent weapons to destroy the living dead! It's the world's first zombie combat rock music video! Watch out, Saddam Hussein... you're no match for Operation "Zombie" Storm and... *The Zombie Army!*

GOBLIN
75 Mins. · Cat. No. 1031 · $20.00

A newlywed couple (Bobby Westrick & Jenny Admire) move into their new house with the help of their friends. But what they don't realize is that twenty years ago, the previous owner of the house—a farmer practicing witchcraft—inadvertently raised a monstrous creature from the depths of hell ...and now it's coming back to make up for lost time! The Goblin, set free from its dark prison within the earth, lays waste to the Missouri countryside, hungry to mangle or kill anything or anyone in its path. The young people, trapped inside the house, are pushed to the nightmarish extremes, forced to retaliate ...or become the next victim of the *Goblin!*

Goblin delivers unbelievable scenes of violence and gore... just pray he doesn't deliver them to your doorstep!

PREHISTORIC BIMBOS IN ARMAGEDDON CITY
70 Mins. · Cat. No. 1032 · $20.00

Welcome to Old Chicago City... the last remaining outpost of civilization after World War III. Though the city is ruled by the evil Nemesis (Robert Vollrath) and his army of cyborgs, the only thing standing in the way of utter post-nuclear domination is Trianna (Tonia Monahan) and her fierce, beautiful tribe of Prehistoric Bimbos! When Nemesis, with the help of the metal-clawed tyrant Salacious Thatch (Deric Bernier) attempts to destroy the Bimbos once and for all, he quickly discovers it's not going to be as easy as he thought! Filled with wacky action, goofy creatures, scenery chewing villains, and enough bimbos to fill two post-nuclear action comedies, this film will blow your mind... Strap yourself in and prepare yourself for... *Prehistoric Bimbos In Armageddon City!*

SHOCK CINEMA VOLS. 1-4
60 Mins. · $10.00 each
Cat. No. 1567/1568/1570/1571

Vol. 1 - Interviews with: Charles Band, Fred Olen Ray, Jeff Burr, Scott Spiegel, David DeCoteau, Courtney Joyner, Ernest D. Farino, Daniel M. Peterson, Chris Roth, J.R. Bookwalter and Mark McGee!
Vol. 2 - Interviews with Forrest J. Ackerman, Robert Quarry, Steve Neill, Deanna Lund, Ted Newsom, Melissa Moore, Joel Bender, Michael Burnett, Gary Graver, Frederick Bailey and John Goodwin!
Vol. 3 - "Bloopers, Babes and Blood" is a hilarious and gruesome sixty minutes chock full of your favorite T&A, action, gore, trailers and bloopers!
Vol. 4 - "B-Movie Makeup Effects" is an in-depth look behind-the-scenes at movie magic performed by some of today's hottest up-and-coming makeup effects artists! You'll see graphic effects as they are created, applied and performed, side-by-side with the actual footage as seen in the films!

HUNDREDS OF OTHER TITLES AVAILABLE FROM $10 AND UP! SEND $1.00 FOR A FULL PRICE LIST!

Tempe Video ad from **Film Threat Video Guide #8** (1993)

the sense that it is usually consumed in the home."[1] This means that subcinema covers the fields of direct-to-video, and by extension, shot-on-video works. SOV horror, as an element of subcinema, is defined by its videobility and its divergence from the theatrical

1 **Lobato, p.117.**

cinematic experience. Excepting **Boardinghouse**, no SOV horror feature saw significant theatrical distribution; these are films that were made *on* video *for* the home video market, eliminating the matter of translation or transfer by and large. One rare example of SOV horror meeting the theatrical model is the case of premiere screenings held in local theaters, a process heavily employed by Kansas City, Missouri filmmaker Todd Sheets.[1] In this case, however, the theatrical exhibition was a limited event, celebratory rather than functional or economic, and the primary emphasis remained on video distribution itself. Sheets offers a fascinating case of an SOV filmmaker who unapologetically embraced and championed analog video as his sole means of independent creative expression. Between 1989 and 1994, Sheets directed and attained distribution for seventeen feature-length SOV films, making him by far the most prolific director in the category during my highlighted period of SOV horror.

ENGLEWOOD 10917 Winner Rd 252-2463 PICK UP OUR NEW CALENDAR!
WORLD PREMIERE • SATURDAY NIGHT 11:00 • VIDEO PROJECTION
ZOMBIE BLOODBATH
Local film producer TODD SHEETS and zombies will be present. Film will be shown on video.

Zombie Bloodbath theatrical premier notice, **Psychotronic #18** (1994)

Sheets exemplifies Lobato's claim that "Subcinema travels via subterranean channels but it is not underground in any deliberate way. It takes little pleasure in its marginal status, and would happily go mainstream if market conditions allowed."[2] While not striving for mainstream acceptance, Sheets was open about his aspiration to be the Roger Corman of the 1990s—that is, a successful, identifiable cult figure making a living by regularly releasing genre films to an established audience via stable means of production and distribution.[3] Through his deals with Cinema Home Video, Tempe Video, and ultimately his own Asylum Home Video label, Sheets found a receptive audience for

1 All instances of these screenings relied on video projection, so these examples are still removed from celluloid cinematic exhibition. This practice has a long history, with adult theaters in the 1980s regularly switching to video projectors for screening pornographic films.

2 Ibid.

3 "Video Outlaw News," p.7.

his ambitions, even as he was regularly attacked in the underground press for the perceived flaws in his work. Despite these numerous pans, personal attacks, and arguments that appeared in the letters pages and columns of several zines, Sheets persisted in his work, improving with each feature. In this way, his legacy also exemplifies the role of the underground press in disseminating news and consumer recommendations on marginal horror cinema in the 1990s. With fewer notable independent genre pictures seeing theatrical release than in the 1980s, the fanzines of the 1990s existed to promote and champion the new wave of amateur filmmaking—even as they worked just as much to denigrate its makers for their technical and personal deficiencies.

For many creators, SOV was aspirational as much as it was utilitarian. Their efforts celebrated video as a fully realized medium recalling Pinion, but the fact remains that many SOV directors intended their early projects as transitional works to the world of higher budget horror. Because of his inexhaustible creativity and enthusiasm for low-budget horror cinema, Todd Sheets is a singular example of a committed SOV auteur. Proudly relying on analog video to realize his ambitious projects, Sheets dispensed with the earlier promotional exploitation of **Blood Cult** to embrace SOV horror as the ultimate avenue of expression for amateur genre filmmakers in the 1990s. More than this, Sheets represents the difficulty in defining the amateur—at what point does one become a professional, especially without formal training despite a self-defined career trajectory? At a certain point, the amount of on-set experience and body of completed work must transform the amateur into the career professional. Because of his voluminous output and prominence in the underground press, Sheets defines the 1990s SOV horror market, as well as its potential for success and legitimate artistic growth. This success includes the creation of a legacy bound to a distinctive filmmaking style. Despite the widespread negativity toward much of his earliest work—a reaction shared by the director himself—a thorough overview of his films between 1989-1993[1] reveals that uniquely video-based horror cinema was a legitimate avenue for artistic development.

1 The films consulted in the following pages are just a sample of Sheets' oeuvre during this period; they are the titles currently in my possession. Other significant features such as **Bloodthirsty Cannibal Demons** (1993) are highly-regarded, but are unavailable for viewing.

Bimbos, Zombies, Dead Things: Todd Sheets' 90s Nightmares

TODD SHEETS' FILMS invariably promise several things: music by the director himself via his metal project Enochian Key, Dario Argento-inspired colored lighting, a cast comprised of a small troupe of regular collaborators, imaginatively cheap gore effects that the camera lingers on for far too long, and credit sequences littered with in-jokes and messages thanking Jesus Christ. Every piece of Sheets' early-to-mid period work bears the unmistakable traces of his personality and interests, and while they are far removed from the world of confessional cinema, they express these elements with more candor than most filmmakers would willingly allow. The earnest sincerity of his filmmaking is a large part of his appeal, as much as the excessive gross-outs and ambitious narratives. This genuine passion for the creation and consumption of horror films also carries over into his understanding of fandom and audience expectations. In one of his many interviews with **The Kansas City Star**, Sheets argues "[h]orror fans don't care about acting...As long as the movie delivers the groceries, they're happy."[1] Standard expectations of cinematic quality are entirely disregarded, a shift that reflects the market turn to direct sales as much as Sheets' own preferences as a fan himself. Given the continued support and inspiration he found during his prolific early period, these observations squarely place him in the roles of amateur and enthusiast, and he rarely failed to deliver his own requirements to audiences.

Shot on ¾-inch video with a shockingly high $40,000 budget, and produced by Sheets' production company Trustinus, 1989's **Zombie Rampage** was by all accounts a failure. Overbudgeted by the first-time filmmaker, guaranteeing a financial loss, and overly ambitious in weaving gang war and zombie invasion storylines, the film still made an impact in certain corners of the genre film world. Sheets personally reached out to filmmaker David DeCoteau, owner of the Cinema Home Video label, hoping to arrange a distribution deal or receive feedback

1 "Blood on a budget."

from someone with connections to the film industry. Intrigued by what was being offered, DeCoteau licensed the film with the stipulation that its title—originally **Blood of the Undead**—be changed, and the film itself be recut. Still a fledgling filmmaker driven more by his passion than any sort of practicality or technical/industrial savvy, Sheets' first film is rough but enthusiastic. Even for DeCoteau, the film was a challenge, but clearly displayed the young director's talents, which inspired Cinema to take a chance on Sheets' following works, a deal that was not particularly lucrative for the filmmaker, but provided opportunities that would build his underground reputation.

In its current state,[1] **Zombie Rampage** is not great cinema, but clearly marks the beginning of Sheets' obsessions on tape. The seventy-five-minute cut of the film (edited from an original run time of eighty-nine-minutes) thrives on its brevity, offering a faster-paced film free of the lagging stretches evident in many SOV features that overstay their welcome. This revisionism shows Sheets' growth as a filmmaker, and his oft-expressed embarrassment with his earliest projects, demonstrated by the pre-credits message that the film is presented in its "director's cut for fans of the original." At this point in time, original versions of many SOV films are inaccessible, relegated only to initial-run VHS copies that remain the domain of hardcore collectors and fans who purchased the films as they appeared. Alternate versions and director's cuts are far from unique in the world of home video, but SOV represents a particularly widespread example of "original" features being made unavailable to modern audiences.

The re-cutting is evident throughout the runtime, which displays choppy edits and several jumps in the narrative's continuity. Even in its truncated state, **Zombie Rampage** is ambitiously conceived despite its lack of innovations. Weaving slasher, street gang, and zombie elements together, the film dispenses with standard notions of plot and characterization (many characters are not even named onscreen), instead placing groups of people into a horrific situation they must survive. As fragmentary as the action is, the director's various concerns

1 No standalone DVD edition has been issued, and VHS copies of Cinema Home Video/Video Outlaw releases are prohibitively expensive. All films made prior to **Zombie Bloodbath** were screened as part of Pendulum Pictures' collection **Decrepit Crypt of Nightmares**, a budget fifty movie collection containing several SOV titles in addition to Sheets' own.

are on display: acting is second thought at best, with outrageous gore scenes receiving the greatest amount of attention, including an infant taken from its carriage and ripped to pieces (achieved thanks to an unconvincing baby doll prop). The make-up effects are cheap, with zombies appearing as little more than pasty-faced people in dirty street clothes. Despite its lack of narrative clarity, several moments do stand out as unique, such as an upstanding bar owner's ad hoc leadership of the various survivors, signifying blue-collar, Christian values resisting adversity. Similarly, a suicide scene is played completely straight and works to engender sympathy, rendering even a minor character as more than fodder for the zombie hoard. Perhaps most tellingly, however, the end credits offer special thanks to Domino's Pizza, Coca-Cola, and "last and most importantly; Jesus Christ, for giving me the determination, the talent and the willpower to make it all work."

Sheets' wholesome outlook is as much a part of his persona as are his gory obsessions. Beyond every film from this era containing some sort of Christian message, most interviews with the director also include details about his lifestyle. Another feature devoted to Sheets in **The Kansas City Star** notes his aversion to profanity, banning explicit language from his sets (in fact, despite their generous bloodshed, his films rarely feature any swearing). Additionally, the director regularly avows his faith, as well as his abstinence from alcohol, drugs, and tobacco in print coverage of his films.[1] Even in the pages of the fanzines covering the underground film scene, Sheets is outspoken and unafraid to express his personal beliefs despite the resistance he was likely to find from the decidedly impious audience. At the same time, the director is articulate about his work and faith, dismissing questions about the contradictions between piety and extreme violence, believing his films are too ridiculous and over-the-top to be taken seriously.[2] As much as he was part of the underground video horror scene during this period, Sheets was decidedly not an underground director in the sense promoted by **Film Threat Video Guide**, never appearing in their pages or courting notice. The earnestness displayed in his films as well as his commentary set Sheets apart from the transgressive films

1 "Blood on a budget."

2 Gallagher, #17, p.29.

of the day, with his art tied more into his subjective identity than any sort of calculated pose for acceptance.

This openness is reflected in Sheets' earliest films themselves, which bear the marks of amateur cinema alongside his increasingly ambitious conceptions. Even as he struggled to evolve his filmmaking techniques to match his vision, there is little doubt or self-consciousness in the films themselves, and Sheets was clear about the role he wanted to play in the genre filmmaking world. Made on marginal budgets provided by DeCoteau largely using ¾" video, the productions spanning 1989-1992 are uneven in appearance as much as content. Working with limited means was no matter of shame, merely a necessary step on the way to establishing his legacy as a modern horror filmmaker. Even DeCoteau felt that Sheets' earliest works were lacking finesse, hence the retitling and re-editing of the Cinema releases.[1] Despite this, the distributor saw both the demand in the direct-to-video marketplace, as well as Sheets' budding talent and assisted the director as a means of benefitting both their careers. Cinema Home Video's deal saw not only foreign licensing for several films, but also late night cable television appearances on the USA Network's cult programming block.[2] For an amateur director with little to no name recognition, Todd Sheets began his career fortuitously and received guidance from DeCoteau which raised his profile over the course of the 1990s.

Zombie Rampage was followed at various points by Sheets' "Bimbos" films, **Bimbos B.C.** (1990), **Sorority Babes in the Dance-A-Thon of Death, Prehistoric Bimbos in Armageddon City** (both 1991), and **Bimbos in Time** (1993). Commissioned by DeCoteau to cash in on the video success of his **Sorority Babes in the Slimeball Bowl-A-Rama** (1988), the films are free of horror elements, but do demonstrate hallmarks of Sheets' developing style (**Bimbos in Time** was released by Englewood Entertainment). Featuring regular collaborators Tonia Monahan, Jerry Angell, Veronica Orr, and Mike Hellman (also Sheets' early effects man), these early Trustinus productions exemplify the films made to meet the demands of the growing direct-to-video market in the 1990s. Nonetheless, the director soon expressed embarrassment with these projects, noting in a letter to **Alternative Cinema** that he hoped

1 "Missouri Invaded," p.22.

2 "Blood, beasties."

TEMPE VIDEO DIRECT

NIGHT OF THE LIVING DEAD 25TH ANNIVERSARY DOCUMENTARY
83 mins. • Cat. No. 8989 • $19.95 • Directed by Thomas Brown
Gathered together for the first time in 25 years are director George A. Romero and the creative forces behind NOLD. Also on hand are celebrity interviews with John Landis, Wes Craven, Tobe Hooper, Sam Raimi and other filmmakers. Officially licensed and produced with the cooperation of Image Ten, Inc.! NEW LOWER PRICE! "Absolutely indispensible to anyone who loves this seminal classic horror film..." - Ron Ford, *Shocking Images*

THE DEAD NEXT DOOR
84 mins. • Cat. No. 8984 • $19.95
Directed by J.R. Bookwalter
A scientist has created the ultimate virus: it takes over and replaces a corpse's cells, using it as a slave to keep supplying its favorite dish...humans! When the virus goes awry, the government fights back with The Zombie Squad. Their mission: save the humans, and seek out and destroy the dead! LIMITED AVAILABILITY! "An epic that surpasses even the scale of Romero's staggering efforts...an example of what can be done outside of the studio system..." - David E. Williams, *Film Threat Video Guide*

DEAD IS DEAD
75 mins. • Cat. No. 1029 • $19.95 • Directed by Mike Stanley
Eric is attacked and partially dismembered by a mutant creature and left for dead. A woman named Laura finds him and uses an experimental drug on him known as Doxital. Eric uses his supply of the drug to pay off a debt, but the Doxital he gives away is a bad batch! Can he get it back in time? "...has a subtle, menacing feel to it, coupled with above-par performances..." - Tom Brown, WHIZ-NBC Radio

OZONE
83 mins. • Cat. No. 8990 • $29.95
Directed by J.R. Bookwalter
AS SEEN IN FANGORIA! "A stylish ride through some cinematic effects that will leave comparable projects in the dust..." - Hugh Gallagher, *Draculina* • "Tremendous! The sense of danger that hangs over this film is highlighted by surprising effects and a moody musical background that softly underscores the on-screen unease. Risky enough to be independent but slick enough to have the feel of a big studio production...it's absolutely worth a look." - Michael Copner, *Cult Movies* • "With a movie like this, Bookwalter is the numero uno choice for cult director of the year!" - *Movie Mania*

WINTERBEAST
80 mins. • Cat. No. 8985 • $9.95 • Directed by Christopher Thies
Something strange is going on up in the mountains of a tiny winter resort community. But this isn't just any mountain...this is the Indian burial ground of the Chakura tribe! Fearless park ranger Whitman and his bumbling right-hand man Stillman are hot on the trail when they meet up with Sheldon, owner of the nearby Wild Goose Lodge who holds dark secret that leads to the Winterbeast! It's action, horror and comedy when *The Evil Dead* meets *Northern Exposure* in *Winterbeast*! NEW LOW PRICE!

GOBLIN
75 mins. • Cat. No. 1031 • $19.95
A newlywed couple move into their new house, but they don't realize that the previous owner of the house raised a monstrous creature from the depths of hell...and now it's coming back to make up for lost time! The Goblin lays waste to the countryside, hungry to kill anything or anyone in its path!

SHRECK
75 mins. • Cat. No. 1033 • $19.95
Roger is a young horror fan living in a house whose previous owner happened to be Max Shreck...a Nazi madman who committed a series of murders in the 50's. On the anniversary of his death, Roger and his friends hold a seance and resurrect Shreck! Now they must battle for their very lives as Shreck attempts to complete a horrifying ritual begun years before any of them were born!

LIMITED VIDEOS $9.95 EACH!
ABOMINATION, THE - Super-gory Super-8mm mutation flick!
ATTACK OF THE KILLER REFRIGERATOR - Ultra-gore!
DISCIPLE OF DEATH - British-made, one of our hottest sellers!
DOCUMENT OF THE DEAD - The classic documentary on the making of George A. Romero's "Dawn of the Dead" and more!
EDGAR ALLAN POE'S MADHOUSE - 3 video tales of terror!
GALACTIC GIGOLO - Ruth Collins! Gorman Bechard directs!
GHOUL SCHOOL - Joe Franklin guest-stars in this romp!
HELLROLLER - Michelle Bauer & Liz Kaitan cameo!
MURDER WEAPON - Linnea Quigley gets naked and kills!
NIGHTMARE ASYLUM - Psychos get their revenge in this epic!
SKINNED ALIVE - It's fun for the whole family...the Mansons!
WOODCHIPPER MASSACRE - Exactly what it sounds like!

BOOKS & OTHER MERCHANDISE
ATTACK OF THE B-MOVIE MAKERS - 2nd printing of this look at films of Fred Ray and David DeCoteau! 100 pgs., $9.95
B-MOVIES IN THE 90'S AND BEYOND by J.R. Bookwalter - The definitive look at low-budget how-to B-moviemaking! 132 pgs., $9.95
ROBOT NINJA & SKINNED ALIVE SOUNDTRACK CASSETTES - 2 for the price of one! 60/50 mins., $9.95 for both!

SHATTER DEAD
84 mins. • Cat. No. 8992 • $29.95
Directed by Scooter McCrae
AS SEEN IN FANGORIA! "McCrae has eschewed the standard trappings of gory zombie movies...emerges as a unique and unsettling entry, mixing religious fervor with our own fears of mortality, desire and belonging. Filled with bizarre and sometimes hilarious imagery as well as extreme but thankfully well-paced and original scenes of violence, *Dead* overcomes its low-budget origins and manages to be both entertaining and disturbingly thought-provoking at the same time. One last warning: devout Christians and pregnant moms will probably be offended right out of the box!" - Art Weingardner, *Alternative Cinema*

ZOMBIE COP
75 mins. • Cat. No. 1572 • $9.95
Directed by J.R. Bookwalter
During what seems to be a routine drug bust, a hardened cop named Gill meets up with a voodoo doctor named Dr. Death. Death is shot while chanting some ritual but manages to kill Gill in the process, cursing his existence for all time! In the following nights, both Gill and Death rise from their graves to carry out life as members of the undead. Gill enlists the help of his human partner and together they track down the ghoulish Death, who is continuing his nefarious plans for world domination!

THE MAJORETTES
92 mins. • Cat. No. 8988 • $9.95 • Directed by Bill Hinzman
Someone's killing the beautiful young majorettes at the local high school! From the first gruesome murder to an ending that literally explodes with violence, you will descend into a high school nightmare where greed, lust and murderous revenge pass for school spirit, where every locker could be hiding a dead body, where the price for being beautiful is paid in blood, and where everyone's favorite subject is the art of survival. From the book by Horror Hall of Famer John A. Russo (*Night of the Living Dead*)! NEW LOW PRICE!

THE SCARE GAME
120 mins. • Cat. No. 8991 • $29.95
Directed by Eric Stanze
Experience a love gone wrong in *The Fine Art*. Valerie meets Bill and a passionate romance begins. Valerie soon discovers that she must not only protect her life...she must defend her mind! *The Scare Game* is contained in its own dimension and is run by a demon who roams the game, collecting the souls of the game's victims. Six players face bloody, violent death with each round of the game. In the final round, the strongest player fights one-on-one with The Game Demon...a fight to the death! Insanity is the game...**death** is the winner!

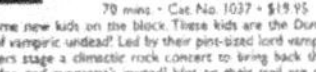

THE WITCHING
72 mins. • Cat. No. 1034 • $19.95
Stewart and Morris think they're about to spend a boring Friday at home watching grandma. But Stewart's house magically becomes the doorway between Earth and Hell, where every closet and refrigerator door hides a portal to a mystical dimension, where they must do battle with evil forces that are both human...and inhuman! It's a wild cinematic broomstick ride!

DOMINION
70 mins. • Cat. No. 1037 • $19.95
There's some new kids on the block. These kids are the Dominion, a battalion of vampiric undead! Led by their pint-sized lord vampire, the bloodsuckers stage a climactic rock concert to bring back their demonic leader, and everyone's invited! Hot on their trail are two unknowing detectives and the terrible tot's sister!

GALAXY OF THE DINOSAURS
75 mins. • Cat. No. 1578 • $9.95 • Directed by Lance Randas
Stopping for a brief lunch break on the planet Gurgon, innocent Zyroxans encounter complete chaos and terror as a race of ferocious dinosaurs are hell-bent on turning a field trip into a full-fledged fright fest! The Zyroxans go head-to-head with these prehistoric psychos! BRAND-NEW REMASTERED DIRECTOR'S EDITION! "A classic of its kind...deserves a nomination for the Golden Turkey Awards!" - Peter Gray, *Cult Movies*

SHOCK CINEMA VOLS. 1-4
60 mins. ea. • $9.95 ea.
Vol. 1 (Cat. No. 1567) - Interviews with Charles Band, Fred Olen Ray, Jeff Burr, Scott Spiegel, David DeCoteau & more!
Vol. 2 (Cat. No. 1568) - Interviews with Forrest J Ackerman, Robert Quarry, Steve Neill, Dearna Lund, Melissa Moore and more!
Vol. 3 (Cat. No. 1570) - *Bloopers, Babes and Blood* is a gruesome sixty minutes chock full of your favorite gore trailers and bloopers!
Vol. 4 (Cat. No. 1571) - *B-Movie Makeup Effects* is an in-depth look behind-the-scenes at movie magic!

THE ZOMBIE ARMY
80 mins. • Cat. No. 1030 • $19.95 • Directed by Betty Stapleford
Army Sergeant Saddow has a problem. The Pentagon bought a former insane asylum to use as a base for the elite female unit The Lethal Ladies. The problem is they didn't check the asylum fallout shelter for leftover inmates! Two were left behind when the nuthouse was abandoned and are now wreaking havoc upon the Army by capturing soldiers and turning them into mindless zombies. Watch out, Saddam Hussein...you're no match for Operation "Zombie" Storm and... *The Zombie Army*!

ZOMBIE RAMPAGE
81 mins. • Cat. No. 1580 • $9.95
Directed by Todd Sheets
A young man is caught in a web of terror when he tries to meet his friends at the train station for a reunion. Unfortunately, he never makes it. What he does do, however, is stumble into a nightmare world full of zombies, inner-city gangs and serial killers. *Zombie Rampage* is full of state-of-the-art makeup effects, some of which are the most graphic ever captured on film. *Zombie Rampage* supplies full-throttle action and graphic violence...it's definitely not for the squeamish or faint of heart!

ZOMBIE '90: EXTREME PESTILENCE
80 mins. • Cat. No. RG02 • $29.95 • Directed by Andreas Schnaas
Guts and gore, splatter and more. A new lesson in real bad taste from the makers of *Violent Shit*. A military machine carrying unrested lethal chemicals crashes into a forest. Two doctors discover the epidemic and take on the hopeless fight against the living dead. A gruelling shocker that sets new standards in the modern gore film, directed by Andreas Schnaas. Dubbed English language version. Theatrical-sized posters are also available (please call or write for price).

BIMBOS B.C.
75 mins. • Cat. No. 1582 • $9.95
A Barbarian woman is attacked while on a routine hunting mission. She pulls herself to a building that turns out to be a fortress for prehistoric bimbos! When they discover that their Queen has been bitten by a radioactive beast, the bimbos begin a quest to find an antidote to save the Queen from the deadly poison.

PREHISTORIC BIMBOS IN ARMAGEDDON CITY
70 mins. • Cat. No. 1032 • $19.95
Welcome to the last remaining outpost of civilization after World War III. Though the city is ruled by the evil Nemesis and his army of cyborgs, the only thing standing in the way of utter post-nuclear domination is Trianna and her fierce, beautiful tribe of Prehistoric Bimbos! Strap yourself in! NEW REMASTERED EDITION!

SORORITY BABES IN THE DANCE-A-THON OF DEATH
75 mins. • Cat. No. 1035 • $19.95
Four sorority sisters conjure up a demon within an ancient crystal ball. To their rescue comes two nerdy frat boys looking for an easy score. But only two elderly antique dealers can rescue them from destruction...until they've taken their ghoulfest to the dance-a-thon of death! The biggest, boobiest bimbo-fest of them all!

KINGDOM OF THE VAMPIRE
75 mins. • Cat. No. 1573 • $9.95
Jeff lives at home with his mother. He has a night job in a liquor store. He looks pretty good for a vampire that's ninety years old. But Jeff's mother is a terrible hag who has a habit of killing children in her bloodthirsty rages. When Jeff meets Nina, mother has other plans for her!

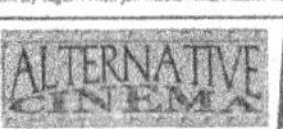

ALTERNATIVE CINEMA

The ultimate B-movie magazine has arrived! Published quarterly, ALTERNATIVE CINEMA is the definitive source for B-movie news, previews and home video & laserdisc reviews. Our first two issues featured exclusive coverage of J.R. Bookwalter's OZONE, Roger Corman's New Horizons Home Video, the films of Andreas Schnaas and Olaf Ittenbach, supporting actor spotlights on Christine Taylor and Ami Dolenz, the making of DARKNESS, Full Moon's new erotic fantasy label Torchlight, SHATTER DEAD, the best in B-movie reviews and editorials and all of the latest and greatest from the independent film world! Each issue is just $2.95 (plus $1 postage); a 1-year, 4-issue subscription is $15, a 2-year, 8-issue sub is $25 (postage included). Make check or money order payable to ALTERNATIVE CINEMA when purchasing magazines.

TO ORDER
Send a check or money order
payable to: **TEMPE VIDEO**
P.O. Box 6573, Akron, OH. 44312-0573.

Add shipping charges: UPS Ground $4.00 for one item, $6.00 for two or more items. UPS C.O.D. orders add $5.00. Sorry, no credit card orders. Overseas shipping is $20.00 for one item, $25 for two or more items in U.S. funds only. OH. residents add 6.25% sales tax. Sign that you are 18 years of age or older and include your phone number. All titles are new, factory-sealed SP-speed VHS NTSC videotapes (please call for PAL versions). No illegal dubs. No refunds, exchange for defects only. Allow 2-4 weeks for delivery. C.O.D. orders may be faxed to (716) 628-4316 or call (216) 628-1950.

Tempe Video Direct ad from **Film Threat Video Guide #11** (1994)

viewers would forget the trilogy and focus instead on his current and future projects.[1] Still working to define his voice early in his career, and hampered by the demands of commissioned storylines, Sheets found himself employed as a journeyman exploitation director rather than creating more personal art.

1 Sheets letter, p.6.

The films released by Cinema are crude even in their revised versions, to the point that many would question their suitability for distribution at all. Writing on the films Sheets completed for DeCoteau under his deal with Cinema, Robert W. Butler of the **Kansas City Star** notes that the early films "are, indeed, pretty horrible, with muffled sound, incomprehensible plots, amateurish acting and violence that would be offensive if it weren't so cartoonish. Unless you're a dyed-in-the wool splatter addict, they're just about unwatchable."[1] In effect, they embody the perception of SOV horror as the ultimate in generic marginalia. **Edgar Allan Poe's Madhouse** (1992),[2] confirms these assertions. Completed in just two days—filming, editing, music, and all post-production elements—the anthology is completely disjointed but nonetheless touches on several of Sheets' recurring aesthetic touches. Comprised of four stories allegedly based on Poe's fiction yet bearing no discernible traces of his influence (the first story cuts in a portion of his later 1992 release **Dominion**, while the third segment is Sheets' own 1986 backwoods horror short **Dead Things**), there is no rhyme or reason to the feature's content. Sheets appears as the host at the start wearing a cape, is replaced midway through by a female storyteller dressed as a witch, and closes the anthology out himself in a new location and wearing a different outfit.

The audio and picture quality are identical to **Zombie Rampage** and the **Bimbos** trilogy, the segments having been filmed around the same time or earlier and sent to DeCoteau for consideration. Gore effects are plentiful but are rudimentary raw meat and Karo syrup displays, lacking any sort of refinement or craftsmanship in their intent to shock. Tonia Monahan and Veronica Orr appear again, reflecting the loyal contributor base Sheets had built to assist with production, and the soundtrack is provided by Enochian Key. The settings alternate between Sheets' own bedroom for his introductory sequence, to an abandoned factory building in the first story, nondescript wooded locales for the second as well as "Dead Things," and a local historical

1 "Blood on a budget."

2 My timeline is approximate and based largely on guesswork; Sheets' own filmography lists the production dates of titles, not their distribution dates—thus **Nightmare Asylum** is credited 1990, but Cinema tapes list a 1992 copyright; likewise, **Goblin** is listed by the director as 1991 despite its 1993 release by Video Outlaw.

attraction for the final segment. Throughout these, however, Sheets makes use of expressive colored lighting which suggests the influence of Dario Argento and would be a hallmark of his later features. Although the urban ruins that defined **Zombie Rampage** are again employed, they nevertheless serve as suitably desolate locations for the horrific events of the tales. By this point, Sheets demonstrated a greater awareness of *mise en scène* and how it contributes to the effectiveness of works limited by their budgets. In particular, the abandoned train station and dilapidated shack featured in "Dead Things" give the story an atmospheric menace denied by the amateur acting and presentation. Even working with recycled content, Sheets reveals a resourcefulness at making what little was available to him as impactful as possible. Expressing disappointment with the film shortly after its release, he nonetheless displays some pride in noting "[for] a movie made in two days, it's OK."[1]

1992 saw Sheets making several additional contributions to the horror video market. **Edgar Allan Poe's Madhouse** was followed by **Nightmare Asylum**, a $500 production taking place entirely in a local haunted house during its off-season. As a result, the film is a rambling series of set pieces relying on the attraction's props and an increased amount of gore effects to drive its limited narrative. Regular collaborator Jerry Angell appears in his first significant role, while Sheets himself plays the patriarch of a cannibal family, complete with a poor southern accent. This is where Sheets' fandom and self-aware humor make their most notable appearances, with not only the obvious nods to Tobe Hooper's **The Texas Chain Saw Massacre** (1974), but easter eggs referencing George Romero, Wes Craven, and John Carpenter. **Nightmare Asylum** is less a coherent narrative film than an excuse for Sheets and his friends to experiment with graphic effects and props given free rein in the local attraction. This speaks to the democratic nature of the direct-sale VHS market, there being no other realm in which a film so elliptical and crude would see release and moderate success.

Nightmare Asylum is a film made for no one save its creator and his collaborators, despite its guaranteed release by DeCoteau. Still, a

1 "Blood on a budget."

number of impressive qualities speak to the director's growing talent for video filmmaking, not the least of which is the resourcefulness of his $500 budget. Sheets again demonstrates a utilitarian ability to get the most from his materials, relying on the attraction's props to populate his *mise en scène*. Similarly, the high key colored lighting and fog machines utilized create a palpable, if no less cheap, atmosphere that is heightened by the confounding construction of the actual haunted house itself. There are plenty of low, canted angles and short takes, with the stark sets rendered surreal (even as the film itself is decidedly not) by their unplaceable appearances. The minimalism of the setting works surprisingly well, with even the cheap rubber haunted house props peppered throughout (bloody mannequins hung on meat hooks, Styrofoam heads littering the floor) proving effective. Ultimately, the presentation veers into the instability implied by the title, even as the film recalls a community theater production of a haunted house walkthrough more than a feature film.

Even as a narrative feature film, **Nightmare Asylum** recalls Laurie Oullette's discussion of camcorder television programming. Writing about amateur video submissions infiltrating American prime time television in the mid-1990s, Oullette argues that the "notion that ordinary people might make TV instead of just watching poses a potentially subversive threat to capitalist control of the media."[1] While Sheets' films and other 1990s SOV productions never posed a realistic threat to the industrial dominance of Hollywood, they nonetheless represent a subversive alternative for those unimpressed with the sanitized mainstream output of that decade. Reaching back further, the earliest SOV features did best the major studios in delivering video product where the corporate industry was hesitant and concerned more with copyright infringement than harnessing the technology's potential for revenue. The surprise success of **Blood Cult** was a legitimate example of alternative video product usurping the mainstream media's control over the film industry. As Lucas Hilderbrand outlines, prior to the introduction of major studio releases on the home video market, pornography was the most notable success of the early video era.[2]

1 Oullette, p.33.
2 Hilderbrand, p.56.

ALSO AVAILABLE FROM TEMPE VIDEO:

1993 · 70 Mins. · Cat. No. 1032
Unrated · Fantasy-Comedy

Welcome to Old Chicago City...the last remaining outpost of civilization after World War III. Though the city is ruled by the evil Nemesis (Robert Vollrath) and his army of cyborgs, the only thing standing in the way of utter post-nuclear domination is Trianna (Tonia Monahan) and her fierce, beautiful tribe of Prehistoric Bimbos! When Nemesis, with the help of the metal-clawed tyrant Salacious Thatch (Deric Bernier) attempts to destroy the Bimbos once and for all, he quickly discovers it's not going to be as easy as he thought! Filled with wacky action, goofy creatures, scenery chewing villains, and enough bimbos to fill *two* post-nuclear action comedies, this film will blow your mind. Strap yourself in and prepare yourself for...*Prehistoric Bimbos In Armageddon City!*

1993 · 75 Mins. · Cat. No. 1031
Unrated · Horror

A newlywed couple (Bobby Westrick & Jenny Admire) move into their new house with the help of their friends. But what they don't realize is that twenty years ago, the previous owner of the house--a farmer practicing witchcraft--inadvertently raised a monstrous creature from the depths of hell...and now it's coming back to make up for lost time! The Goblin, set free from its dark prison within the earth, lays waste to the Missouri countryside, hungry to mangle or kill anything or anyone in its path. The young people, trapped inside the house, are pushed to the nightmarish extremes, forced to retaliate...or become the next victim of the *Goblin!* *Goblin* delivers unbelievable scenes of violence and gore...just pray he doesn't deliver them to your doorstep!

A Division of Tempe Video

Tempe Video Ad from **The B's Nest #11** (1993)

Long equated by detractors, horror and pornographic films shared the common trait of early arrival on the home video market and found success to the surprise of all major parties. Though Oullette's essay avoids discussion of video-lensed feature films of any nature, there is a clear connection to the potential of features shot-on-video seeing legitimate distribution.

Removed from the heyday of early video pornography as well as the open market of the 1980s video store boom, Sheets' films released through Cinema, Video Outlaw, and his own labels were all part of this tradition of subversive media realized through the analog video medium. Recalling the earlier legal wrangling surrounding Beta and VHS technology, Oullette argues that "usually privatized domestic images created by non-professionals are worthy of broader public exposure [which] has been emphasized from the beginning."[1] Sheets' films proved successful enough among the growing underground horror audience of the 1990s to see release regardless of their contents. Their quality notwithstanding, the many tapes bearing his name were fixtures on the genre scene, existing alongside dozens of like-minded works to fill the place of mainstream horror cinema. As much as they were honest expressions of the directors' creativity

1 Oullette, p.37.

and visions, these films were legitimate outliers to the traditional cinematic studio system. Their subversive nature rests not so much on their chances of financial success as their sheer existence and dissemination through a grassroots network established by other fans and artists.

Watching Sheets' earliest films in sequence, their inherent videobility becomes readily apparent: limited by numerous constraints (budgetary, technical, and performative), they never falter in their commitment to the material, transforming their low-grade, consumer video origins into positive attributes. His next 1992 release by Cinema, **Dominion**, represents a moment of legitimate filmmaking growth, taking Sheets' stories out into the world of suburban homes and businesses rather than downtown alleyways and abandoned industrial spaces. At the same time, **Dominion** most strikingly presents his filmmaking as a matter of personal expression, the work of an amateur still driven by passion and fandom as much as careerist aspirations. The entire film builds to a performance by Enochian Key, which includes Jerry Angell in addition to Sheets himself, who takes a break from his traditional cameo roles to concentrate on behind-the-scenes work and lets his growing cast of regulars tell his story. At one point, Sheets' protagonist expresses her desire to attend the concert to her skeptical parents, who dismiss Enochian Key as dangerous, satanic metal. She insists on the band's positive qualities and messages, arguing "they sing against Satan." Sheets inserts his own beliefs directly into his film, reinforcing his faith by centering the argument on his own band and presence. Underneath this, the scene imbues the film with a believable generational tension and family drama that is far more successful due to its proximity to the director's own life.

This more personal approach is complemented by relative aesthetic maturity, indicating his progress over just a few short years. Ostensibly a straightforward vampire story, **Dominion** manages to bring the atmospheric touches that were developed in earlier videos to the forefront, delivering a work that is consistent in its approach rather than offering a smattering of allusions and reference points. The narrative of a sect of vampires living in tunnels beneath Kansas City, led by ageless child Cabal, is imaginative and ambitious beyond the scope of anything Sheets had previously made. The scenes set in the vampires' underground lair are spare, employing the setting for mood rather than the utilitarian approach to abandoned spaces just a few films prior. Interior scenes in suburban homes are supplied with muted lighting that is naturalistic, but also adds a grim and foreboding mood to the entirely nocturnal proceedings of the film. Of course, these atmospheric touches are also tempered with a heightened amount of onscreen carnage, featuring dissolving vampire corpses and fists rammed through torsos with gruesome results. At this point, Sheets finally struck the balance between genre aesthetics, personal expression, and hardcore bloodletting that had defined his own fandom if not yet his art.

The following year brought the release of Sheets' most infamous and ambitious films. **Goblin** is an odd step backward from the subjective elements of **Dominion**, occurring in a single setting and featuring the filmmaker's most extreme gore effects to date. Beginning with Jerry Angell swearing while cutting weeds in the dark, the film is a bizarre meditation on mundanity and its disruption, filtered through the lens of a supernatural slasher. Following Angell's death by the titular creature—who wears denim shorts and light washed blue jeans in alternating scenes—the plot shifts to a group of friends helping two members of their circle move into their new home, an abandoned farmhouse. The act of moving initiates everything that follows, this banal chore leading to the Goblin being summoned from a spell book discovered in an old trunk. Late in the film, one character even expresses the sentiment that the house is "a symbol of you guys fighting and winning." Much like **Dominion's** generational strife, the quiet domesticity of everyday life undergirds the supernatural action of the film. This effect is also heightened by the film's ability to capture a particular time and place convincingly and down to the smallest details. As much as it serves as an exercise in gross-out effects, **Goblin** is ultimately a portrait of average people doing ordinary things and finding their comfortable lives disrupted by horrific circumstances.

The ¾" video is as rough and grainy as each of the previous films, denying any technical refinement. The editing is Sheets' most proficient to this point, intercutting between the survivors unaware of the violence outside and the elaborate kills with surprising fluidity. Despite this, the kill scenes revel in prurient bloodletting, with each murder receiving extensive close-ups as the Goblin disembowels his prey; several scenes last a number of minutes as the creature smashes cuts of meat between its claws and frothy brown gore sputters in the background. There is also a pronounced obsession with anal and genital trauma, with multiple characters receiving scythes and claws in their crotches before being disassembled. This particular fixation led one later reviewer to call the film "68 minutes of a monster pulling stuff out of people's holes while other people walk around the exterior of a house."[1] In fact, this onscreen violence proved to be a breaking point for the distributor, with Sheets noting that the film was originally made for DeCoteau, who found it "too gruesome even for him."[2] J.R. Bookwalter's Video Outlaw ultimately stepped in to release the feature, cementing the director's alliance with one of underground horror's most identifiable labels of the 1990s.[3]

If **Goblin** is the most notorious of Sheets' early-90s SOV releases, then **Zombie Bloodbath** (1993) is his most highly regarded work. Accumulating equipment as his career progressed by investing film revenues into his next productions and working toward improving his technical craftsmanship, Sheets finally had the means to match his growing cinematic talents. The communal aspect of Trustinus further encouraged this progress, as cast and crew members agreed to work for free until significant profits were generated.[4] Each film through 1993 served its purpose of contributing to the director's legacy and making his name on the home video market, with an eye always on future endeavors. Expressing disappointment with his previous work, while also providing the sort of honest self-assessment that is rare in the world of underground cinema, Sheets notes that he had not been completely satisfied with any film prior to **Zombie Bloodbath**, but was generally pleased with their outcomes considering their limitations. Prior to its release, the director announced **Zombie Bloodbath** as something special, his first truly serious project, and his most ambitious. Made on a budget of $26,000 thanks to local investors

1 Ziemba, **1990s**, p.115.

2 "Blood, beasties."

3 Around this time, Tempe/Video Outlaw acquired the rights to the Cinema Home Video catalog once DeCoteau folded his company to focus on his own filmmaking once more, making Bookwalter the distributor of several of Sheets' films ("Tempe Adds," p.1).

4 "Invasion of the incredibly cheap."

as well as the profits from his earlier releases, the film was a massive event in Kansas City as well as the broader horror underground. Self-deprecating and good-humored as always, Sheets joked "you could say I'm out of the trash can now and sitting on the rim. I still make trash, but now the acting and effects are good."[1] Never intended as serious art, Sheets's largest production was meant to deliver the most satisfying, entertaining movie possible while elevating his own reputation.

The film's budget is important to note regarding Sheets' commitment to video filmmaking. Despite a claim that it was budgeted at $8,000 in the pages of **Alternative Cinema** (still a huge leap over **Goblin's** $800-900 finances), the film's actual budget cements it as one of the more

BIMBOS IN TIME
Cat. No. 13501 • $29.95
From the video hits *Bimbos B.C.* and *Prehistoric Bimbos in Armageddon City* come these ferocious female warriors out to smash all evil that comes their way! When Salacious Thatch starts up an old nuclear reactor, it opens a time door, sucking our favorite buxom beauties into another dimension and spiralling them through time! Full of action, girls and exciting special effects, this is one hilarious film that will keep you laughing out loud from beginning to end!

ZOMBIE BLOODBATH
Cat. No. 13502 • $29.95
Zombie Bloodbath will shock and scare you like no other zombie film can! A non-stop rollercoaster ride that will keep you on the edge of your seat and leave you breathless! Gory state-of-the-art special effects and exciting action will leave you screaming for more! The dead rise and begin tearing through a small town...can they be stopped? Watch this exciting horror film and see!

BLOODTHIRSTY CANNIBAL DEMONS
Cat. No. 13503 • $29.95
A group of crazy teenagers break into an abandoned old theatre and kill the owners. They dump their bodies in the basement and wake up the *Cannibal Demons* that have been locked there for over a hundred years. The demons attack the teenagers one by one until only a handful are left. But that's not the worst part...the people killed by the demons will return to life as demons! As the evil population grows, it's up to these brave teens to save the future of all mankind. Will they make it? Watch this film and find out!

❑ BIMBOS IN TIME ❑ ZOMBIE BLOODBATH
❑ BLOODTHIRSTY CANNIBAL DEMONS
$29.95 for ea. tape. Shipping add $3.50 per video, $5.00 for two or more videos. Mail orders to: TEMPE VIDEO, P.O. Box 6573, Akron, OH. 44312-0573.

Name ______
Address ______
City ______ State ______ Zip ______

Ohio residents add 6.25% sales tax. UPS C.O.D. add $5. Check or money order in U.S. funds only. Make all checks payable to TEMPE VIDEO. For UPS C.O.D. delivery, please call (216) 628-1950 or FAX your order to (216) 628-4318. Allow 2-4 weeks for delivery. Sorry, no credit card orders. Videos are VHS NTSC only.

Asylum Home Video/Tempe ad from **Alternative Cinema #1** (1994)

1 "Zombie Bloodbath."

expensive SOV horror projects of its time.[1] Comparable to the production costs allotted by United for **Blood Cult** eight years earlier, yet just over half the sum required to make **Zombie Rampage**, the director by now had a clear understanding of the financial elements of filmmaking. In order to make a more "serious" film, Sheets knew that heightened production value would contribute to the overall success of the finished project, especially as far as audience and personal satisfaction. A $26,000 (or even $8,000) budget was by far enough to shoot on film, giving the production a more traditionally acceptable appearance and pedigree. Leif Jonker's **Darkness**, another gory underground horror sensation from 1993, was shot on Super 8 film with a $2,000 starting budget (that ballooned to nearly $20,000 by the end of post-production).[2] Whether due to his own comfort with video as a medium and his accumulated equipment, or the start-up costs of beginning in film production, Sheets stuck with his previous format and stayed devoted to SOV production.

The leap in production quality is immediately evident, as the video picture and audio qualities are markedly improved. Now shot on Hi-8 video, the image is clear, a step beyond the murky ¾" image quality of the previous releases. The film's lighting is also much more effective, with Sheets employing his trademark filtered color lights to add depth to scenes rather than mere accents of color, providing a deeper palette than previously seen. The massive cast, which saw over 700 extras employed to portray the horde of zombies throughout the film, also reflects his growing ambition and comfort on set. While Auggi Alvarez, Jerry Angell, Tonia Monahan and other regulars still comprise the primary cast, their performances are more convincing, clearly a result of Sheets' own growth as a director, now able to elicit stronger showings from his team. The audience is not thrust into the film's action as in previous features but instead presented with an inciting incident and offered detailed explanations of just why the outbreak is occurring. Introductions to characters and plot developments are measured, given serious consideration and built upon continuously rather than offered as simple asides. A large reason for the film's narrative clarity is its use of a broader world, from

1 "Missouri Invaded," p.50; Gallagher, #17, p.28.
2 Collins, p.4.

Ad for Leif Jonker's **Darkness, Film Threat Video Guide #9** (1993)

military boardrooms (filmed in a local municipal building) to suburban homes and open exterior spaces. These elements all work to give the film a feeling of legitimacy, playing as a cinematic production with cross-audience appeal rather than an amateur passion project.

The plot is fairly simple: a reactor meltdown at a military facility forces evacuation after zombies kill the site's personnel. Five years later, public housing is built on the property, and a gang terrorizing the city dumps bodies in the underground tunnel leading to the former power plant which houses zombies. A group of teenage friends and their parents flee several zombie attacks and must unite to survive the onslaught of undead creatures. Later, it is revealed that the reactors were built on a Native American burial ground after the tribe's descendants lost a court battle for the land and placed a curse on the area. Despite the potential for social commentary on the United States military, ecological issues, and American relations with indigenous populations, most of these elements pass without much comment. Where Sheets does add surprising depth is in the interactions between his characters, who appear as well-rounded people rather than victims. Sheets manages to legitimately engender sympathy and attachment to his characters, with the parents sharing stories of loss and grief that are stunted but succeed in their sincerity and effort. When Angell's character, Larry, is killed midway through the film, it represents a significant moment, one met with grief and actual consideration of his and his family's lives. His wife and children are shown in shock, delusional and devastated to the best of the actors' abilities. The film slows for several minutes to express their agony; Larry's death is not just another gory thrill. Incredibly, this all occurs despite the fact that his intestines are ripped out through his anus (recalling **Goblin's** anal violence fixation). Later, his wife kills her youngest children and then herself in a startling murder-suicide that is not played for shock effect.

In its most readily available version, as part of Camp Motion Pictures' **Zombie Bloodbath Trilogy** collection, the revised **Zombie Bloodbath** distinctly bears its alterations. The credits have been redone using digital technology and the runtime is truncated by nearly fifteen minutes to remove portions the director was unhappy with initially. Much like the Polonia brothers' Camp DVD release of **Splatter Farm**, Sheets has taken a revisionist approach to his film's legacy. In reworking his film, Sheets was clear that his intention was "making it closer to what I wanted. Maybe there was an effect that didn't come out right...with the digital revolution, I'm able to go in and remove those [mistakes]."[1] Here, Sheets' SOV projects diverge, albeit

1 "'Zombie' auteur."

retrospectively, from Lyotard's definition of acinema. The original edit of **Zombie Bloodbath** "produces true, that is vain, simulacrums, blissful intensities, instead of productive/consumable objects," a statement just as true of the extant versions of his previous productions.[1] SOV horror often revels in excess, whether it be extreme gore and juvenile scatology as in the case of **Goblin**, or the meandering stretches of **Nightmare Asylum**. As much as Sheets and his contemporaries embodied acinema in their enthusiastic naivete, they did not aspire to it, and made no conscious decisions to create works bearing the intensity of incongruity that Lyotard praises.

Underground cinema as a whole, and the horror genre in particular, are natural exercises in vanity; although Sheets relies upon his crew and collaborators, his name is centered, marketable and recognizable to SOV fans. While the 2007 re-envisioning of **Zombie Bloodbath** suits his aspirations as an amateur filmmaker turned professional, remedying the mistakes that were never intended for release, it deprives the work of some rough charm. Erika Balsom, speaking on the question of authenticity and the reproducibility of film/video media, notes that the copy "offers greater access and availability but also threatens to liquidate uniqueness and historicity."[2] Now out of print, Camp's DVD release is still the most accessible means of viewing Sheets' signature film, and provided him with his widest distribution and exposure, with advertisements in genre bible **Fangoria**, which routinely excluded his works from coverage at the time of their initial releases. This retrospective appreciation is overdue given the director's tenure in the genre industry, but without the original rough edits of his features, it is unlikely that Sheets would have attracted such devotion.

The re-release does not make **Zombie Bloodbath** any less notable, nor does it undermine his commitment to the video format. In particular, the matter of video-as-filmmaking connects to a debate that raged between the fans and creators of horror features at the height of the direct-to-video era. SOV horror by nature has a limited appeal, from its amateurish acting and presentation to its often-grating

1 Lyotard, p.54.
2 Balsom, p.26.

incoherence. Throughout the 1990s, there were discussions about just how to present one's work as something distinct and valuable against the perceived disposability and glut of lesser features that flooded the market. In an interview with Hugh Gallagher for **Draculina**, Sheets expresses his pride in being a horror filmmaker working and succeeding with video, before calling out his contemporaries who make "films where some 17 year old (sic) went out in the back yard with Aunt Martha and his best buddy and shot a movie called **Splatter Farm**...that shit's gonna go, it's making a bad name for me."[1] Sheets was aware of his unique and marginal place in the horror film world, but aspired to a standard of quality that was rarely attainable. His valuing of his own work over the Polonia brothers' debut ignited a good deal of controversy in the magazine's pages that lasted through the next several issues. Responding to Sheets, Mark Polonia challenges his comments, noting that **Splatter Farm** was by then almost ten years old, a movie made by teenagers for $100 that was fortunate enough to see release and launch his and his brother's careers. Challenging Sheets' Christian charity, as well as the shoddy construction of **Goblin**, Mark suggests that Todd contact him directly as they are acquaintances. Writing in the same issue, Sheets apologizes for his comments, noting "we must all stick together...today's independents need to grow up and learn the business...some of my film's (sic) were real trash, but they were entertaining trash!".[2]

Sheets later apologized for his negativity, taking a deprecating stance on his own previous releases. Noting that they made money and seemed better at the time of completion, they are still "trash" bearing his name, a fact that embarrasses the director but is unavoidable. Sheets closes by stating that all he truly meant was to "pull us all together to make some quality work...We can and will get better with each film."[3] This call for unity among SOV filmmakers was necessary, as craftsmen working on the fringes of the already marginal independent film industry. Even the underground press seemed poised to attack Sheets and other SOV directors regardless of their successes and best efforts. Despite a long profile on the director

1 Gallagher, #17, p.30.
2 Sheets letter, #18, p.5.
3 Sheets letter, #19, p.51.

Main Force Pictures ad from **Draculina #18** (1994)

in its premiere issue, **Alternative Cinema** includes a review of **Zombie Bloodbath** that ends by proclaiming it "Sheets' best movie...but he's going to have to do better than this if he wants to bring his own brand of homegrown gore to today's very jaded gore movie fans."[1] Sheets recurs throughout **Alternative Cinema** as a regular whipping boy, with

1 Griffith, #1, p.50.

writer David Wagner's Worst of 1993 films list consisting entirely of Todd Sheets films.[1] A review of 1993's **Bloodthirsty Cannibal Demons** notes the film's "amateurish acting, amateurish writing, amateurish direction, amateurish camera work, and amateurish effects...the same old *crap* you've seen in every other Todd Sheets movie."[2] Perhaps most damning, an op-ed section on "Camcorder Movies" derides rival publication **Independent Video** as "the Todd Sheets of magazines."[3] While other SOV directors (particularly Todd Cook) drew similar ire from the supposed champions of independent genre cinema, Sheets himself was made an example of all that was wrong with the cycle of films in the 1990s.

In his "Center Stage" review of **Zombie Bloodbath 2: Rage of the Undead** (1995), Bookwalter remarks on the "complaints and outright condemnations I've received from other filmmakers who feel [Sheets'] presence in **Alternative Cinema** makes the rest of us look bad."[4] At the same time, Sheets' omnipresence in the pages of **Draculina** and **Alternative Cinema**, as well as his films' distribution by Bookwalter's labels, reflects the fiscal nature of the underground horror marketplace. Despite the constant ridicule from contributors and even publisher Bookwalter, the director attracted his widest audience through their coverage. Issues of **Alternative Cinema** lambasting Sheets' work feature Tempe ads for his tapes, and Bookwalter was inspired enough by his efforts to offer constructive criticism as a legitimate act of goodwill. As a crucial, prolific fixture on the SOV horror scene, Sheets delivered product regularly and had a recognizable aesthetic as well as a growing resume, which did not absolve him of perceived cinematic wrongs. That said, his films would have fallen into obscurity like countless other titles reviewed in the magazines if they were not proving successful for the distributors. Sheets also found success abroad, with his films attracting audiences in Asia, resulting in licensing deals in Japan and Malaysia.[5] Not only did his efforts secure a loyal fanbase at home in Kansas City via his

1 Wagner, #4, p.37.
2 Wagner, #2, p.51.
3 "Taking Sides," pp.57-58.
4 Bookwalter, #4, p.56.
5 **ZB** Making Of

"The Home of the Killer B's!"

P.O. Box 6573 · Akron, OH. 44312
Phone & FAX: (216) 628-1950
Toll-Free Orders: (800) 666-4679

TEMPE VIDEO is our main distribution label which caters to the horror/sci-fi/fantasy crowd, featuring quirky movies big and small--*all unrated*--that we exclusively package and market to video retailers and collectors. In addition, we are feature producers! Our credits include such films as *The Dead Next Door*, *Robot Ninja* and many more. *Night of the Living Dead* co-creator John A. Russo has recently joined up with us to distribute his horror hits *Heartstopper* and *The Majorettes* as well as to co-produce *Midnight 2: Sex, Death and Videotape*.

To cater to the more daring video viewer, we have introduced VIDEO OUTLAW...a sister label catering to offbeat shot-on-video features from all genres. VIDEO OUTLAW has been formed to offer only the most unique and *unrated* video-lensed features we can find, giving a new generation of filmmakers an outlet to have their product packaged and marketed with the dignity and respect it deserves!

All of our TEMPE VIDEO/VIDEO OUTLAW titles include *The B's Nest Video Magazine*, which includes celebrity interviews and behind-the-scenes footage of all of the low-budget features we distribute. This exclusive video bonus also features coming attractions, merchandise for sale and more!

But TEMPE VIDEO is also your home for one-stop mail-order B-video buying! In addition to our own titles, our product list includes over 500 videos from all genres: horror, sci-fi, comedy, T&A, action, black and much more, **all priced from $10 and up!!**

Send $1.00 today to receive a FREE sample issue of our newsletter The B's Nest which includes a price list and much more or call today to order any of our TEMPE VIDEO or VIDEO OUTLAW product!

COMING SOON:
The Majorettes ✦ Quest for the Monkey God
J.R. Bookwalter's Ozone ✦ Goblin ✦ Shreck
Prehistoric Bimbos in Armageddon City
Sorority Babes in the Dance-A-Thon of Death
Dominion ✦ "Night of the Living Dead" 25th Anniversary Documentary *and much more!*

Tempe Video/Video Outlaw Ad promoting forthcoming Sheets titles from **The B's Nest #11** (1993)

regular collaborators and the local media, but his business savvy put Sheets in a unique position to capitalize on his efforts and reach greater audiences than many SOV filmmakers working at the same point in time.

As much as he suffered in their pages, Sheets' legacy was largely made through the coverage of these fanzines. More importantly, however, his relentless prolificacy and commitment to his art above all else (even when vocally not considering it to be "Art") allowed Sheets to establish himself as a crucial voice in the world of horror on home video. His reliance on video was not a purely economic means of production, and neither was it a matter of familiarity or training, as some of his earliest shorts had been completed using Super 8, mirroring the trajectory of many SOV directors throughout their careers. Without the low cost and high flexibility of analog video, there is no doubt that Sheets would have been unable to sustain such a tireless stream of releases throughout the early 1990s. The format itself enabled his productivity as much as his own creative impulse, and his mastery of the technology contributed to his growing proficiency as a filmmaker.

Video as Longevity

SHEETS' COMMITMENT TO the video format continued throughout the 1990s, with other notable titles **Moonchild** (1994), the ambitious **Zombie Bloodbath 2: Rage of the Undead** (1995), and **Violent New Breed** (1997) numbering as just a few examples of his continuing output. To this day he continues to work with digital video, with this career-long usage of the format mirroring the path of horror auteurs treading similar ground. Oullette suggested that home recorded content and camcorder antics were the future of popular entertainment, yet low-budget would-be auteurs have long appropriated the technology for their own ends. While the successes of the 1980s laid the foundation for Sheets and his contemporaries, the filmmakers working within the SOV cycle in the 1990s harnessed the ultimate expression of video's accessibility and in many ways revolutionized the mode of cinematic production. Resistant as audiences were to the look of analog video, the evolution of the technology gradually led to its widespread adoption by even the dominant filmmaking industry.

Of course, this shift was slow, largely reserved for independent and low-budget features throughout the late 1990s and early 2000s. In fact, digital video's industry dominance and the death of the celluloid standard did not fully take effect until years after the production of analog video and VHS had ceased. With the majority of film releases now made using high-grade video equipment, it is important not to overlook

Ad for J.R. Bookwalter's **The Dead Next Door, Film Threat Video Guide #3** (1991)

the filmmakers working in the horror genre alongside Sheets who recognized video's potential as a means of egalitarian production. These men and others realized that adopting video was not only an acceptable continuation of their previous celluloid efforts, but also the most plausible means of extending their careers as low-budget filmmakers.

Prior to the founding of the Tempe and Video Outlaw labels, not to mention the publication of **Alternative Cinema**, J.R. Bookwalter made his name in the underground film scene with his own Super 8 zombie epic, **The Dead Next Door** (1988). With assistance from **The Evil Dead's** Sam Raimi, and a budget that grew to $125,000, Bookwalter knew firsthand the limitations and tribulations associated with producing works on film. Following the release of his debut, Bookwalter lived hand to mouth making horror films however possible, sustaining his passion for the genre above all else. This led to a series of commissions for DeCoteau and Cinema Home Video, largely shot on 16mm film and released to the DTV market contemporaneous to Todd Sheets' work. By 1992, however, Bookwalter had adapted to the demands of low-budget cinema production, embracing video as the most practical format for his own style of films. That year, he produced the so-called "Six Pack" series of features for DeCoteau—six total films, with two filmed back-to-back on a two-week schedule each, for a total budget of $5,000 per pair.[1] This model outdoes even the workaholic habits demonstrated by Sheets, a natural concession to the commissioned nature of the projects and their existence as products above all else. The films, beginning with 1992's **Kingdom of the Vampire** and **Zombie Cop**, suffered for their rushed, constricted productions, and Bookwalter himself was largely displeased with the results.

Noting the ease of shooting video over film, as well as recognizing the economic realities that privileged the former, Bookwalter began work on his "turning point" feature, **Ozone,** in 1994. Shot on S-VHS-C equipment to give it a professional sheen despite the $3,500 budget and incorporating digital effects that stood out from the low-grade practical work of his contemporaries, the film was a step forward from every previous effort he'd made.[2] In his own words, **Ozone** was "the culmination of all my hopes and dreams for the shot-on-video way of life."[3] Made for a fraction of the cost of **Zombie Bloodbath**, **Ozone** was a cause célèbre within the world of direct-to-video horror, attracting notice from every major and minor publication catering to fans of SOV cinema. This was all capped by the debut issue of the filmmaker's own **Alternative Cinema** devoting the cover and ten-page feature story to the film. Arguably more a reflection of the publication's inherently promotional nature than a conflict of interest, the issue's "Center Stage Review" also highlighted the film, calling it "a virtual thrill-show of lightning intensity and savage drama...good stuff!."[4] Proving that his own magazine's coverage was not simply biased hyperbole, **Film Threat Video Guide** (who at one point called out **Alternative Cinema's** nepotistic promotional tactics) gave **Ozone** a rave review, expressing amazement at its professional sheen despite its budget and the typical prejudice against SOV features in the publication. Interestingly, that review also asks the question, "When does one stop classifying someone as an 'amateur'?", reflecting Bookwalter's elevation above his unschooled status, something never awarded to Sheets in print despite

1 **B-Movies, pp.148-149.**
2 Ibid, p.205.
3 Ibid, p.177.
4 Brown, "Center Stage," p.53.

his similar journey.[1] Emboldened by the success of his most satisfying project, as well as his video labels and magazine, Bookwalter continued making SOV features throughout the 1990s and remains a staunch supporter of others working within the cycle.

B-Movies in the 90's and Beyond ad from **Independent Video #3** (1992)

Publisher and editor of essential zine **The Splatter Times**, Donald Farmer also had ambitions of horror filmmaking. Emboldened by the potential of early video technology, Farmer adopted the format for his first film, 1986's **Demon Queen**, and shot almost entirely on video for the remainder of his career. Carrying his zine's fixation on all manner of cinematic violence over into his filmmaking, Farmer packed his features with cheap gore effects and ample nudity. Catering to traditional exploitation audiences with his subject matter and promotional tactics, Farmer was an early proponent of analog video as a continuation of the badfilm lineage explored simultaneously by Vale, Juno, and their contributors (his 1993 release **Savage Vengeance** was an unofficial sequel to 1978's rape and revenge hit **I Spit on Your Grave,** featuring original star Camille Keaton). Farmer's conscious decision to channel these earlier exploitation influences suggests his use of video technology was as much a calculated aesthetic choice as it was an economic necessity. These parallels between the cycles of classic exploitation filmmaking and

1 Norman, p.30.

Cover for **The Splatter Times #7** (1985/86)

SOV amateurism are fully on display in his films, which reveal "a first-time filmmaker utilizing the fundamentals of backyard horror as a basis for dreamy disengagement."[1] Though not an established celluloid filmmaker, save his early experimental shorts, Farmer remains an important figure in the development of analog video as a means of independent expression.

San Francisco director Nick Millard had a successful run of celluloid productions in the realms of both hardcore pornography as well as horror/exploitation cinema. His 1975 release **Criminally Insane** bears many of the attributes of SOV horror in its approach to mundane life interrupted by brutal violence, but is still a work that "resembles something that could actually take place in reality."[2] By the 1980s, Millard had shifted his output to video production as a means of extending his career while delivering films quite different from those that had established him on the grindhouse and drive-in circuits.[3] Each of Millard's eight SOV features (produced between 1986-1999) displays a similar aesthetic, often featuring the same actors and sets—similar

1 Ziemba, **1980s**, p.51.
2 Ibid, p.48.
3 Ibid.

to **Criminally Insane** and other 1970s works utilizing Millard's own home as a primary location—as well as endlessly recycled footage from earlier projects, be they celluloid or video. In approaching filmmaking from such an idiosyncratic perspective, recalling cinema *vérité* with little regard for audience satisfaction or comprehension, Millard provides the most thorough connection between the SOV cycle and traditional exploitation filmmaking.[1] Enabled by camcorder technology to realize his ideas with greater freedom and ease, Millard carved out a peculiar niche for himself that coincided with the death of independent exploitation screening nationwide and the rise of the video store. The hallmarks of Millard's films, "shockingly terrible compositions, non-stop jump cuts, complicated plotlines about nothing in particular," are one and the same with those of many SOV amateurs.[2] His professional successes of the 1970s and pedigree as an established genre director meant little in the open market of video creativity. If anything, Millard's visions of rampant mundanity were better suited to the SOV cycle, fitting in with the aesthetics of that movement far more than they did celluloid traditions. Not as outspokenly devoted to video as Sheets, Bookwalter, or Farmer, Millard nonetheless adapted to the changing industry of the 1980s and re-established himself as a notable voice in a crowded scene.

There are many other instances of exploitation and horror filmmakers adopting video technology for their independent productions in the decades before its widespread adoption within the industry. Cult exploitation director James Bryan and producer Renee Harmon utilized video for their surreal 1990 collaboration, **Jungle Trap**, which remained unfinished until 2017, when crowdfunding initiated by BLEEDING SKULL! and the American Genre Film Archive enabled its completion and release. This retrospective project also touches on the growing cult appeal of SOV horror, with the donation model reflecting the base of vocal fans willing to support alternative horror cinema and its restoration. Also explicit in this instance is the participatory nature of cult fandom, now even accorded to SOV horror which had long languished as subcultural refuse. On this point, there is a connection

1 Ibid, p.49.
2 Ibid, p.48.

back to Sheets' earliest productions, the ones that established both his filmmaking legacy as well as his devoted base of friends and collaborators. Laurie Oullette notes "[w]ith their relatively low cost, ease of use, high image quality, and general availability, camcorders increase the potential for the development of a more inclusive, participatory medium."[1] Sheets' cinema, not to mention plenty of other SOV works, indicate a distinct brand of participatory film production. Emboldened by the aesthetic disappointments of **Blood Cult** and other visible SOV releases, hundreds of would-be filmmakers across the country were empowered to take a chance at moviemaking, feeling their efforts could be no worse than what they had just seen. With this came an entirely hands-on approach to filmmaking, with anyone interested or willing to show up being included.

As roughshod as his earliest films may be, Sheets tapped into this enthusiasm behind the scenes in each of his tapes. While its affordability and easy learning curve were major components in his dedication to the format, video proved to be just as much a form of encouragement and positive communal interaction. The outtakes and behind-the-scenes features on the **Zombie Bloodbath Trilogy** DVD set reveal a crew of people having fun with their work, undaunted by the traditional anxieties of film production. Wasted takes are chances for laughs, not money down the drain, and any mishaps on set are embraced for their entertainment rather than causes for stress. Above all, for Todd Sheets, allegiance to analog video production meant freedom from the constrictions of industrial filmmaking practice and even the wear of daily life. That he succeeded against his limitations as well as the backlash he faced serves as one of the most inspiring cases of SOV horror as a force of legitimate oppositional cinema. Unconcerned with outside perspectives and every negative force working against him, Sheets trawled through the world of acinematic creation to arrive at the point of legitimate talent and respect from the community he participated in himself. While his features are unlikely to convert any skeptics to the charms of SOV horror, they unquestionably account for one of its most distinctive bodies of work.

1 Oullette, p.33.

04

SOV HORROR AND THE UNEXPECTED AVANT-GARDE

SOV HORROR, LARGELY the cinema of outsiders—generically, technically, and even socially—during its 1984-1994 period was defined by the prominence it gave to amateur artists. Fragmentary, nonsensical narratives, rudimentary grasps of framing and editing, and especially the insistence on unvarnished script and performative elements marked the most visible amateur video efforts as impenetrable cinematic detritus. While these characteristics make the cycle inherently difficult to appreciate, they are not without precedent in film history. Much as earlier celluloid exploitation efforts were singled out for their idiosyncrasies, the realm of experimental film has largely remained outside the mores of popular entertainment. Avant-garde cinema has historically been defined in terms of opposition to the commercial mode of filmmaking, instead embracing independent, amateur models of production and distribution. While there are countless varying definitions of the term, avant-garde cinema is generally understood to encompass works bearing fragmentary, non-linear structures, innovative visual and technical qualities, and a greater tendency towards formal experimentation. This emphasis on autonomy and independence has permitted greater personal freedom and the creation of more subjectively significant works.

Many of the attributes that mark avant-garde cinema as challenging to widespread consumption are shared by broader film works produced by amateurs. Clive Young defines fan films as "unauthorized amateur or semi-pro film[s], based on pop culture characters or situations, created for noncommercial viewing."[1] This definition emphasizes the imitative aspect of amateur filmmaking, with the author lovingly noting the

1 Young, p.4.

"incredible lack of quality, craftsmanship, or even understanding of how to make a moderately coherent movie...it's all those 'faults' that make fan films exciting."[1] For Patricia Zimmerman, a more studied approach helps to understand amateur cinematic production: "Professionalism and amateurism traverse this dichotomy between the public sphere of the economy and the private sphere of the home and personal life in very specific ways...The difference between professional film and amateur film, then, marks a social distance sustained through the specialization of technique."[2] In each instance, amateurs work out of passion, motivations outside of the capitalistic Hollywood system, even if in the case of Young's definition, they rely on its properties for inspiration. These two texts represent, respectively, the two poles of amateur cinema as it is commonly understood: the unabashed enthusiasm and unpolished presentation of fan-made imitations, and the meandering *vérité* realism of home video recording. Even as affordable 8mm, Super 8, 16mm, and analog video technology enabled a growing number of would-be filmmakers to capture their visions and daily events, unskilled film production was long the realm of hobbyists rather than craftsmen.

The American experimental film scene, however, openly embraced the techniques of amateur production. With the emergence of Maya Deren in the 1940s, the amateur cinematic tendency was fully validated and welcomed for its contributions to filmic art. For Deren, the amateur filmmaker is "one who does something for the love of the thing rather than for economic reasons," and is privileged due to greater "freedom—both artistic and physical." Thus, amateur films are motivated by true passion and are more aesthetically valuable due to the lack of formal restrictions placed upon them by any established systems. P. Adams Sitney classifies Deren's work into the specific category of "trance films," a style which greatly influenced later avant-garde cinema. In Sitney's terms, the trance film "deals with visionary experience...The protagonist wanders through a potent environment toward a climactic scene of self-realization."[3] Trance films often make use of dream narratives, ritualistic practices, and other devices to establish separate planes of reality and awareness. Linking the advent

1 Ibid, p.1.

2 Zimmerman, p.2.

3 Sitney, p.18.

of the trance film with the progression of the American cinematic avant-garde, Sitney speaks on the highly personal nature of the style, "true psycho-dramas."[1] The trance film evolved from surrealism, but stakes its territory through an absence of metaphor, revealing instead the psychological concerns of the filmmaker alone. Of Deren's cinematic debut, he concludes that the influential and innovative work "begins with a dream unfolded within shifting perspectives."[2]

Conceived as a "kind of home movie" between Deren and her then-husband, Alexander Hammid (listed in the credits as "Hamid"), **Meshes of the Afternoon** (1943) employs elements of horror cinema within its trance film framework to create nightmarish fragments of psychological distress.[3] Unbelievably complex and rich for its fourteen-minute runtime, the film employs a number of devices including point-of-view shots, handheld cinematography and disorienting close-ups to render its investigation of a woman's subjective experiences. Deren, playing the woman, finds herself haunted by a cloaked, mirror-faced figure as well as doubles and triples of herself. Events recur, from the appearance of Deren's doppelgangers, to the repetition of actions across indistinct temporalities and settings. The film is imbued with an ever-present sense of menace, as the woman is haunted by the cloaked figure, finds a knife threateningly placed in every room of the house, and drifts in and out of sleep witnessing her own image inhabiting the home. The film concludes with a man (Hammid) returning to the house for a second time, finding the woman dead in the living room, a smashed mirror in her lap and shard of glass clenched in her fist, as well as seaweed wrapped around her head, recalling an earlier shift in setting to an empty beach. For Sitney, Deren's haunting short condenses the "experience of an obsessive, recurrent series of dreams into a single one by substituting variations on the original dream for what would conventionally be complete transitions of subject within a single dream."[4] The film carries Deren's subjective vision onto the screen, a circuitous, coiling nightmare of discovery and internal confrontation.

1 Ibid, p.14.
2 Ibid, p.15.
3 Rhodes, p.47.
4 Sitney, p.11.

Another major figure in American avant-garde cinema and advocate for amateur production methods, Stan Brakhage formulated his own approach to this concept. Brakhage considered himself an amateur as opposed to an artist, arguing that "the amateur photographs the persons, places, and objects of his love and the events of his happiness and personal importance."[1] While they share some similarities, Brakhage's theory of the amateur diverges from Deren's in his desire to honestly capture the qualities of his life which are the most meaningful. Artistic freedom again allows a more varied, personal expression. Sitney defines Brakhage's early-to-mid style as "lyrical film," characterized in how it "postulates the filmmaker behind the camera as the first-person protagonist of the film. The images of the film are what he sees, filmed in such a way that we never forget his presence."[2] Thus, in Brakhage's films, he is always present as the capturer of the moving image, and accordingly, what is projected onscreen has great personal significance. The lyrical filmmaker "affirms the actual flatness and whiteness of the screen, rejecting for the most part its traditional use as a window into illusion."[3] Sitney's point here again locates the emphasis of this experimental style on subjective expression, now concerned with the concept of vision rather than psychological inspiration. Brakhage's work demonstrates this by allowing him to "compress his thoughts and feelings while recording his direct confrontation with intense experiences of birth, death, sexuality, and the terror of nature."[4] Thus, the lyrical film presents the manifestation of the filmmaker-subject's engagement with the sensorial world they inhabit, rejecting narrative or artifice as a means of conveying honest experience and expression.

Sitney identifies **Anticipation of the Night** (1958) as Brakhage's breakthrough film in the lyrical style, describing "the doomed quest for an absolutely authentic, renewed, and untutored vision."[5] The film is a series of events and images captured by Brakhage's handheld camera, with placid suburban scenes fractured by rapid edits and

1 Brakhage, p.149.
2 Sitney, p.160.
3 Ibid.
4 Ibid, p.168.
5 Ibid, p.165.

a perpetual sense of motion. Wholly unconcerned with narrative or linear structure, the images instead form several sequences: a man leaves his house, a rose in a bowl of water is shaken, a camera held while running captures jumbled images of neon signs and streetlamps overhead, sprinklers water a backyard, an infant crawls across the grass. Interior and exterior spaces are explored, as driving footage captures indiscernible outdoor areas just as close-ups examine the details of a suburban home. These daylight moments are split with nocturnal scenes alternately frantic and prolonged in their forward momentum, Brakhage proposing "camera movement as the elementary figure of film structure."[1] Scenes at a carnival occupy much of the film's middle section, the rapid, sped-up motions of the rides continuing the swirling, neon cityscapes of the earlier segments, the recurrent circularity of the day emphasized yet again. The film, originally intended to conclude with Brakhage's actual suicide caught on camera, instead ends with his staged hanging, and suddenly the repeated low-angle shots of trees come into focus and coalesce.[2] The final image is Brakhage's shadow swinging from a rope against the house's exterior. Scores of amateur SOV filmmakers have similarly asserted their perceptions by recording the particularities of their worlds in equally distinctive and innovative manners.

Deren and Brakhage likely could not have predicted their theories would find a most apt expression via the underground cycle of SOV horror. Because of their nonexistent production values, and especially the filmmakers' absolute lack of formal training, these movies remain bizarre outcasts among genre films, proudly or unconsciously displaying more ambition than technique or talent. As a result, moments of surreal, discomforting disconnection and accidental visual innovation emerge, which complicate their classification as merely horror films. While mainstream horror cinema utilizes instances of extraordinary events to play upon the audience's fears, the most personal amateur SOV works address the insecurities of no one but the creators and their cohorts. The best amateur productions employ tenets of both Deren and Brakhage's theories, demonstrating

1 Ibid, p.163.
2 Ibid, pp.164-165.

a significant bond to Sitney's categories of trance and lyrical film styles. That this was generally unintentional on the part of the amateur horror directors is all the more impressive.

Charles Pinion's **Twisted Issues** (1988) and Carl Sukenick's **Alien Beasts** (1991) are unique among amateur SOV horror films. Each director has their own idiosyncratic style and expresses personal concerns through techniques and methods that recall the innovations of avant-garde art cinema as much as low-budget horror moviemaking. Their similarities with more highly regarded experimental films were often noted within the confines of the underground press. Some important revelations emerge when they are examined as works of avant-garde art, even when this is at odds with their intended functions. Stephen Thrower's suggestion of an alternate viewing method "where all the 'shortfalls' of technique are actually artistic achievements... art-in-negative" gets close to the striking nature of these elements.[1] These films can be re-contextualized alongside Deren and Brakhage's work to read them as explicitly avant-garde works of art, uncovering commonalities that should not remain ignored. Pinion's feature reads as a clear example of the trance film, recalling Sitney's definition in its employment of mythic dream and trance imagery, manipulating genre conventions to establish its unique role as an experimental horror film. Sukenick's movie bears more in common with Brakhage's lyrical sensibility, albeit in a decidedly perverse manner at odds with his philosophy. Its worldview and the peculiarity of its existence are documented in unsettling, often confessional detail, even as it largely retains a traditional narrative structure. Not only do these two films exist as explicit works of avant-garde art, but they suggest the ways that other amateur SOV narratives can stand as legitimately meaningful and innovative projects.

Twisted Issues: Media as Entrancement

CHARLES PINION'S **TWISTED Issues** is one of the most difficult SOV titles to categorize: proudly shot on consumer-grade video, it features

1 Thrower, p.43.

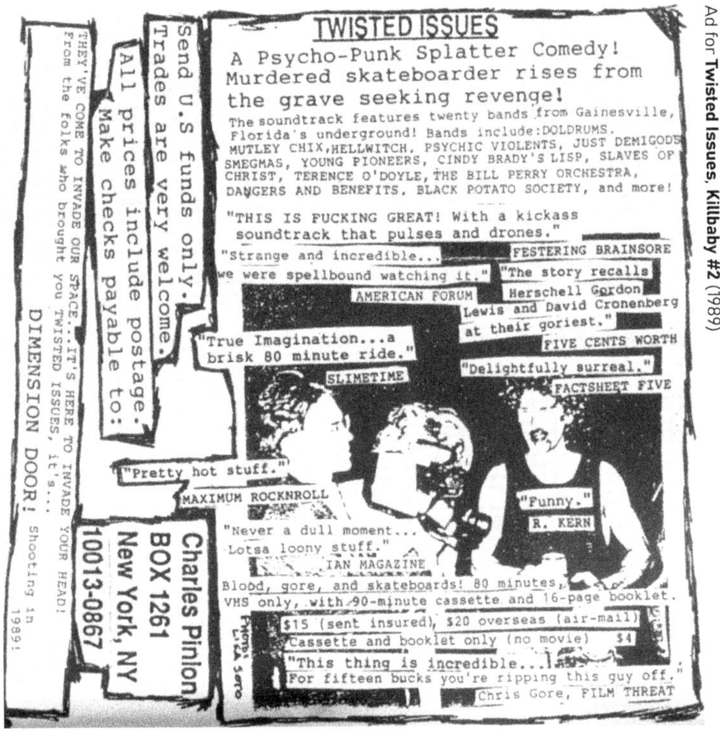

Ad for **Twisted Issues**, **Killbaby #2** (1989)

documentary footage of the local Gainesville, Florida punk scene, a narrative concerning an undead punk seeking revenge after his murder, and scenes of Pinion watching his own movie and assorted found footage on television. Conceived as a documentary-cum-farewell to the independent music scene that had fostered his artistic expression for years, **Twisted Issues** is a mesh of disparate elements both real and staged. This is an undeniably amateur production, from the use of an early single-system camcorder to the legitimate punks that comprise the cast, and at no point does it obey the rules of traditional narrative filmmaking. Despite this, the segments featuring the director himself establish an undeniable connection to the trance film style pioneered in Deren's work.

Sitney argues that directors working with the trance film style often cast themselves as their protagonists so the "film becomes a process of self-realization."[1] Whether or not Pinion is the film's protagonist, he is certainly its most striking and important character due to the way he impacts the narrative progression. In fact, the first original image shown in the film after a series of news clips has Pinion's own blood-soaked eyes watching this footage on television, establishing his constant task from the opening seconds. Pinion's role as the character of Charles is never explicitly explained, though in the first few minutes a group of punks attempt to contact him at his home. This establishes Charles as part of the film's narrative space but also signifies his willful removal from that realm as he ignores them, disengaging himself with the more linear elements of the plot. Charles features prominently throughout the movie, embarking on a visual, "psychotronic" journey, isolated with his girlfriend until the film's climax. The majority of his scenes concern the transmission of images, both found and manufactured, via television, and Charles is transfixed by the video picture. The use of appropriated footage acts as commentary on mainstream 1980s society, while integrated scenes from the movie's own narrative emerge as a discussion on the nature of filmmaking and the omnipotence of the creator.

Pinion articulates a serious, pro-video philosophy in his "Pulp Video Manifesto," which serves as a theoretical apotheosis of the format. At the time of **Twisted Issues**' production, Pinion noted that "no one in Gainesville, or most places in 1987, was going to shoot a narrative feature on VHS. It just wasn't done. It's easy to forget how absolute the bias was toward film back then."[2] While this wasn't entirely true, given the earlier work of David Prior, Chester Turner, and especially **Blood Cult**, each of these presented more straightforward narratives, with considerably less interest in formal experimentation. Pinion's insistence on not only utilizing cheap VHS technology to make a feature-length work, but also his fetishization of the video image itself reflects the deeper significance of Charles' trance state. The character's hypnosis insinuates a subversive seductiveness engineered for the movie itself; he is entranced by the image because of its unharnessed potential as a disseminator of artistic content. This emphasis on the capabilities of video reflects Pinion's adoption of the format to create legitimate art.

1 Sitney, p14.
2 Everleth.

Twisted Issues ad from **Killbaby #1** (1989)

The director "never wanted the viewer to forget what it was shot on...VHS had that added quality that I've never found since, which is an intrinsic aesthetic pugnacity."[1] Charles' onscreen role and visual journey is suggestive of Pinion's own quest for legitimacy as a creator of narrative, noncommercial cinematic works utilizing a highly unpopular medium.

Only two characters directly engage with Charles and his girlfriend in their home: their friend Steve who stops by for a beer run, and the mysterious, shamanistic Hawk. Steve is the only character in the film who is privy to Charles' omnipotent television, stumbling into the room as it broadcasts Paul, the doomed skateboarder, being murdered in a parking lot. Charles quickly changes the channel once Steve recognizes Paul, the screen switching to a blurry video image of a strange Eastern totem sculpture later revealed to be in Hawk's possession. Shortly after this, Steve gets in a car with the four people who have killed Paul, clearly uneasy after what he saw on the television. As Paul's reanimated form appears to exact revenge for his death, Charles reveals himself in the car's driver side mirror and commands Steve to get out and flee. Charles is capable of controlling elements beyond his own space, and his appearance in the glass recalls the mirror-faced figure in Deren's **Meshes of the Afternoon**.

Hawk's role complicates the single protagonist reading of the trance film proposed by Sitney, seeming to occupy an equally powerful role

1 Hunchback, p.17.

in the film's universe. Not appearing until near the film's conclusion, Hawk is a spacy, gaunt figure to whom the murderers turn for help despite their discomfort around him. In Hawk's apartment, the camera lingers on the Eastern sculpture, investing it with an unspoken totemic power reinforced by its unexplained appearance on Charles' television throughout the film. Charles even calls Hawk to confront him about his collusion with the murderers, and later sneaks into Hawk's apartment to destroy the figurine. While its presence is never explained, the object invests Hawk with the same abilities as Charles' television, granting him seeming immortality and omnipotence; its destruction is what ultimately triggers Hawk's violent revenge spree against Charles and his girlfriend that ends the film. This final scene is the only one in which Charles and his partner are exposed to the film's rampant violence, having previously been mere observers while enacting their own form of comic brutality against one another. Throughout the film, Charles and his girlfriend kill and maim each other in several graphic set pieces, always surviving and regenerating their health just a short time later. They exist within the film's narrative space, but are removed from it, with violence enacted against their bodies serving as a means of reinvention rather than finality. Only Hawk seems to pose a legitimate threat to their mythic status, but even he is unable to kill them—as Steve watches on, disturbed but unfazed—until Charles acts upon the television that enables his film itself.

Late in the film, Pinion makes his strongest claims toward a mythology of the video image. Jack Sargeant identifies a recurring "fascination with mytho-poetic thematics," in Pinion's works, which here takes the form of the television screen's omniscience.[1] Pinion instills his visuals with a poetic substantiality heretofore unheard of within the medium's usage. Unlike earlier trance films such as Deren's **Meshes of the Afternoon** or Kenneth Anger's **Fireworks** which realized the trance experience through dreams, Pinion employs the viewing of video media to initiate a journey to awareness. At the film's climax, the television assumes an all-powerful role, capturing the onscreen action live in the manner of closed-circuit video. The final confrontation occurs in Charles' home and suggests that only what is

1 **Cinema Contra**, p.95.

visualized on the television screen is legitimate in the context of the film's art. Only when Charles himself shuts off the television is there a moment of self-realization: the picture cuts abruptly to black, denying the viewer any actual moments of closure, and driving home the point that the journey itself has been entirely artificial and manufactured for the screen. Thus the all-encompassing role of television "is identified as a window/eye onto another world...an altered sense of mind... which offers the spirits a distorted perception of material reality."[1] Rather than use the trance film form to probe his own psyche or arrive at a moment of inner development, Pinion appropriates the style to advance the case for his art. Sitney identifies the subjective power in **Meshes of the Afternoon** in Deren's representation of herself encountering "objects and sights as if they were capable of revealing the erotic mystery of the self."[2] Pinion encounters the very medium that he employs, locating the erotic pull of the material not within himself, but the very art form he has undertaken to construct.

Sitney comments that the trance film "offers us an extended view of a mind in which there is a terrible ambivalence between stable actuality and subconscious violence."[3] Regarding the violence in **Twisted Issues**, Pinion was motivated by his then-recent exposure to splatter and exploitation films, wanting to fill his debut feature with easily accomplished effects with broader commercial appeal.[4] Charles and his girlfriend's ambivalence toward the violence they view on television and in their own interactions reflects their disconnect from the exterior world. They may be transfixed by the splattery violence onscreen, but apart from Charles' warning to Steve, never act on it directly. Only when Hawk enters their home to end the cycle of murder at the conclusion are they spurred to react and defend themselves. Prior to this, their bemusement with the numerous murders represents stability, the reflected chaos of the society around them reduced to a numbing background noise they must navigate internally. In this sense, the film (as well as Pinion's subsequent video features) "gleefully explode[s] the psychedelic underpinnings of the

1 Ibid, p.96.
2 Sitney, p.11.
3 Ibid, p.12.
4 **Cinema Contra**, p.101.

TWISTED ISSUES
A PSYCHO-PUNK SPLATTER COMEDY

"An eighty minute excursion into an insane world."
GOREFEST

"One of the, uh, sharpest satires on the Michael/Jason/Freddie brethren of bloodletting bad guys to hit the slasher genre... It's a great movie and a lot of fun!"
Eric Danville, HIGH TIMES

"A combination of slasher type narrative with Decline of Gainesville Civilization type hardcore documentary... We raved about it."
SLAUGHTERHOUSE

"The story recalls Herschell Gordon Lewis and David Cronenberg at their goriest."
FIVE CENTS WORTH

"This thing is incredible... The gore is cheap, but it's good. A real crowd-pleaser and it'll make some squeamish folks leave the room... I'd like to see what this guy could do with a budget. Maybe the world is safer so long as Charles doesn't have one."
Chris Gore, FILM THREAT

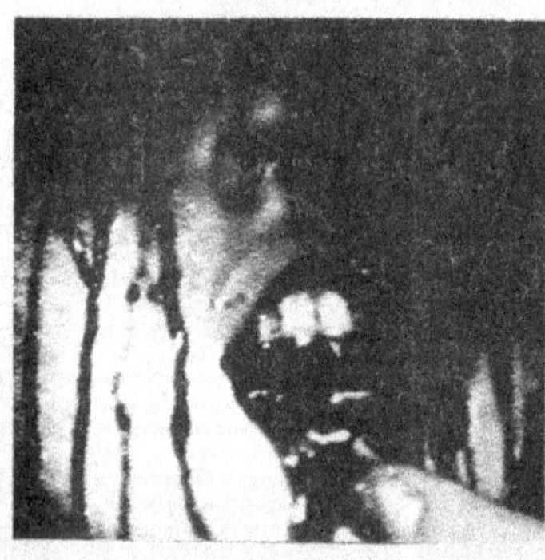

a film by
CHARLES PINION

80 MINUTES
FEATURE-LENGTH • SHOT ON VIDEO
$15

AVAILABLE FROM

Film Threat Video ad for **Twisted Issues**, **Film Threat Video Guide #1** (1990)

commonplace, depicting the turbulent chaotic maelstrom that exists at the fringes of the real world."[1]

Drawing further parallels to Deren's **Meshes of the Afternoon**, both that earlier film and **Twisted Issues** end with the deaths of the

1 **Deathtripping**, p.247.

filmmakers themselves—or at least their onscreen representations. Deren's psychological mirror of herself is found dead after a series of nightmarish confrontations with her own image and the dangers of the domestic world she inhabits. In Pinion's case, the very means of representation are what bring about this destruction, suggesting without the author there can be no art itself, the journey a cyclical form of self-immolation that also reflects Pinion's decision to leave Gainesville for New York City. In both instances, this end of the journey is the only possible resolution, the visions of Deren's film and the narrative of Pinion's are unable to conclude in any other manner. The moment of realization is the difficult coda to the painful and personal process of self-examination and representation that defines their trance film styles. The violence of both works, whether internal or external, acts as a creative force as much as a subconscious one, stripping the author of all that they control even as they have guided the course of the action over the preceding minutes.

Pinion's willingness to experiment and take risks to elevate his work beyond the industrial imitations of so many other SOV releases of the late-1980s clearly resonated with underground audiences. A reappraisal of the film in **Film Threat Video Guide** as one of twenty-five essential underground films notes "[o]nly a handful of filmmakers have been able to use video for anything other than boring, meandering pointlessness. Charles Pinion is one of those people."[1] In a surprisingly enthusiastic review, Charles Kilgore of the **Ecco** fanzine, no great champion of video-based filmmaking, praises Pinion's film as "however self-indulgent and technically crude, **Twisted Issues** transcends its limitations with unexpected imagination, stylistic audacity, and a flair for story-telling."[2] Even without explicitly connecting the film to avant-garde cinema, Kilgore echoes the sentiments often expressed by the 1980s underground in decrying experimental cinema, namely self-indulgence and idiosyncratic construction. Similarly, Rick Sullivan's **Gore Gazette** ends its brief mention of the film by pointing out that "Nihilist N.Y. film lobster-director Nick Zedd has been quoted as saying 'I really hated **Twisted Issues!**', so it's probably worth a look-see."[3]

1 "Assault," p.52.

2 Kilgore, p.2.

3 Sullivan, p.7.

Twisted Issues storyboard from soundtrack booklet

Pinion's film is removed from the Cinema of Transgression movement he was often placed alongside, as well as the horror community's belligerence toward that cycle's pretensions, straddling as it did art, experimental, and exploitation film styles.

In a retrospective appraisal of the director's oeuvre, Jack Sargeant mentions the revelatory approach taken to the format itself: "By mobilizing his work under a supposed stylistic and micro-political banner, Pinion embraces the notion of a production process that exists separate from film: that of video."[1] Even as Pinion continued to work exclusively with video through the 1990s, refining both his technical approach and his overt engagements with experimental film, his debut remains his most strikingly ambitious and personal work. From its near-documentary origins, to its all-hands-on-deck collaborative approach and especially the centering of the first-time director as his own protagonist, it remains a significant moment in SOV history, one of the first times when so-called visionary film and trash-pulp art were forced to meet on their own terms. In Pinion's hands, video filmmaking seized the lyrical style, observing "with accuracy the way in which

1 **Cinema Contra**, p.96.

the events and objects of the day become potent, then transfigured, in dreams as well as the way in which a dreamer may realize that she dreams and may dream that she wakes."[1] Substituting dreams for cinematic entrancement, **Twisted Issues** relies on its format as much as its content to probe the subjective identity of its creator. While **Twisted Issues** adopted fragmentary techniques and insular references to great acclaim, other experimental passion projects from the SOV cycle were met with complete derision and bewilderment, meaning their revelatory contents often went unacknowledged at the time of their release.

Alien Beasts: Personal Struggle as Lyricism

THE ONLY QUALITY connecting the work of Stan Brakhage with Carl J. Sukenick's **Alien Beasts** is the expression of a subjective mindset, including a lyrical presentation of personal elements. In fact, Sukenick's film is so maddeningly personal, delirious, and incomprehensible that it is incomparable to any other cinematic works in existence. One reviewer in **Alternative Cinema** was so confounded that they noted the film's mere existence was some sort of miracle, that it should be permissible in the same sense as the Ebola virus.[2] **Alien Beasts** is unquestionably a passion project of great personal importance, but also represents how subjective expression can render works "foreign to life as we know it on every level imaginable."[3] Just as Brakhage used his lyrical films to record crucial moments in his life, such as the birth of his children and his mourning a family pet, Sukenick's narrative feature captures the things and ideas that were prominent in his life at a particular moment in time. It may not be a lyrical film in the strictest sense, but that lens offers the best means of extracting some sort of meaning from its contents.

Sitney conceives of the lyrical film as involving the filmmaker as protagonist, unseen behind the camera but present in every frame

1 Sitney, p.11.
2 Beesley, p.51.
3 Ziemba, 2014.

Alien Beasts ad from **Film Threat Video Guide #7** (1993)

of film via the presentation of their literal worldview.[1] In Brakhage's lyrical films, "the screen is filled with movement, and that movement, both of the camera and the editing, reverberates with the idea of a person looking."[2] Sukenick's film, concerned with the act of seeing through its security camera footage (as told to the viewer by the director's narration) presents the insular world of his New York neighborhood populated by characters of his creation. The world is revealed not through movement, but static, unblinking long takes, inverting the motion of Brakhage's films to arrive at a frustratingly slow-moving presentation that nonetheless reveals the filmmaker's concerns through its terminal pacing. The film's lyrical approach to the world within a fantastic narrative recalls Marie Menkin's "delicate mesh of observation and imposition" that inspired Brakhage previously, offering both lived experience and constructed strangeness.[3]

The film's plot is threadbare, and only begins to make sense after multiple viewings, which was likely unintentional. Aliens and mutants have invaded a military base, a woman named Sara loses her family, and the world is somehow irradiated. None of these things save the aliens are shown onscreen, emphasizing the narrative's secondary

1 Sitney, p.160.
2 Ibid.
3 Ibid, p.161.

Space Robot Warriors ad from **Independent Video #3** (1992)

function to the movie's aesthetic affectations. The VHS photography is barely passable, the military base is a suburban home, and the only fatigues to be found are presented in a still image of two men. There are countless long, static takes of Sukenick himself shouting at his actors, ostensibly in character, and groups of people sluggishly fighting on his front lawn comprise what seems like half the movie's runtime. These extended reaction shots, typically filmed as Sukenick directs his cast in front of the camera, often recall Andy Warhol's **Screen Tests** in their unwavering intimacy. Other long stretches of the movie are merely stills of people who never act or text offering scant plot details; these are all overlaid with Sukenick's shouted narration. From the start, the film plays like a transmission from the world beyond traditional filmmaking.

The difficulty in understanding **Alien Beasts** is confounded further by the existence of **Mutant Massacre 1** and **2** (released before and after **Alien Beasts**, respectively). These three films are not distinct projects or parts of a series as their titles would imply, but are instead three separate film works comprising the same roughly two-and-a-half hours of footage. Unique scenes, clearly filmed during the same period of shooting, feature in each of the three titles, and repeated footage is chronologically altered, creating elaborately disjointed narratives from a limited number of component parts. As much as these re-

Carl J. Sukenick's
MUTANT MASSACRE 2
"Blood, Nudity, Violence"
C.J.S. FILMS
c/o Sukenick
305 W 28th Street #12D
New York, NY 10001
$29.95
Make check payable to
Carl J. Sukenick

Mutant Massacre 2 ad from **Independent Video #11** (1995)

edits confused and frustrated audiences, there is a clear acknowledgement of the mutability of video and the embrace of plasticity on Sukenick's part. A paid advertisement for the title **Space Robot Warriors** in **Independent Video** carries the editorial note "If the photograph in this ad looks familiar, it should be (sic), it was in our article about 'Mutant Massacre'".[1] Meanwhile, a review of **Alien Beasts** in **Draculina** begins "Remember my review back in issue #13 of Sukenick's **Mutant Massacre**? Well, look it up and change the name to **Alien Beasts** and you'll have my same review, because basically—it's the same video."[2] Even unintentionally, Sukenick's formal experimentation with a limited set of materials defied all expectations of underground audiences at their time of release.

Sukenick's naïve defiance of every rule of production acts as a sort of lyricism-in-negative, recalling Thrower's discussions of "bad" movies operating on an entirely different spectrum. He fervently pursues the vision in his head, creating a work of anti-art that mirrors Sitney's claim that a lyrical filmmaker must film "what he actually sees, not what he has been taught to see or thinks he should see."[3]

1 **Independent Video**, #3, p.25.
2 Gallagher, #16, p.47.
3 Sitney, p.168.

CARL J. SUKENICK'S

"MUTANT MASSACRE"

C.J.S. Films
P.O. Box 340
Nanuet, NY
10954

WARNING:
BLOOD
VIOLENCE
NUDITY

$29.95

Mutant Massacre ad, **Film Threat Video Guide #3** (1991)

While Sitney intends this literally via the mechanism of the camera as eye, Sukenick's technical limitations and struggles with mental illness distort this sentiment to offer the clearest possible expression of his internal state, how he experienced the world at the time of filming and the act of creation as the sole means of exorcising his inspiration. This dogged pursuit of his ideal vision opens his world to the viewer, putting every miniscule element of his life on display. Sukenick features himself prominently in the movie, ultimately saving the day in a long, improbably impressive stop-motion animated sequence. This scene in particular is revelatory, featuring shots of Sukenick's childish drawings and action figures, as well as his voiceover narration cheering himself on in the fight. This detached feeling leaves everything and everyone completely open and vulnerable, and each actor onscreen save Sukenick is clearly uncomfortable during their scenes. Despite this, Sukenick exposes himself completely over the course of the film, giving a candid view of his life that one review compared to Jonas Mekas' diary film **Walden**.[1] Sitney describes the diary film as "*quotidian lyrics*, spontaneous, perhaps tentative, records of a sensibility in the

1 Ziemba, 2014.

midst of, or fresh from experience."[1] They are similar to home movies, but emphasize the subjective over the collective, lacking conventions of wider appeal or mundanity freed from conflict.[2] **Alien Beasts** may appear as a home movie and is certainly subjective in its operations, but its intended appeal as a commercially-inspired work places it in the realm of the communal. Sukenick's honest expression of his passions rather than mere recording of personal events aligns his work with Brakhage's sensibility above Mekas'.

The film's most notable moments are its concluding portions, which feature the most extensive visual effects, as well as the director's strongest assertion of his own role as heroic protagonist. After another long take of a fight in a backyard, a purple-faced mutant is shot with an arrow, catches fire, and spews viscous liquid from his wound. Suddenly the picture switches to a negative image, a low-budget means of representing the radiation attack occurring onscreen. For the next few minutes, images repeat: the mutant slowly dies under a freeway overpass, a Styrofoam head smokes and catches fire, the figures previously shown fighting are frozen in a still moment. This montage of visual effects renders everything in expressionistic relief, resulting in even greater free-form chaos onscreen as the audience struggles to adjust to the cheap video effects. Finally, a frame of Sukenick's leering, grinning face is revealed, and the picture switches back to a positive image. The previous visuals are asserted as the inner workings of his mind, the cheap effects the realization of his visionary expression playing out before the director's watchful eye, his presence in front of the camera as intrinsic to the workings of his art as his vision through its lens.

Following this is a nearly-five-minute stop-motion animated sequence depicting Sukenick's personal struggle as his character kills the remaining mutated enemy agent. Through clay models, a rubber alien mask, articulated action figures, and even crude colored pencil drawings, Sukenick uses a cross section of media to recount his spectacular battle with the creature. A sculpted model hand is hacked into a bloody mess with a hatchet, just as a shrieking clay

1 Sitney, p.424.
2 Ibid, p.425.

Alien Beasts ad featuring creature's mask from **Independent Video #5** (1993)

face is constructed piece-by-piece and squashed into an oozing puddle. Film images of Sukenick in an outdoor area are spotlighted and panned, alternating the animated actions with more tangible, corporeal elements. These moments in particular reveal the director's control over his medium and his knowledge of the mechanical-technical properties of a film camera. Several minutes later, after the credits have begun to roll, Sukenick intones in a final narration, "Carl, you destroyed the enemy agents and the alien extradimensional monsters. Everything is destroyed, you won!" The entire process of the film has been Carl's personal journey, his own progression toward artistic validation. This concluding experimental detour is a technical milestone in his aesthetic progress from narrative creation to the projection of a more internal, personalized art form. Where Brakhage's **Anticipation of the Night** ends with the director's own suicide by hanging, Sukenick's concludes with his triumph over an evil force of his own creation. In cheering himself on throughout the final moments of **Alien Beasts**, Sukenick recognizes that he is his own star, the force driving his work onscreen and behind the camera, and if no one else is able to connect with what he has created, then his own satisfaction is the most important outcome of his efforts. While he has found an appreciative audience in retrospect, **Alien Beasts** represents the significant risks of personal filmmaking and the difficulties in exposing such honest work to the world at large.

No review or coverage of Sukenick and his movie seems entirely comfortable in approaching it, because there is no precedent for its content. An early review in **Draculina** dismisses the film as "a confusing piece of nonscense (sic) that can't be taken seriously by anyone with a brain."[1] More recently, Joseph Ziemba, who notes its disturbing insularity, pegs **Alien Beasts** as "a child-like experimental document in the guise of a backyard horror movie." This is perhaps the most apt summation of what the film accomplishes, without even addressing the particulars of its presentation. Other critics directly acknowledged the opposing paradigms of art and trash filmmaking, noting that Sukenick "never hides behind the 'art-film' disclaimer, making it that much more honest...and strange."[2] In calling the film "honest," the reviewer gets to the point of why the film is so off-putting and original because there is no doubt at any point that Sukenick's intentions were earnest in unleashing his all-too-revealing vision. Beyond its disquieting proximity to Sukenick's life, the movie is also noted for its aesthetic quirks being "so badly done to the point where they were beyond badly done. They were art."[3] The central concern for reception is the film's inability to fit into any predetermined categories, emerging as an entirely new form. While his presence and vision are on the screen far more than behind the camera, Sukenick managed to present the particularities of his existence in the clearest possible terms, reflecting Brakhage's inspiration by the commonplace elements of domestic life.[4] **Alien Beasts**, even against its creator's intentions, emerges as a work of all-too-personal avant-garde art by accident as opposed to design, and remains a singular documentation of personal creative inspiration.

Despite the candid openness of **Alien Beasts** and the impression one forms of Sukenick in watching it, a familiarity with the director's life and subsequent works goes a great way toward clarifying his intentions. This reliance on "extratextual information...to 'enhance or enrich' [the] engagement" with Sukenick's film is outlined by Sconce

1 Gallagher, #16, p.47.
2 Williams, #3, p.21.
3 Nirenberg.
4 Sitney, p.150.

in his discussion of paracinematic readings.[1] In this particular case, biographical information is crucial to unlock **Alien Beasts'** lyricism, asserting the camera lens as the filmmaker's eye. By the early 2000s, Sukenick's mode of production had shifted entirely, with his residence in a care facility providing him with not only a pool of ready and willing collaborators but also an entirely different approach to video making.[2] These more recent features still contain supernatural and generic elements, but are often given over to equal amounts of personal reflection, recalling the video diaries of underground legend George Kuchar. Sukenick is often distressingly candid about himself in these solo video segments, detailing his lifelong battle with schizophrenia, the devastating loss of his mother which required his move to the facility, and his daily anxieties surrounding food and sex. Of course, these nuances and confessional elements were completely unavailable to the audiences who stumbled upon **Alien Beasts** in the early 1990s. Confused and intrigued by the stark, half-page advertisements that appeared in the pages of **Fangoria**, **Film Threat Video Guide**, and other zines of the day, early audiences could make little sense of these confusing films. Carl's mental illness may not define his first three features, but it necessitated their creation as a means of expression that would have been denied to him in any other manner.

Returning to Brakhage, **Alien Beasts** offers a different metaphor of vision—one of how Sukenick himself sees the world, the expression of his visions onscreen with no regard for precursors or tradition. This is oppositional, outsider art in every sense, vital for its revelations. As a work of self-contained personal expression, it is unmatched in its feverish imagination and distinctive flow. That its sought audience was the underground horror fanbase speaks as much to its exclusion from any sort of canon or serious appraisal as to its supposed flaws. Each of Sukenick's countless video releases offer variations on the themes contained here (as well as the **Mutant Massacre** duology). His concerns as an artist never change, even as his expression of them has shifted in recent years. Much as Brakhage's lyrical films

1 Sconce, "Trashing," p.389.
2 Nirenberg.

often centered on the director's personal life, his family and their home—with **Anticipation of the Night's** early moments of seeming suburban tranquility almost predicting **Alien Beasts**' various lawn brawls in a bizarre manner—Sukenick's personal world, interior and exterior, subconscious and spatial, is what ultimately drives his style of production. Behind every video work is a lyrical sensibility that connects for no one save the director, not for his lack of effort, but his idiosyncratic approach, so at odds with every conception of cinema as an art form. Much like his predecessor in lyricism, the images in Sukenick's films are bizarre, uncomfortable, and all but unrecognizable to outsiders, yet there is no question that they are invested with the importance of the life he leads, his filmmaking the only possible expression of their impact; indeed, his relentless prolificacy recalls Brakhage's nearly ceaseless output on film.

Sukenick's earliest available films, shot largely on Super 8 and unavailable to the public until their VHS releases by Poser Rot Productions in the 2010s, reveal more linear narratives. They still display the same fractured worldview and reliance on Styrofoam props to illustrate narratives of espionage and interstellar conflict, but lack the monotonous editing and repetition of **Alien Beasts**. **Ninja Dream**, a mid-1980s production, again centers Sukenick himself as a special agent working to defeat an insidious invading force. Read against one another, **Alien Beasts** can be seen as a progression in Sukenick's filmography, coupled with the earlier **Mutant Massacres**, his arrival at the point of filmmaking freed totally from the confines of traditional narrative and the demands of mainstream cinematic production. Even if, as Matt Desiderio argues, Sukenick was attempting to create films with mass appeal, no longer were the forms of his works defined by his influences.[1] **Alien Beasts** signifies the arrival of his own personal filmmaking style, centering his experiences and ambitions while disregarding the expectations of his target audience and the very concept of cinema as entertainment. This film was the breakthrough point, the shift from the traditional constraints of aboveground cinema that had limited his expression much as Brakhage's earlier attempts at trance films had hindered his groundbreaking concept of personal filmmaking.

1 Nirenberg.

Conclusions

ALTHOUGH THEIR WORKS are distinctive, both Pinion and Sukenick owe a debt to avant-garde pioneers Deren and Brakhage for creating new methods of unconventional personal expression. In fact, Carl Sukenick's artist profile for his Community Access artist page notes Brakhage's **Mothlight** as one of his favorite films, suggesting that his own avant-garde techniques are more intentional than his critics would admit. Even where these disparate styles do not conform completely, they stand as a unified cinema in opposition to traditional, mainstream films. As examples of genre cinema above all else, these films retain traces of common narrative structures as well as the direct influence of more commercially popular works than Deren and Brakhage's own projects. This is not necessarily a negative quality, as the true element emphasized in both filmmakers' essays is the freedom of expression unique to amateur production. Just as avant-garde films have a limited appeal to some audiences, so too do horror films of particularly modest means.

There's no question that the majority of amateur horror films shot-on-video bear no formal connections to the avant-garde. That the works discussed here do share some connections signifies the potential of video to create something more unique and daring than what has come previously. Despite their crude, simplistic appearances, these are rich, complex films that reflect the identities and interests of their makers, mirroring the essential qualities of critically-lauded works by Deren and Brakhage. Films as uncompromising as Pinion and Sukenick's deserve readings that are similarly unique, given their unprecedented expressions of subjective experiences. Approaches such as Thrower's recall the functionality of terms such as outsider and *art brut* to assess art that is wholly self-possessed, encapsulating both the avant-garde and amateur horror styles. Non-normative cinema is not merely the result of artistic failings or outright ignorance on the part of the creators. It can be the product of an entirely alternative sensibility, one that exists at odds with all conceptions of standard filmic art and entertainment. As discussed earlier regarding the films of Chester Turner and Todd Cook, many viewers of SOV horror erroneously attribute to them elements of surrealism and avant-garde techniques. While these are convenient means of describing the bizarre representations on display, they do a disservice to the numerous films that legitimately contribute to experimental film discourse.

Neither feature discussed here is an example of a "pure" trance or lyrical film, as Sitney would posit for several experimental films that followed **Meshes of the Afternoon** and **Anticipation of the Night**. It is also important to remember his assertion that "[trance] films in general...tend to resist specific interpretation."[1] Even lyrical works can be dense and difficult to interpret, even for those familiar with their essential components. Challenging all concepts of genre films as easy entertainment, Pinion and Sukenick too resist easy analysis. This is not only a result of their ambitions, but also a matter of their contents being so overwhelming, even in conflict with their low-budget presentations. By offering their inherently subjective projects to even the niche audiences of the underground, these directors rewrote the rules of video expression to suit their own needs.

1 Sitney, p.20.

05

SPLATTER VIDEO: MUTATING THE SLASHER FILM

IN HER 1992 study of gender in the horror film, **Men, Women, and Chainsaws**, Carol Clover begins her chapter on the slasher film by stating "[a]t the bottom of the horror heap lies the slasher (or splatter or shocker or stalker) film."[1] This echoes the widespread critical revulsion toward the enormously-popular slashers of the 1980s—most visibly the **Friday the 13th**, **Halloween**, and **A Nightmare on Elm Street** franchises, as well as countless standalone releases from both major and independent studios. Perhaps the most famous critical backlash of the era was Gene Siskel's review of the first **Friday the 13th** (1980) in **The Chicago Tribune**, which savages the film and refers to director Sean S. Cunningham as "one of the most despicable creatures ever to infest the movie business." Roger Ebert reviewed **Friday the 13th: Part 2** (1981) with a half-star out of four, claiming it to be "a cross between the Mad Slasher and Dead teenager genres; about two dozen movies a year feature a mad killer going berserk, and they're all about as bad as this one." Ebert also accuses the film of ruining his childhood and fond memories of the theater in which it screened. Slasher films were as divisive as they were profitable, a tension that served as a particularly potent example of the divide between high and low art among genre films.

Clover succinctly defines the slasher film as "the immensely generative story of a psychokiller who slashes to death a string of mostly female victims, one by one, until he is subdued or killed, usually by the one girl who has survived."[2] Preoccupied with creative

1 Clover, p.21.
2 Ibid.

kill scenes, rising body counts, and repetitive nudity from its young cast, the slasher film cycle of the 1980s was formula-bound to a fault. This didn't stop the immense financial returns garnered by both the aforementioned series and numerous one-off features employing the stalk and slash equation defined by John Carpenter's **Halloween** (1978). Because of its gendered violence and reliance on nudity and retribution for sexual transgressions, the slasher film, per Clover "gives a clearer picture of current sexual attitudes, at least among the segment of the population that forms its erstwhile audience, than do the legitimate products of the better studios."[1] In their artless usage of exploitation techniques, slasher films are often more culturally revealing than tasteful major studio productions. This quality, however, does not come without its costs, and the surface-level offenses of slasher narratives saw great backlash from all variety of film critics.

This early critical disapproval set the tone for the mainstream press' reception of the hundreds of slasher films produced throughout the 1980s. Even the underground had grown tired of repetitive serial killer narratives, not to mention the ceaseless cycle of sequels and imitations. In the debut issue of his **European Trash Cinema** fanzine, Craig Ledbetter offered his mission statement for the new magazine, noting that he would be covering European genre films on video exclusively, in reaction to the glut of disposable slashers and direct-to-video films of the time.[2] Editor Steve C. of British zine **In the Flesh** declared his publication a "FREDDY and JASON FREE ZONE" and expresses displeasure with the regular coverage of slashers in other publications.[3] Other zines such as Charles Kilgore's **Ecco**, Cecil Doyle's **Sub-Human**, and noise musician Keith Brewer's **A Taste of Bile** emerged as conscious reactions to the overexposure of slasher films in other American publications, something of which the mainstream **Fangoria** magazine was particularly guilty.

In his discussion of para-paracinema, Matt Hills assesses the **Friday the 13th** series because of its immense popularity, particularly among latter-day audiences. As corporate products engineered by major

1 Ibid, p.23.

2 **ETC** was created following the deliberate ending of his earlier **Hi-Tech Terror** publication, a result of the editor's disgust with the current American home video market.

3 **In the Flesh**, p2.

Forgotten SOV slasher: ad for **Deven's Room, Independent Video #7** (1993)

studios, yet also incredibly popular works of "non-art," the **Friday the 13th** franchise was too "obviously a commercial success at the time of its initial release to be feted as underground trash, too historically recent to be recuperated as archival exploitation cinema, too standardized or proficient in its direction to be 'bad,' and yet possessing its own cult fan following."[1] These resources, as well as a growing number of popular and academic studies on the subgenre, reflect the constant popularity and reinvention of these films for audiences of all stripes. One area of appraisal that has largely been neglected is the crossover between SOV horror techniques and slasher film conventions, films which are a subcategory within a subgenre.

SOV horror covered every variation of subgeneric material, but it was through the established conventions of the slasher film that the cycle found its earliest and greatest success in United's release of **Blood Cult**. As previously discussed, that feature was a calculated attempt on the part of the distributors, running with the immensely

1 Hills, p.232.

popular and successful slasher template and adapting it for the home video world. Even before this, David Prior's **Sledgehammer** demonstrated an awareness of the commercial potential in imitating current trends. In these early examples, commercial success was the evident inspiration, rather than the subjective motivations evident in other SOV projects such as **Black Devil Doll from Hell**. While the slasher film cycle experienced its financial peak by the mid-1980s, the style never went out of fashion, with numerous titles produced yearly since the form's official inception in 1978. SOV horror, always ready to capitalize on the successes of the past, followed suit and churned out countless threadbare stalk and slash films long past the genre's mainstream relevance.

Inspired by several factors, some prominent SOV slashers took the generic formula and twisted it into something more bizarre, revealing, and challenging, revising the dominant narrative of that style. Gary Cohen found notable success with his 1987 debut feature, **Video Violence**, a small-town-with-a-secret slasher that attempted to inject criticism about the consumption of violence and horror film conventions. However, because of the film's reliance on the sort of misogynistic violence decried by mainstream critics, its conceptual aims fall far short of its intended commentary. Mark and John Polonia's **Splatter Farm** (1987) offers no intentional critique or higher purpose than commencing the brothers' filmmaking careers. As a result of their youthful energy, splatter film fandom, and especially their naivete surrounding extreme content and the representation of sexual violence, **Splatter Farm** is a disquieting and unintended subversion of the slasher. Clover utilizes the term mutation to refer to the evolution of the slasher film formula between the years 1974-1986.[1] **Video Violence** and **Splatter Farm** offer mutations of this standardized operation, subversions and deviations from even the formulaic impulses of the stagnant genre.

While she did not have SOV horror in mind, Clover admits her affection and impression of low-budget exploitation filmmaking. Regarding mainstream horror productions like **Silence of the Lambs** and others, she "cannot help thinking of all the low-budget,

1 Clover, p.26.

often harsh and awkward but sometimes deeply energetic films that preceded them by a decade or more—films that said it all, and in flatter terms, and on a shoestring."[1] **Splatter Farm** may not have made its points better than later mainstream productions, but "harsh," "awkward," and "energetic" are words that aptly describe the Polonias' debut. Likewise, Cohen's film displays a great deal of ambition, as well as particularly polished technical elements that elevate it above lesser SOV productions, but is still of a piece with their "low" appeals to consumers. Neither film attracted mention in the mainstream press, and very little within the underground, drawing none of the widespread derision inspired by mainstream slasher films; due to their subcultural status and lurid existences as cheap video store fodder, Cohen and the Polonias' films were beyond even the scope of slasher backlash. Because of this, their ambitions and even their flaws have not been fully appreciated by anyone save diehard cult film fans. **Video Violence** may fail at realizing its noble ambitions due to its overindulgence in exploitation, but retains its visceral power as one of the SOV cycle's most visible titles. Meanwhile, **Splatter Farm** exceeds its humble origins and remains a work that is profoundly offensive and distressing, yet successfully challenges the slasher film paradigm in ways that recode the form's rules.

Profoundly Disturbing Mutations

INSPIRED BY A video store customer's concern for her children viewing sex but not violence in a rented tape, Gary Cohen's **Video Violence** was the most financially successful and visible SOV title of the 1980s, next to **Blood Cult** itself.[2] The film better demonstrates the fascinating failings of the shot-on-video horror cycle than most other films of its kind, and it does so from within the rental industry itself. The film exists because of Cohen's insider's perspective of the home video market, which is decidedly not a fan's perspective. Cohen made the movie as a video store clerk who seemed to resent his very

1 Ibid, p.20.
2 Ziemba, **1980s**, p.212.

customer base and their attitudes, or at the least was bewildered by them. In the film, this latter detail subverts his very function as a business owner. Though its inspiration would seem to imply that **Video Violence** offers a critique of the wanton violence in both slashers and SOV horror videos, it falls notably short of this goal and instead wallows in the sort of debased cruelty that inspired its creation. Its violence and generic elements are too unpleasant and distressing to enjoy from even a detached perspective, depicting an unpolished ugliness that reflects the video market's freedom from censorship and MPAA regulation.

The film is undeniably mean-spirited, and fully "aware of the atmosphere it creates" through the framing device of a small-town video store's customers returning their own homemade snuff tapes.[1] Scenes of family members renting **Blood Cult** and extended moments in the shop itself are intermixed with prolonged scenes of misogynistic violence, in particular one taped sequence where Howard and Eli, two of the town's killers, torture a woman on camera. Eli taunts his victim, strips her, and ultimately carves his name into her chest. The argument criticizing the belief that sex is more offensive than violence is entirely invalidated by the film's introduction of sexualized violence as a major narrative device. Despite the crude analog video presentation, Joseph Ziemba argues that "**Video Violence's** discordant sexual content can't be justified with a laugh. It's too invasive. Which is ironic given Cohen's demure intentions."[2]

For all of its undeniable misogyny and various excesses, **Video Violence** demonstrates a strange sort of vitality by placing viewers almost entirely within the actual retail spaces of 1980s America. Moreover, given Cohen's own role as a video store owner and the film's metatextual rescripting of this reality, it reveals at least some form of awareness as a capital-driven exercise more than a serious artistic statement. This is not to say that the film lacks more enlightening material—consider the anti-film within the narrative, **The Vampire Takes a Bride**. A take-off on the snuff tapes driving the plot as well as an example of their very existence, the mock-art film offers a subversive

1 Ibid, p.214.
2 Ibid.

glimpse at the terrifying potential of home video better than the rest of the feature containing it does. Even with its fantastic subject matter, the vampire film is a biting and startling attack on aesthetic violence, offering the violent act-as-terror without any juvenile excesses. It reveals how the technology which permitted Cohen to make his film can be used to create works that are more real than much of life itself, even as fanciful and staged as they may appear. This is a world that would never exist on film, and that immediacy and proximity to the authentic is what makes **Video Violence** occasionally successful as a horror film.

The film's approach is too mannered and competent to provide base entertainment in the manner of inepter SOV works. At no point are there lapses in logic or judgement that derail the narrative or veer into the realm of the bizarre. There is no justifying the film's gendered violence, and Cohen was a grown man when **Video Violence** was produced. As awful as his violence may be, there's an awareness in it that denies simple pleasures of grotesque spectacle and emerges as something more troubling. There is nothing so rigorous as to suggest a critique of audience attitudes, and no way to resolve the disconnect between simple entertainment and troubling social criticism. Cohen has much to say about the consumption of violence but offers few answers to justify the extremity of his depictions. The nihilism of the film's conclusion is convincing and disturbing, particularly given the calm setting and stifling atmosphere of 1980s consumerist excess. **Video Violence** may display some gloss that separates it from other SOV features, but it also has an unseemly quality that still makes it stand apart as a negative example. As troubling as it is fascinating, Cohen's film remains a powerful signifier of a particular era in film history.[1]

Discussing the subgenre's appeal during its heyday and beyond, Clover notes that "[y]oung males are...the slasher film's implied audience, the object of its address."[2] What would she make of **Splatter Farm**, an amateur effort made by and almost entirely comprised of, yet not necessarily made *for*, adolescent males? While admittedly an expert on genre cinema by the time of her text's publication, Clover

1 This section is a revised and updated version of an essay that appeared in my own self-published volume, **When Renting is Not Enough** (2020).

2 Clover, p.23.

writes that hers was a process of conversion, a coming to terms with the peculiar affects and charms of genre cinema that was not natural to her cinematic consumption initially.[1] Twin brothers Mark and John Polonia began their film obsession, and resultantly, their careers, as fans of horror cinema, the very slashers and sequels that defined Clover's arguments five years after their film's video release. Through a series of backyard and basement lensed Super 8 efforts, the Polonias were self-taught amateur filmmakers who became professionals. Their experimentation with celluloid in their first projects—unintended for commercial release, but nonetheless seeing distribution in the mid-2010s after their cult reputation had grown—gave them the confidence to pursue increasingly ambitious endeavors, honing their technical skills while amassing a body of impressive special effects that would reappear in subsequent features for years to come.

As with so many other amateur filmmakers of the era, the brothers were emboldened by the runaway success of **Blood Cult**, realizing that the floodgates had opened for low-budget horror on video, and that competence and even audience satisfaction were no longer the object. Their first commercially-released film, and still their most notorious work, is 1987's **Splatter Farm**, which drew the industry attention they desired. Loaded with a number of violent set pieces that outdid most commercial releases of the time, the film quickly gained notoriety among cult horror fans. Made for an alleged $100 and displaying a striking mix of technical inventiveness with naïve attitudes toward representing extreme violence, **Splatter Farm** is unlike any other slasher film produced during the 1980s. Although the brothers were only eighteen at the time of filming, the film is a challenging clash of low-budget aesthetics, relentless energy, and disquieting excess that twists generic conventions into a work as innovative as it is unpalatable.

Twin brothers Alan (Mark) and Joseph (John) decide to spend the summer with their elderly aunt Lacey (Marion Costly) on her farm. Alan is kind, sympathetic, and generous, while his brother is crude, abrasive, and standoffish. Joseph teases Alan en route about Aunt Lacey's unnatural affection toward him, something she later acts on in

1 Ibid, p.20.

one of the film's many offensive depictions of degeneracy. On the farm, Aunt Lacey proves to be the least threatening presence, as they find a strange young handyman, Jeremy (Todd Michael Smith), has taken up residence with her. Jeremy is established as the film's antagonist from its opening minutes, which show him dismembering a corpse in the barn before masturbating with its severed hand. The film proceeds as a series of mundane events—the twins doing chores for Lacey, eating tense meals with her and Jeremy—interrupted by disturbing acts of violence. After several grueling sequences, and following both brothers' murders, Lacey reveals to Jeremy that he is the product of incest via her brother, whose putrefying corpse has been propped in a chair in the barn throughout the film. Outraged, Jeremy kills her with a firework to the crotch and escapes the film's violence unscathed.

The Donna Michelle VHS cut of **Splatter Farm**, technically speaking, the "original" version released in 1987, remains the most shocking commercial SOV release of the initial cycle. Though it is not the preferred or intended form of the film, it is the one that first saw commercial release, attracted infamy, and was in distribution for the longest period. The Donna Michelle cut is also notably more graphic than the 2007 Camp Motion Pictures directors' cut. Despite Mark Polonia's assertion that the Donna Michelle edit was an assembly cut that the company insisted on releasing without additional post-production work, it is responsible for the film's current reputation. It is also far more revealing in its various excesses, representing the unfettered teenage male id on tape, offering an unrestrained peek into the minds of the filmmakers that is unmatched by any other SOV slasher. Unlike **Video Violence**, which was made by adults within one sector of the video industry, **Splatter Farm** is the work of fans, amateurs despite their impressive pedigree of shorts, and displays no high-minded posturing despite its careerist ambitions. For these reasons and others, it fulfills ambitions previously not seen in even mainstream slasher films and stands as a significant deviation from the formal constraints of that style.

As detailed above, the film introduces its tastelessness from its earliest moments, with Jeremy's corpse-assisted masturbation initiating the cycle of mounting degeneracy. The film's most extreme moments are also its most revealing, reversing the gendered conventions of slasher film violence, though they are no less offensive

Splatter Farm-centric Camp Motion Pictures DVD ad, **Rue Morgue #69** (2007)

for this accomplishment. While much of the transgression rejects conventional slasher film misogyny, it remains highly disturbing regardless of the course taken. Joseph Ziemba asserts that "the idea of teenagers crafting a gore film that relies on abhorrent sexual acts to keep things rolling is unsettling. It's a little too revealing."[1] Writing on what she terms "body genres"—pornography, horror, and melodrama—Linda Williams notes that "the fun of 'gross' movies is in their display of sensations that are on the edge of respectable."[2] While the crude presentation and challenging sexual violence of **Splatter Farm** would seem to prevent spectatorial entertainment, there is a definitive value in its willingness to go to such lengths. Williams also

1 Ziemba, **1980s**, p.182.
2 Williams, p.2.

notes that "analyses of systems of excess have been much slower to emerge in the genres whose non-linear spectacles have centered more directly upon the gross display of the human body...Pornography is the lowest in cultural esteem, gross-out horror is next to lowest."[1] The Polonias delivered a work that is seemingly at odds with serious criticism due to its very nature and content, which makes it even more worthy of reconsideration.

The clearest deviation from slasher film convention is the film's lack of any female characters, save Costly as Aunt Lacey and a brief appearance by a door-to-door missionary. The question of the Final Girl, one of the most traditional slasher elements, is rendered moot from the very start; in fact, there is no heroic figure whatsoever in the film. Both Alan and Joseph are ultimately revealed to be powerless, doomed to ignoble deaths as the film careens toward its bleak conclusion. Clover defines the concept of the Final Girl as the survivor of the slasher film, "the one who did not die...the one who encounters the mutilated bodies of her friends and perceives the full extent of the preceding horror and of her own peril; who is chased, cornered, wounded; whom we see scream, stagger, fall, rise, and scream again. She is abject terror personified."[2] The Final Girl character defines the slasher film as much as its unstoppable antagonist. **Splatter Farm**, however, negates the concept itself by featuring no prominent female characters as victims, save Aunt Lacey's murder after our protagonists have already been dispatched. In fact, the film's reversal of the gendered dynamics of slasher violence instead offers a perverse emphasis on male victimhood that exceeds the savagery of traditional subgeneric narratives.

Another major point Clover makes regarding the male victims of slasher films notes that they "are shown in feminine postures at the moment of their extremity."[3] This codes the recipients of violence in terms wherein even male identification is rooted in a gendered reading by the spectator. Slasher film violence is inherently misogynistic in its traditional representations, but the Polonias reject this through their literalized representations of male victimhood. Untangling **Splatter**

1 Ibid, p.3.
2 Clover, p.35.
3 Clover, p.12.

Farm's psychosexual preoccupations would require a psychoanalytical analysis far outside of the reach of this book. However, the kill scenes and other gory indulgences can be examined within the context of the genre itself, emphasized for their divergence with convention and what they accomplish through their sheer excess. To a fault, **Splatter Farm** is a film without repression, every abhorrent and transgressive act is realized to the fullest extent enabled by the limited budget. Sexual transgression is not a condition for vengeance or punishment, but is in fact the sadistic impulse that results from the killing urge itself. Here the Polonias invert Clover's claim that in slashers, "violence and sex are not concomitants but alternatives."[1]

The most notorious scene in the film, and the longest alteration between the two released versions, is Joseph's excruciating torture and death at Jeremy's hands. Lasting several minutes, but noticeably longer in the VHS cut of the film, this sequence is the height (or nadir) of SOV cruelty and is viscerally effective despite its outrageousness. Frustrated with Jeremy after several bizarre encounters, not to mention Jeremy's obvious and unwelcome attraction to him, Joseph confronts and fights the handyman. The following torture scene reads as a catalog of horror: Jeremy forces fellatio on Joseph (complete with semen spit into the grass), beats and urinates upon him, and inserts his fist into latter's anus before smearing feces on his face. This is the longest portion of the scene, extended so that Joseph's near-fatal stabbing with a pitchfork comes as a relief. Following this, Aunt Lacey discovers Jeremy with her nephew's body, only becoming upset when Jeremy knocks over his father's skeleton in an assertion of his newfound masculinity. She then helps him bury Joseph alive, a scene John Polonia performs fully naked and exposed as he is pelted with actual dirt in a shallow grave. This long sequence is a parade of degradation and horror, far more upsetting than its cheap presentation should allow.

This section of the film bears a number of revelations, which extend beyond the puerile shock of the actions rendered. Joseph's humiliation and violation exceeds any standard of acceptable violence in commercial cinema (and **Splatter Farm**, despite its low profile, was

1 Ibid, p.29.

intended as a commercial work), and even if none of the effects are convincing in the least, the very conception and depiction of such abhorrent acts itself is unsettling. The scene engages the sexual violence typically spared of male characters in slasher films, and literalizes the assault metaphorically inflicted upon female victims via the phallic intrusion of the knife or similar weapons. Joseph's face while he is being tormented is the portrait of abject terror Clover reserves for her Final Girls, but he is not fated to survive, and is forced to confront this nihilistic conclusion in the moments leading up to his death. John Polonia, for his part, does not shy away from his depiction of this debasement, rolling around pantless on the dirty floor of the barn, covering himself in viscous liquids to represent his character's vital fluids, and subjecting himself to a literal burial, his genitals exposed to the camera. The phallocentric violence of even female-centered slasher film narratives is complicated, the Final Girl "a male surrogate in things oedipal, a homoerotic stand-in."[1] The Polonias subvert this gender reversal by literalizing the violence against a male character, as well as emphasizing the homoeroticism in their film. Rather than requiring a male reading of the slasher conventions to unpack the complexity of male identification, **Splatter Farm's** torture scene forwards an actualization of these subtextual elements.

Another revealing moment from this scene immediately follows the torture. Jeremy props Joseph, slowly bleeding out, in a lawn chair next to the house and enters the barn. Confronting his father's skeleton, he berates the corpse: "I'm the man of the family now, daddy!". Teased throughout the film, Jeremy's murderous impulses originate from his feelings of inadequate masculinity, not to mention the guilt associated with his alleged murder of his father figure. Interestingly, the corpse still occupies a position of power in the household—likely a nod to the withered grandfather figure of **The Texas Chainsaw Massacre**—which implies the patriarchal control overriding the twisted family of the narrative. Jeremy, later revealed to be the product of incest between Lacey and her brother, fits the long line of slashers derived from troubled familial lineages, but ultimately resists the controls of his upbringing, contrasting the murderous devotion demonstrated

1 Ibid.

INSANITY PRODUCTIONS

presents

THE GROUNDHOGS DAY MASSACRE 2

The VIOLENCE!

The BRUTALITY!

The STUPIDITY!

(Warning: This movie may cause mental distress & discomfort)

For a copy send $15 + $3 p/h to:

INSANITY PRODUCTIONS
PO Box 46074
Bedford, Ohio 44146

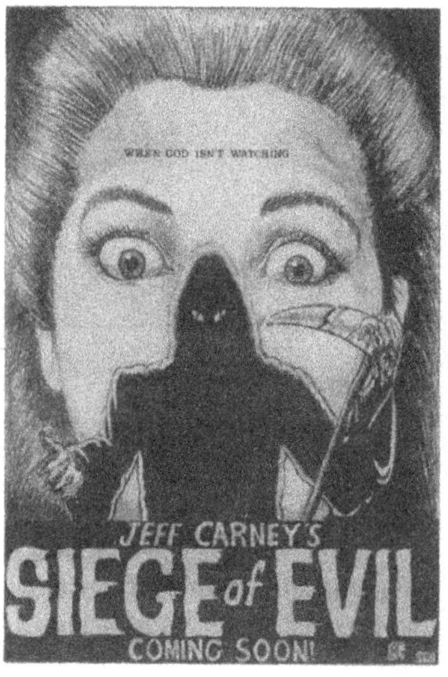

More forgotten SOV slashers: ads for **Groundhog Day Massacre 2** and **Siege of Evil**, **Independent Video #5** (1993)

by Leatherface and his brothers and especially the ur-slasher, Norman Bates. As an amalgam of the Polonias' various slasher film influences, Jeremy is not typical of the killer archetype, save in his actions. He is not childlike, disabled, or disfigured, like Leatherface, Jason Voorhees or countless others. Instead, he is unrestrained in his violence, allowed to freely indulge his murderous passions. As a standalone film, **Splatter Farm** dispenses none of the mythmaking (even retrospective) of many other works in the subgenre. It is self-contained, bringing piecemeal elements of its influences, adding to the uneasy tension of its extremity and naïve origins.

As is often the case with slashers themselves, there is more to Jeremy's character than is immediately apparent, a depth evident beneath the crude surface of the film itself. Jeremy is frequently shown with a red gloss on his lips, suggesting the application of lipstick, likely referencing the gender confusion displayed by Leatherface. He is also brazenly sexual rather than repulsed by the act itself, revealed during his first appearance, as well as the lunch scene following Alan and Joseph's arrival at the farm where he masturbates under the dinner table. Mark and John Polonia express their intention with this scene, as well as several other moments, as establishing Jeremy's homosexual attraction to Joseph, which culminates with the torture scene discussed above. If depictions of rape are rare in slasher films, then representations of outright homosexual desire—regardless of context or execution—are nearly as uncommon. Jeremy's psychosexual behavior is not a matter of confusion as he acts on every desire his body expresses. Clover notes that "[k]illing those who seek or engage in unauthorized sex amounts to a generic imperative of the slasher film."[1] The Polonias yet again flip the convention, placing the execution of sexual desire as the imperative in the act of violence itself.

Returning to Williams' discussion of body genres and her noting the fun of gross movies and their lack of respectability, **Splatter Farm** is nothing if not obsessed with bodily functions and fluids: vomit, feces, urine, semen, and blood are all major elements of the film's narrative. Whether or not it is fun is another matter entirely, but the film's representation of such effluvia clearly transgresses the lines demarcated by so-called "safe" cinema. John Polonia's exposure of his genitals also breaches lines of acceptable sexual representation in mainstream cinema. Not only does **Splatter Farm** break the rules of the slasher film in its failure to conform the expectations of the victims' genders and behaviors, but it also confronts the standards of gendered representation inherent in mainstream filmmaking. None of this was the intended function of the work, but beneath the disturbing surface of the film's acts are more startling moments of innovation.

Alan is not spared the sort of horrific sexual violence his brother suffers, something hinted at in the early driving scene where Joseph mentions Aunt Lacey's unnatural affection toward his brother. Late in the film, after several passes made toward him, Aunt Lacey makes Alan a cup of tea laced with a drug and takes advantage of him while he is unconscious. The brothers, again noting their discomfort with their film's shock tactics do remark that this scene is surprisingly chaste given the horrific nature of the act itself.[2] The assault lasts only a matter of seconds, represented by two figures moving under a heavy blanket as the camera shakes in and out of focus, interrupted by several shots of Alan's sleeping face in a medium close-up. In contrast to Joseph's death, this scene is more disturbing in its

1 Ibid, p.34.

2 "Back to the Farm."

conception while its representation reads as innocuous if not tasteful. Why it was deemed necessary is another matter entirely, but it is far less graphic than countless similar scenes in other exploitation films. Yet again reversing the gender dynamic of the slasher film, not to mention the rape and revenge titles also analyzed by Clover, the rape is exploitative in its inclusion but not its realization. While this incestuous reversal may not validate the presence of the scene—and in fact renders it more disturbing—it does deviate from held expectations of trash filmmaking in its desire to offend.

Aunt Lacey suffers no consequences for this specific transgression, but she does suffer both onscreen and off as a result of the film's deranged attempts at entertainment. Late in the film, Alan is abruptly shot in the head attempting to avenge his brother's death. Aunt Lacey, frustrated more than horrified at the murders, confronts Jeremy, revealing the incestuous nature of his conception. Enraged, Jeremy murders his mother by stuffing a firecracker into her vagina, causing her entire body to explode. The effect could be comical—provided by a fake foil-wrapped rocket and meat-stuffed mannequin—but after the film's parade of anal-genital violence, this act too is difficult to endure. There is also something distressing about the intrusive violence the two female characters face—the missionary has her chest torn open and her heart eaten, and Aunt Lacey is violated in a manner recalling her assault at her brother's hands, seemingly punished for his violence by her own offspring. Earlier, however, Lacey spends a quiet moment with her brother's corpse, longing for his presence and attempting intimacy with his corpse by reaching into his open zipper. His genitals have withered to dust, which seeps through her fingers as she expresses disappointment and sexual frustration.

As disturbing as the film's male-oriented violence may be, it does not relent when it comes to Lacey's character. This was the first Polonia film to even feature a female character due to the brothers' admitted awkwardness throughout high school. Furthermore, later films, such as **Lethal Nightmare** (1991) and **Bad Magic** (1997) feature no female victims nor any of the deranged sexual violence of their first film. Still, **Splatter Farm's** complete disregard for both the handling of sexual violence and Lacey's own trauma reveals the filmmakers' ignorance and inexperience. The brothers express this sentiment themselves in the commentary track for the film's DVD recut, noting that the scene of incest is in especially

CREATIVE CONCEPTS UNLIMITED
RD #1 Box 275
Mansfield , PA 16933

"SPLATTER FARM"

Shot on 1/2" VHS, full length 90 min - Explicit docu-drama. Distributed by Pheonix Home Video (over 2000 copies sold).

"LETHAL NIGHTMARE"

Shot on Super 8, full length 90 minute - Horror. To be released by Pheonix Home Video in October 1993

"HOW TO SLAY A VAMPIRE"

Shot on 3/4" video with Filmlook. 90 minute - Comedy. To be released by Milestone Entertainment Inc. in the fall of 1993

"HELL SPAWN"

To be shot on 3/4" video with Filmlook. Full length aprox. 100 min. Now in production

John Polonia, Todd Michael Rimatti and Mark Polonia

Creative Concepts Unlimited promotional material from **Independent Video #7** (1993)

poor taste, and that they regret the extremity of the torture scene, recognizing the potential reality of the horrific acts it depicts. As with so much of the film's shocking power, its most infamous moments resulted from youthful disregard for standards of good taste and acceptable representation. Were the brothers not teenagers at the time of production, there's no doubt that the work would lack the shocking acts it unashamedly flaunts. That said, it also would lack much of the unintentional innovation and impact that it carries through its subversion of genre tropes.

Accustomed to shooting on film via their earlier Super 8 projects, the Polonias admit that they were slow to embrace video's potential, and relative novices with the technology at the time of production. In this sense, **Splatter Farm** recalls Jean-François Lyotard's concept of acinema, including every error by necessity rather than conscious decision simply because no alternatives existed. Illustrating this in their commentary on the film, the brothers note that the early driving scene was shot as though they were conserving celluloid stock: one brother's line was filmed from the opposite seat, before switching camera subject and position to capture the subsequent dialogue. Completely unaware of the potential to shoot coverage of the entire scene and construct the edits in post-production, the Polonias added a greater amount of labor in their production. Other scenes were shot with no coverage, simply beginning and ending a take exactly as scripted. Only two scenes were redone later to achieve better versions, and many scenes were completed with only single takes.

Despite their accumulated knowledge of filmmaking, the directors filmed **Splatter Farm** in the manner of consummate amateurs. This accounts for much of the film's roughshod appearance, even in its revised DVD edition, along with its budgetary limitations.

Even independent celluloid slasher films bear the sheen of professionalism, featuring none of the technical and performative errors of **Splatter Farm.** In the Polonias' case, commercial demands actually necessitated the release of the imperfect cut. Rather than Lyotard's conception of excessive, revealing moments lost to the capitalistic requirements of cinema, the booming home video market itself demanded more product, inspiring Donna Michelle to distribute **Splatter Farm** in its roughest possible form to satisfy customers. This hastiness preserved the most shocking and revealing moments of the film, along with its more unprofessional touches. The film's status as acinema is what defines its innovations—because of its imperfections, its creators' naivete, and its unexpected release, **Splatter Farm** is more than a slasher film, it is a mutation of that form. These deficiencies, not to mention the perversity on display in the initial release, did not deter the commercial success of the film: a 1993 promotion in an issue of **Independent Video** notes that the film had sold over 2,000 copies by that date.[1] These are not significant figures against any form of mainstream cinema, but they are no less impressive given the film's alleged $100 budget and humble beginnings. Moreover, the film's unlikely success granted the Polonias the name recognition to continue directing low-budget SOV features and build a devoted cult audience. Clearly, acinematic content need not interfere with the aims of commercial cinema production, even on a reduced scale.

Affect and the SOV Slasher

SPLATTER FARM BELIES its simple façade to prove that the slasher genre could offer innovations as late as 1987, and regardless of its filmmakers' intentions, it reads unlike any other film of its sort. While cheap entertainment and shock were the intended responses at the

1 "Creative Concepts," p.30.

time of production, in many ways **Splatter Farm** negates such a notion. Everyone in the film suffers, much as unprepared viewers are still likely to have trouble with its visual assault. There is no identification in effect for the spectator: Jeremy is revealed from the opening moments to be a perverse murderer, Aunt Lacey's well-meaning exterior is shattered through her incestuous lust and harboring of Jeremy (though a case could easily be made for her as one of the film's victims due to the abuse suffered via her brother), Alan is well-meaning and kind but inspires little sympathy, and Joseph is crass and abrasive. One reason for the film's off-putting nature—in addition to its catalog of aberrations—is its lack of traditional filmic identifications. These elements of the film prove that even in acinematic works, the parts truly constitute the whole.

As with many paracinematic readings of trash as art, **Splatter Farm** would offer little beyond puerile shocks if the directors did not invest it with legitimate creativity and skill in its presentation. Insert shots of Jeremy dancing nude in a field, holding a skinned human face up to his own head, inject moments of nightmarish near-surrealism that give the rest of the film's brutality a starker context. Mark and John Polonia note that this moment was included as an intentional nod toward their notions of art cinema, citing Todd Smith's obsession with David Lynch's **Blue Velvet** as their direct inspiration. Elsewhere, the camera work suggests a greater ambition than typically on display in SOV projects, with an impressive dolly shot across Aunt Lacey's dining room table during her final confrontation with Jeremy startling as much as the earlier inept gore in its skillfulness. After this scene and Lacey's death, Jeremy dances nude in the field, finally freed of his familial restraints and emboldened to continue his deranged lifestyle unencumbered. Just on the other side of filmic function and the strictures of good and acceptable cinema is complete liberation. The Polonias may have displayed an early fascination with the slasher film—again embodying the adolescent male audience cited by Clover—but they evolved beyond these trappings to advance their filmmaking style. Embarrassed by the prurience of this film and eager to move beyond it in their dedication to their careers, the brothers progressed.

Much like the gendered violence in Cohen's film, the conception rather than the execution of **Splatter Farm's** brutality is shocking. Even for fans of the film, it remains "one of the most vile, unbelievable,

Another forgotten SOV slasher: **Tortured Soul II** ad, **Film Threat Video Guide #13** (1995)

sickening, hypnotic and perverted horror films imaginable; tempered with a charming slice of teenaged honesty."[1] The violence was admittedly an afterthought, often improvised in the moment of filming, something not true of **Video Violence**. This does little to reconcile the base impulses of the film with its aims at simple entertainment, but does speak to the deeper cultural representations of the slasher film style and the brothers' understanding of them. This is not to say that it is progressive in its attitudes toward gender roles, homosexuality, and violence in slasher films—far from it in fact, given the above lack of consideration. This is a film that is immature and vile in its very existence, but bewilderingly sincere in its conception. Even—and sometimes especially—clumsy and offensive art can challenge the very systems it tries (and often fails) to imitate.

1 Mogg, p.129.

06

EXCESS AND OUTRAGE: THE TRANSGRESSIVE SOV UNDERGROUND

SPLATTER FARM'S YOUTHFUL transgressions may push the limits of acceptable representation, but excessive shocks were hardly unique among SOV horror features. Several earlier films crossed the line from mere bad taste into willful offense, straddling the poles of naïve exuberance and a genuinely antisocial embrace of video's unregulated creative potential. Perhaps unsurprisingly, many of these titles have proven to be among the most lasting and popular films to emerge from the cycle. As a truly independent art form, SOV horror answered to none of the enforced restrictions regulating mainstream cinema. Directors reported to no one but themselves, ratings boards were completely removed from consideration, and in many cases, there were no producers or investors to appease with marketable products. For all the freedom imparted upon the creative process itself, there was also a blatant disregard for notions of good taste or sensitive depictions of horrifying material. For every wholesome **Tales from the Quadead Zone** or **Demon Dolls**, there were just as many examples like **Video Violence** that carried on the exploitation tradition of outright offense.

In fact, while **Splatter Farm** offers valuable if uncomfortable insights into the minds of adolescent horror fans, many of the Polonias' contemporaries deny this sort of critical reevaluation. Unintentional as they may have been, the brothers' innovations represent a legitimate destabilization of the subgeneric slasher film style. To assume or argue that all SOV features are critically valid or valuable is a misrepresentation of the cycle, one that ignores its roots in the exploitative practices of earlier trash filmmaking. Despite their shared technical properties, the full body of SOV horror films is too disparate and diverse to approach as an enlightened form. Many films revel in outright obscenity and outrage for the sheer sake of provocation, attacking notions of decency rather than simply challenging them.

In these cases, the aesthetics of trash filmmaking are adopted not for enlightenment, or even entertainment in some cases, but to elicit visceral reactions from viewers and critics alike. These are examples of filmmaking as an uncompromising, even anti-artistic, means of expression; no regard is paid to mainstream standards of decency, just as the question of entertainment is often rendered irrelevant. In cases where extreme representations of sex and violence operate as means of incitement, trying to salvage the reputations of the films themselves is a failure to take the works on their own terms. They cannot be read as high-minded or even socially worthwhile because to do so is a violation of their very functions.

Critic and theorist Arthur C. Danto articulated the concept of disturbational art, referring to works which were not merely offensive or disturbing, but legitimately threatening to both spectator and creator alike. Largely concerned with performance art, to Danto "these various arts, often in consequence of their improvisational and shabby execution, carry a certain threat, promise a certain danger even, compromise reality in a way the more entrenched arts and their descendants have lost the power to achieve."[1] There is a barrier here regarding filmmaking, as the chances of legitimate danger arising from screening a feature film, particularly shown in the home as most SOVs were, are nil. Danto is clear that works that are simply offensive to notions of good taste cannot be truly considered disturbational, but does offer other spaces where this boundary can be crossed. He argues that "in disturbational art, the artist is not taking refuge behind the conventions: he is opening a space which the conventions are designed to keep closed."[2] Thus, the acinematic properties of many SOV features, particularly when coupled with extreme contents and nihilistic worldviews, are what impart them with the power of true disturbation. In representing forbidden acts and events in ways that themselves are prohibited by arbiters of proper filmmaking, certain SOV horror films cross from mere agitation into the realm of art as a legitimate threat.

SOV horror's fascination with confrontation was evident from its inception, with early releases like **Blood Cult** reveling in exploitation

1 Danto, p.119.
2 Ibid, p.125.

for its own sake. The films of Chester Turner, Wally Koz, and especially underground provocateur Joe Christ, indicate that the expression of bad taste was not merely a stylistic component of SOV filmmaking, but in many cases its *raison d'être*. Charles Pinion also demonstrated that punishing content could be employed by underground filmmakers; however, he did so in a manner that proved extremity can have an undeniable purpose, even if it is no less pleasant to encounter. These films, even where obnoxious and uncompromising for no distinct reason besides provocation, remain important pieces of the SOV horror underground. The continual pushing of boundaries has proven influential on the recent video horror filmmaking movement. Now working almost exclusively with digital video, today's extreme horror filmmakers take inspiration from these notable transgressors, creating an entire subgenre of filmmaking containing little but the most horrible, previously unfilmable aberrations. While I can't redeem the contents of the films to follow, they are nonetheless important in setting a precedent for the current generation of underground production.

Precursors in Extremity

CHESTER TURNER'S PIONEERING 1984 release **Black Devil Doll from Hell** remains one of the cycle's most infamous works. Both lambasted and celebrated as an "early SOV cesspool...Easily the most vile, deranged, and hysterical film to ever be scored with a Casiotone" the film remains divisive.[1] Concerning devout Christian Helen Black and her chance encounter with a cursed ventriloquist dummy, Turner's debut embraces a *vérité* approach to homemade filmmaking that wallows in misogyny. Helen finds her deepest desires realized as the puppet comes to life, sexually assaults her in an extended scene, and awakens her innermost urges, causing her to seek a lover who can satisfy her as the puppet did. The film offensively forwards the notion that all women need sexual contact–even when forced—to find satisfaction and even the most chaste secretly desire degradation. At the same time, it also bears a twisted sense of Christian morality, with Helen punished at

1 Ziemba, **1980s**, p.11.

555 advertisement, **Deep Red #6** (1989)

the end for her promiscuous ways. The tension between misogynistic ignorance and simplistic morality tale is a result of Turner's amateurish techniques, assuming every technical duty himself during production and casting friends and family in every role. The $8,000 feature is both undermined and enhanced as a result of its threadbare production: it is so inept in appearance and execution that it succeeds as an unintentional comedy. Simultaneously, its grubby home video look imparts a sense of genuine derangement and claustrophobia. Easy as it may be to laugh off a puppet conceived by the director as resembling "Rick James as a farmer," this hilarity is less digestible when the noxious rape scene lasts as long as it does. Richard Mogg finds these excesses both laudable and despicable, calling Turner's debut the point "where SOV horror goes completely off the rails...the most unapologetic example of camcorder misuse I have had the pleasure of viewing."[1] Because of his naivete and the film's ignorant rather than malicious worldview, it succeeds as a traditional badfilm—terrible by accepted standards, but an unintentional comedy, enlightening in its failures. As the 1980s progressed, however, several more horrific examples would emerge as well.

1 Mogg, p.37.

Wally Koz's **555** (1988) was inspired by the director's disdain for SOV releases like **Blood Cult** garnering success despite their lack of redeeming qualities, making it an exercise in bad taste meant to cash in on earlier examples of the same. Seeking imitation rather than innovation, Koz's slasher depicts his killer practicing necrophilia with each of his female victims. More upsetting than this is the film's rampant and vocal misogyny, from the mistreatment of victims to the gendered epithets employed throughout. Turner may have unknowingly imbued his film with regressive gender roles, but Koz embraced the misogyny of his screenplay without concern. Subsequent films such as Jon McBride's **Cannibal Campout** (1988) and David Schwartz's **Las Vegas Bloodbath** (1989) go even further in their depictions of misogyny, both featuring scenes of fetuses being removed from their mothers' bodies after extensive torture scenes. These late examples of slashers proved that amateur filmmakers were willing to wallow in shock and degradation for its own sake in the hopes of making a name on the video market.

Writing on obscenity, Danto notes that "its use erases a boundary between imitation and reality, and the art is disturbing because the reality it releases is itself disturbing."[1] The above films may be offensive, and arguably obscene, but they contain few traces of reality beyond their "[capturing] surroundings like a documentary time-capsule of the early '80s."[2] Turner and others may have had deranged visions to realize via filmmaking, but they did not live the acts they depicted onscreen, and their works compromised at some level to meet the commercial market. As offensive as the scenes described above may be, there is a measure of comfort in knowing that their perversity was staged rather than actualized. One may struggle to justify their excesses, but they are not disturbational in the truest sense. Unfortunately for viewers, a handful of underground filmmakers seemed to believe that these works did not go far enough and began making more troubling and indefensible work. As Jack Sargeant outlines regarding the progression of the subterranean film landscape, "[if] the nineties underground built upon previous

1 Danto, p.122.
2 Mogg, p.37.

undergrounds, then one of the most influential ideas was that the underground film should embrace transgression."[1]

That's Just Wrong: True Underground Filth

DATING TO THE first decades of cinema itself, transgressive content has a long history in film, and proved especially appealing to underground and genre filmmakers. From the early innovations of Salvador Dalí and Luis Buñuel's surrealist landmark **Un Chien Andalou** (1919), as well as the groundbreaking homoerotic experiments of Kenneth Anger, the underground was well-versed in shocking content. The gore films of H.G. Lewis and the early bad taste comedies of John Waters also made distinct impressions upon later genre filmmakers. It was the Cinema of Transgression, however, that had the greatest impact on the SOV underground. Vowing "to go beyond all limits set or prescribed by taste, morality or any other traditional value system...There will be blood, shame, pain and ecstasy, the likes of which no one has yet imagined," the films of Nick Zedd, Richard Kern, and others proved particularly influential on the new wave of extreme filmmaking.[2] As Jack Sargeant argues, the most lasting influence of the Cinema of Transgression was its "understanding of the importance of confrontation, often manifested through depictions of psychological dislocation, sadism, violence, and what was culturally deemed 'perverse' sex."[3] This emphasis on shock was taken by some as a challenge, and the 1990s saw an influx of films ready to exploit this device to its fullest extent, regardless of what reception they might attract.

Filmmaker and musician Joe Christ arrived just after the Cinema of Transgression's peak years but was to be inextricably associated with that movement throughout his career. His debut release, 1988's **Communion in Room 410** was filmed on Super 8 and transferred to video for post-production, reflecting the celluloid loyalty of the 1980s

1 Sargeant, **Flesh**, p.109.

2 Jeriko, pp.3-5.

3 Sargeant, **Flesh**, p.66.

Ad for Nick Zedd's films, **Film Threat #10** (1986)

underground. Advertised in an issue of **Film Threat** as "a hideous parody of the last supper" and celebrated by the filmmaker as "THE REAL THING! No stage blood here," Christ's confrontational methods were immediately apparent.[1] True to the ad, the short is seventeen minutes

1 "Videos by," p.43.

Ad for Richard Kern's **Manhattan Love Suicides**, **Film Threat #10** (1986)

of Christ and two female acquaintances sitting in a dim motel room taking turns slicing one another's flesh and drinking the blood. There is no variation of content, minimal editing or technical finesse, and nothing to indicate an aesthetic justification for capturing the mutilation on film. A review in **Film Threat** addresses the work as having "no plot, no dialogue, just slash and gore, with mind numbing sound effects" before noting that Christ and his co-stars' antics left a mess of blood in the motel room to horrify the building's staff.[1] From the start of his career, Christ made it clear that his excesses were not safe, that he was not concerned with artistic validity or popular reception, only the realization of his deranged worldview onscreen.

Communion in Room 410 ad from **Film Threat #16** (1988)

To the consternation of the underground press, Christ continued producing and self-distributing shorts throughout the 1990s, increasingly embracing the "death drive" identified by Sargeant. Refining his techniques, but delving further into transgressive bad taste, Christ's featurettes from the 1990s represent the most offensive, outrageous, and indefensible excesses of the underground to that point in time. Now working exclusively with video, Christ's subsequent shorts followed in swift succession, embodying Sargeant's claim that "the ready availability of video technologies allowed [the Cinema of Transgression's] successors to shoot and edit film with an even greater ease."[2]

Speed Freaks with Guns (1991) operates within a loose narrative frame and effectively establishes the concerns of Christ's oeuvre. Starring the director himself, the film recounts the Manson Family-inspired killing spree of Joe and his followers, Kitten, Muffin and Poontang. This is accomplished through several flashback sequences of home invasions and gruesome murders. The majority of the footage, however, is scenes of Joe himself walking the streets of New York, rambling and reminiscing directly to the camera, and being vomited

1 Shapiro, p.8.

2 Sargeant, **Flesh**, p.109.

on by a priest. The film manages to outdo **Communion in Room 410** in confrontation, opening with Joe ranting and shouting racial slurs regarding a plot to poison him with radioactive materials. The coupling of wanton violence, antisocial behavior, and racist humor impart a deeper sense of Christ's sensibilities and reveal his commitment to offense at any cost. The film is pervaded with a "sense of genuine danger, nihilism, and recklessness...Pure exploitation. Filth for the sake of filth."[1] The outrage generated by the film is exacerbated by Christ's role, ostensibly playing a more unhinged version of himself, never comforting his viewers by making clear what he believes or has truly done. In disturbational art, "the subject represented actually entered into its representations," and although viewers may be spared any danger via direct contact with Christ, the worldview offered is noxious enough to cause legitimate unease.[2]

Yet more troubling in Christ's filmography is his third short, **Crippled** (1992), which occurs in a single room, adding a claustrophobic squalor to its story of abuse. A disabled woman (played by Christ regular Nanzi Regalia) seeks a new caretaker after her previous steals from her and neglects her needs. Christ answers the want ad himself, and quickly makes his deranged intentions clear. He taunts and neglects her, places a bobblehead of Adolf Hitler on her nightstand, and finally sexually assaults her before the short abruptly ends. The film exists for no reason other than to offend, reveling in utter debasement and cruelty as an expression of Joe's sick sense of humor. Intended as a dark comedy, but reading as utter abject horror, **Crippled** is an exercise in crossing every possible barrier of good taste to arrive at a point of indefensible trash filmmaking. One review comments "[it's] been a long time since I saw something that made me feel like I shouldn't be watching it, and **Crippled** did that for me. A revolting piece of provocative trash by a professional provocateur."[3] Christ's intention to make comedies, reflecting his own dark, nihilistic humor, is especially troubling. While Waters reveled in the potential of bad taste and camp, his earliest films were meant as entertainment. Christ assuredly had the same goal, but gives a distinct impression that

1 Cobb, #7, p.7.
2 Danto, p.127.
3 Cobb, #7, p.6.

his post-Cinema of Transgression provocations were made for the purpose of dispensing with all rules of acceptability. In fact, regarding an early (pre-filmmaking) stunt where Christ and his friends mocked the JFK assassination in Dallas, the filmmaker notes that even Waters found his antics to be in excessively poor taste.[1] Every detail of his constructed persona, in music, filmmaking, and even his personal life, reveals Christ's commitment to transgression, pushing his life and art to the very limits.

Though outside my time frame, later shorts follow much of the same pattern, with **Is it Snuff? You Decide** (1997) and **Amy Strangled a Small Child** (1998) demonstrating the increasingly disturbational tactics of Christ's filmmaking by further incorporating sexual abuse, murder, and defecation. The former is little more than a staged casting call with a prospective actress, who is ultimately assaulted and strangled by Christ (behind the camera for the majority of the short) and a female cohort. This piece is the nadir of Christ's filmmaking, devoid of any appeal save the director's own aesthetic of confrontation. Completely irredeemable and almost impossible to watch, the short nonetheless serves as a prescient indication of the future of extreme horror in the new millennium. Of the latter film, Steve Puchalski proclaims that it "offers no redeeming social values, and even less filmmaking skill...This is a truly rancid view of humankind."[2] Puchalski also notes that Christ "continues cranking out his crude 'n nasty work on a regular basis," remaining a fixture on the bottom tier of the underground film world, long after his predecessors like Zedd and Kern had stopped working or lost their initial notoriety.[3] Billed by the director as "A comedy about repressed memory flashbacks," Christ was far less concerned with explorations of trauma than he was offending, exemplifying the legitimately dangerous edge of marginal filmmaking to an increasingly unreceptive audience. At this late stage of his career, Christ more than ever exemplified Danto's argument that disturbational art engages "a regressive posture."[4]

Danto writes that "reality must in some way then be an actual

1 Shapiro, p.8.
2 Puchalski, #14, p.40.
3 Ibid.
4 Danto, p.126.

component of disturbational art, and usually reality of a kind itself disturbing: obscenity, frontal nudity, blood, excrement, mutilation, real danger, actual pain, possible death. And these as components in the art, not simply collateral with its production or appreciation."[1] Each of these elements are present at various points in Christ's films, often commingled into the same sequences. Though every act save those in **Communion in Room 410** and his short documentary **Sex, Blood, and Mutilation** (1995) is staged, the veracity of their depictions and corporeal minutiae are more realistic and challenging than any other SOV films of their era. Christ may not have been a legitimate threat to his viewers or even society, but his attempts at provocation offered little chance of entertainment or pleasure in their representations of gendered violence and excessive brutality.

William Brown, in discussing the noncinematic works of Giuseppe Andrews, identifies John Waters' employment of bad taste as a foundational component of American independent filmmaking. Largely abandoning his career as an actor in mainstream Hollywood films, Andrews chose to live a hermetic life in a small trailer park, where he made low-budget digital video features starring the other residents, bringing a surreal scatology to his films, much in the manner that Christ did only a few years prior. On the crudeness of the dialogue and imagery, Brown argues that "this is a cinema that shows aspects of the world and the body that many might consider unbecoming, in the sense of being unfit for polite society."[2] Andrews uses bodily functions as unpretentious devices, closer to reality than any sanitized depictions found in mainstream cinema and employs these elements as humorous asides. Christ also embraced scatology and crudity, albeit of a psychopathic nature, for comedic purposes. The key difference is that Christ's realistic representations of degeneracy are too offensive, criminal even, to be justified. Andrews' cinematic poverty demonstrates that marginal digital filmmaking, though "illegitimate," is ultimately "alive and entitled to live."[3] Transgressive video filmmaking likewise demonstrates its illegitimacy, as well as a tenacious grip on the later generations of underground artists who took it as a rallying call.

1 Danto, p.120.
2 Brown, p.176.
3 Ibid, p.175.

Red Spirit Lake: Justified Outrage[1]

CONCURRENT WITH JOE Christ's most notorious films, Charles Pinion, now relocated to New York City, began work on his second feature. Following the failure of the overly ambitious **Killbillies**, which remains unfinished and lost, Pinion was inspired to simply make another film in the hands-on style of **Twisted Issues**. Though his debut drew regular comparisons to the Cinema of Transgression, Pinion was unfamiliar with those works at the time of its release. After several years in New York, however, he had become acquainted with several contributors to the movement and absorbed their aesthetics into his own cinematic approach. His 1993 film, **Red Spirit Lake**, was not only more experimental and atmospheric than his first, but engaged extreme subject matter in a far more direct and challenging manner. Bringing an ever-present violence that propels every narrative event,

1 This section is a revised and updated version of an essay that appeared in my own self-published volume, **When Renting is Not Enough** (2020).

Charles Pinion DVD flyer (2018)

haunting the characters and interrupting their private moments, each act of brutality in **Red Spirit Lake** is based in violation and sexual deviance. The mean-spiritedness of these events is rooted in the real world analogues they signify rather than their crude execution onscreen. As admittedly exploitative as the film may be, there is a function and purpose to its nastiness.

The narrative begins with protagonist Marilyn's aunt suffering horrifically at the hands of several thugs hoping to wrest the titular property from her possession. Her death brings her niece to the lake house, where she soon encounters the same team of villains that murdered her aunt. Two caretaker brothers make their best efforts to protect her while dealing with their own trauma after being visited by "angels." Soon, the secret of Marilyn's family and the land they inhabit is revealed, tracing back to the brutal torture of a coven of witches who once lived on the land. This is represented through a number of hallucinatory flashbacks and dream sequences that disrupt the realistic violence of the story, adding a touch of surreal unease to the film's proceedings. Marilyn's friends come to visit her, hoping to enjoy their vacation at the lake, and find themselves caught up in the horrific events that result from the dispute over the land, culminating in more degradation and bloodshed, with no character spared.

By beginning the film with an act of violence and allowing it to define his narrative arc, Pinion's film speaks on generational trauma and the devastating impact of gendered violence. At the same time, the work reaches further back, with the torture of the witches reflecting on a history of misogyny and its lingering consequences. The violently sexual comeuppances received by the male aggressors—possession-induced autocastration, anal fisting—do not betray the same hollowly retributive sadism on display in more traditional rape and revenge films. Pinion has gone on record that the film and much of its content were the result of an equal collaboration with star (and his then-partner), Annabel Lee. Pinion notes that the most graphic sexual acts and violent moments were largely her contributions to the film.[1] Like Richard Kern's own troubling collaboration with Lydia Lunch on 1986's **Fingered**, **Red Spirit Lake** offers a view of sexual violence

1 **Cinema Contra**, p.107.

from a female artist's perspective. Pinion's own role as director and editor can be debated, but in their initial intent, the many heinous acts depicted onscreen are cast in a light that is wholly at odds with the misogynistic titillation that defines pure exploitation films like **I Spit on Your Grave** and **Thriller: They Call Her One Eye**.

The film pairs the visceral nature of its actions against a lush, almost psychedelic beauty that utilizes the rawness of analog video to illuminate the world it creates. The lake of its title is almost irrelevant, given that the film is set in the heart of winter, the entire grounds of the property cloaked in heavy blanket of snow. The scenes of the witches dancing and holding rituals outside are stark and harsh, their exposure nearly bleached into the magnetic video itself. By contrast, the film's interiors utilize heavily stylized colored light gels, drenching the rooms of the lake house in neon saturation and giving the horrifying things that occur there a starkness that is almost physically painful to look at as much as they are repulsive ideologically. The violence accounts for much of the movie's runtime, an intentional pacing between acts underscoring their challenge to viewers. The film never compromises its representations, seeking confrontation inspired by earlier transgressive art but informed by discourses removed from underground horror at large.

In selecting the rural setting of its title, Pinion and Lee address the reality that women are not safe from violence or invasion even when removed from the stereotypically dangerous clutter of urban areas, something demonstrated when protagonist Marilyn's memory is triggered back to an assault in the city. There is no illusion of safety, whether from places themselves or the very concept of history and what mankind must be held accountable for over its course. The land itself represents a space of independent women, and its violation by the male antagonists extends to a critique of gendered protection roles. Pinion, with much assistance from Lee, complicates standard underground reception of sexual violence and makes it legitimately uncomfortable to encounter, not mere exploitation fodder. Unlike Christ's films, there is genuine artistic intent inherent in the excesses because their aims are not mere shock or disgust, but inciting honest contemplation of violence and its consequences on bodies and minds.

Pinion exceeds Christ's onscreen transgressions at one point, filming himself masturbating to the point of orgasm, entirely on camera. Speaking with Mike Hunchback, the director states that "putting something as real and un-fakeable as a male orgasm in Red Spirit Lake set the viewer up for the shocks to come."[1] This admission centers his intent on shock, but the fact remains that Pinion revealed far more of himself onscreen than any of his female characters. In enacting an event tantamount to hardcore pornography, the director showed a willingness to expose himself and his own conceptions of extremity in the most graphic manner possible. While the scene was excised from all later editions of the film, its initial inclusion provides an intimate depiction of the filmmaker while signifying his willingness to bare all alongside his performers. Clearly by 1993, the fabric of underground filmmaking had surpassed all prior notions of transgression, a factor that would only mount in the coming years.

Amateur Video Enthusiasts and Hardcore Horror

AS THE 1990S progressed and the underground was flooded with more abrasive content, a number of filmmakers turned to this new trend of extremity in defiance of their earlier works. Missouri filmmaker Eric Stanze made two highly regarded SOV features during the 1990s, **The Scare Game** (1992) and **Savage Harvest** (1994), before working with Super 8 for 1999's avant-garde horror statement **Ice from the Sun**. In 2000, Stanze released his most notorious work, **Scrapbook**, shooting again on video. Concerning a woman who is kidnapped, raped, and tortured by a serial killer, the film reaches levels of debasement not evident in any of his earlier features, including graphic nudity and unsimulated sexual acts. James Aston cites the film as the earliest example of the emerging trend toward hardcore horror cinema in the new millennium.[2] In its rejection of Hollywood's sterile treatment of serial killer narratives, the film quickly became a notorious underground work, and opened the doors for other filmmakers willing to go even further. Stanze's transition from "safer," more entertaining SOV features to the horrifying digital video assault of **Scrapbook**

1 Hunchback, p.14.
2 Aston, p.83.

Salt City Home Video ad from **Alternative Cinema #5** (1995)

represents a turning point in the subterranean horror landscape. The abjection unintentionally achieved by Turner and Koz, and gleefully pushed by Christ, came to the forefront and emerged as a distinctive subgeneric category.

Christ's most offensive films can be easily mapped into the history of extreme horror cinema. **Is it Snuff? You Decide** clearly prefigures later POV simulations such as Fred Vogel's mock snuff tape **August**

Underground series and Shane Ryan's **Amateur Pornstar Killer** films. David Kerekes writes of the custom-made fetish videos of Factory 2000, one of many companies operating in the early 2000s to produce short video works from customer requests. Kerekes cites William Hellfire's 2000 release **Virtual Kidnapper** as a particularly distressing example of the style, operating as a first-person kidnapping and abuse scenario meant to actualize the violent fetish.[1] The short includes a seven-minute-long simulated rape scene, shot from the perpetrator's perspective (portrayed by Hellfire, operating the camera), recalling Christ's earlier feature. Hellfire claims his work is a challenge to his regular customers, arguing "people *should* look at it and see this pro-rape video and be upset by it."[2] Kerekes leaves the quote without comment, segueing instead to an interview with Misty Mundae, the star of the segment, who says of the film, it "was supposed to be repulsive, but the fan base for that kind of thing wouldn't see that element of it. They would be turned on by the gratuitous sex, and the misogyny."[3] Christ's film may be equally horrifying, and potentially more so for its lowbrow comedic intentions, but it was marketed as little more than another piece of his transgressive journey, not legitimate sexual entertainment for misogynists. Despite the minimal print coverage they received, clearly by the early 2000s the most extreme incarnations of SOV horror had made an impact on the underground horror landscape. As with the earlier examples of filmmakers galvanized by **Blood Cult**, these recent directors began as fans foremost and took the egalitarian promise of video to deliver their own uncompromising assaults on viewer sensibilities.

The most common thread through every example of underground transgression in this section is the extensive, unrestrained misogyny on display. There are unfortunately few female directors of SOV horror, robbing the cycle of perspectives to counter the gendered violence so rampant throughout its history. Interestingly, one rare

1 "Small World," p.208.
2 Ibid.
3 Ibid, p.210.

W.A.V.E. TITLES

THUNDER AND LIGHTNING
Lady Thunder (Pamela Sutch) and her less than bright sidekick, Lightning Girl (Tina Krause), face deathtrap after deathtrap set by the evil Black Ghost (Deana Enoches). From being freeze dried to being mannequinized, our intrepid heroines struggle on. Sexy Action and a special guest star make this a must see!
$29.99

VIRGIN SACRIFICES
A man seeking eternal life instead finds himself decapitated, but alive! Four virgins must die in order for him to get a new body. Stars Pamela Sutch, Tina Krause, Dawn Murphy and Clancey McCauley. Nudity, Violence, Wet T-Shirts.
$29.99

LEGAL ENTRAPMENT
Debbie D and Dawn Murphy star in this supernatural thriller! Features voodoo, black magic and swamps, quicksand, nudity and violence!
$29.99

SLAUGHTERED SOCIALITES
Sal Longo gets a "throaty" grip on Tina Krause as ARTIE, the janitor from SLAUGHTERED SECRETARIES. Features nudity, violence and
$29.99

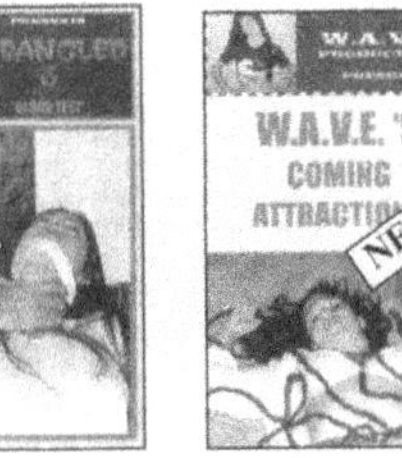

PSYCHO SISTERS
The Original W.A.V.E. shocker! Pamela Sutch, Christine Taylor and Tina Krause star. When Janice Sicole (Krause) is raped, strangled and killed by thugs, her two sisters (Taylor and Sutch) are out for revenge! Contains rape, strangulation, violence, underwear. Contains test screenings of the original demo tapes and footage from the upcoming JJ North remake! $29.99

STRANGLED 3
A madman kidnaps six beautiful women because he thinks that only their blood can save his life! A great violence and nudity-ridden sequel to STRANGLED!
$29.99
Also Available:
STRANGLED $29.99
STRANGLED II $29.99

W.A.V.E.S. COMING ATTRACTIONS
The ultimate PARTY TAPE! Hang out and watch trailers to W.A.V.E. movies.
$19.99

TRAPPED 6
Finally here! The last episode in the TRAPPED SERIES!
$29.99
also available:
TRAPPED $29.99
TRAPPED 2 - $29.99
TRAPPED 3 - $29.99
TRAPPED 4 - $29.99
TRAPPED 5 - $29.99

W.A.V.E. titles distributed by **EI, Alternative Cinema #11** (1997)

example of a distinctive female-lensed SOV work, W.A.V.E.[1] regular

1 W.A.V.E. is a New Jersey-based production company owned and operated by Gary Whitson that films and distributes custom video features from scripts submitted by customers. Centering on fetish material, but encoded within the context of SOV horror narratives, the company is the precursor to the custom fetish videos exemplified by Factory 2000 and others and served as a direct inspiration to Hellfire's New Jersey operation. See **Mail Order Murder: The Story of W.A.V.E. Productions** (dir. by Ross Snyder and William Hellfire, 2020).

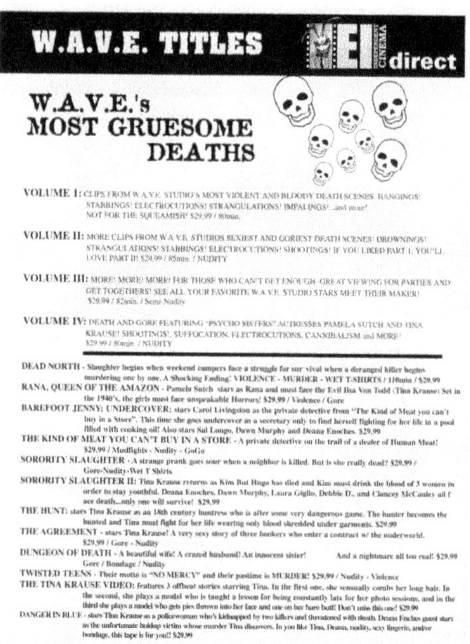
W.A.V.E. TITLES — EI CINEMA direct

W.A.V.E.'s MOST GRUESOME DEATHS

VOLUME I: CLIPS FROM W.A.V.E. STUDIO'S MOST VIOLENT AND BLOODY DEATH SCENES. HANGINGS! STABBINGS! ELECTROCUTIONS! STRANGULATIONS! IMPALINGS! ...and more! NOT FOR THE SQUEAMISH! $29.99 / 80min.

VOLUME II: MORE CLIPS FROM W.A.V.E. STUDIOS SEXIEST AND GORIEST DEATH SCENES! DROWNINGS! STRANGULATIONS! STABBINGS! ELECTROCUTIONS! SHOOTINGS! IF YOU LIKED PART I, YOU'LL LOVE PART II! $29.99 / 85min. / NUDITY

VOLUME III: MORE! MORE! MORE! FOR THOSE WHO CAN'T GET ENOUGH. GREAT VIEWING FOR PARTIES AND GET TOGETHERS! SEE ALL YOUR FAVORITE W.A.V.E. STUDIO STARS MEET THEIR MAKER! $29.99 / 82min. / Semi-Nudity

VOLUME IV: DEATH AND GORE FEATURING "PSYCHO SISTERS" ACTRESSES PAMELA SUTCH AND TINA KRAUSE! SHOOTINGS!, SUFFOCATION, ELECTROCUTIONS, CANNIBALISM and MORE! $29.99 / 80min. / NUDITY

DEAD NORTH - Slaughter begins when weekend campers face a struggle for survival when a deranged killer begins murdering one by one. A Shocking Ending! VIOLENCE - MURDER - WET T-SHIRTS / 110min / $29.99

RANA, QUEEN OF THE AMAZON - Pamela Sutch stars as Rana and must face the Evil Ilsa Von Todd (Tina Krause) Set in the 1940's, the girls must face unspeakable Horrors! $29.99 / Violence / Gore

BAREFOOT JENNY; UNDERCOVER: stars Carol Livingston as the private detective from "The Kind of Meat you can't buy in a Store". This time she goes undercover as a secretary only to find herself fighting for her life in a pool filled with cooking oil! Also stars Sal Longo, Dawn Murphy and Deana Enoches. $29.99

THE KIND OF MEAT YOU CAN'T BUY IN A STORE - A private detective on the trail of a dealer of Human Meat! $29.99 / Mudfights - Nudity - GoGo

SORORITY SLAUGHTER - A strange prank goes sour when a neighbor is killed. But is she really dead? $29.99 / Gore-Nudity-Wet T Shirts

SORORITY SLAUGHTER II: Tina Krause returns as Kim But Hugo has died and Kim must drink the blood of 3 women in order to stay youthful. Deana Enoches, Dawn Murphy, Laura Giglio, Debbie D., and Clancey McCauley all f ace death...only one will survive! $29.99

THE HUNT: stars Tina Krause as an 18th century huntress who is after some very dangerous game. The hunter becomes the hunted and Tina must fight for her life wearing only blood shredded under garments. $29.99

THE AGREEMENT - stars Tina Krause! A very sexy story of three hookers who enter a contract w/ the underworld. $29.99 / Gore - Nudity

DUNGEON OF DEATH - A beautiful wife! A crazed husband! An innocent sister! And a nightmare all too real! $29.99 Gore / Bondage / Nudity

TWISTED TEENS - Their motto is "NO MERCY" and their pastime is MURDER! $29.99 / Nudity - Violence

THE TINA KRAUSE VIDEO: features 3 offbeat stories starring Tina. In the first one, she sensually combs her long hair. In the second, she plays a model who is taught a lesson for being constantly late for her photo sessions, and in the third she plays a model who gets pies thrown into her face and one on her bare butt! Don't miss this one! $29.99

DANGER IN BLUE - stars Tina Krause as a policewoman who's kidnapped by two killers and threatened with death. Deana Enches guest stars as the unfortunate holdup victim whose murder Tina discovers. In you like Tina, Deana, nudity, sexy lingerie, and/or bondage, this tape is for you!! $29.99

W.A.V.E. titles distributed by **EI, Alternative Cinema #11** (1997)

Tina Krause's **Limbo** (1995), is an experimental film confronting sexism and male violence. Though it is not extreme in content, the film stands as a landmark contribution by a marginalized voice within a scene not to be celebrated for its diversity. More than anything, the nihilism of these works is their most alarming quality, the inspirations behind their offenses reflecting the regressive postures emphasized in Danto's discussion of disturbational art. No amount of theoretical analysis can redeem the contents of **Is It Snuff?** or the later fetish tapes, and these are films that have remained subterranean for good reason. Aston's study ably navigates the extreme contents of these films in an attempt to contextualize their excesses, meeting the films on their own demanding terms. Indeed, when rampant misbehavior and transgression is perpetrated onscreen for its own sake, the films can be taken at little other than face value. Unpleasant as they may be, these examples are nonetheless a crucial component of the SOV underground that cannot be overlooked in a comprehensive study.

Danto feels that disturbational art at its core is a representation of the "dionysiac ritual."[1] This bacchanal sense of revelry and expulsion is clearly in effect in Christ's films, which exist to provoke viewers and

1 Danto, p.128.

little else. SOV films are an acquired taste, too rough and amateurish to find widespread embrace. These later digressions are even more difficult to contextualize and defend, though their popularity and the growing number of releases speak to the increasing audience for less complacent, more provocative filmmaking in the new millennium. By the end of the initial SOV cycle, fans alone constituted the viewing and production cultures surrounding these films, and they would sustain underground horror for the coming years. Ultimately, these devotees of bad taste would bring SOV horror back to public consciousness.

07

UNDERGROUND ECONOMIES: SOV RECEPTION IN THE 2020S

THE LATE 1990S and early 2000s saw more horror productions embracing video technology as their format of choice, reflecting the growing prohibitions of celluloid costs. Extreme underground horror continues to thrive through the efforts of companies such as Unearthed Films and Massacre Video. The latter is responsible for the widespread DVD releases of several important SOV productions from the 1980s, including **555**, the films of Chester Turner, and Carl Sukenick's **Alien Beasts** (a co-release with Horror Boobs). Camp Motion Pictures released notable SOV features **Splatter Farm, Zombie Bloodbath,** and **Cannibal Campout** on DVD in 2007. Along with Intervision's release of **Sledgehammer**, these companies revived interest in SOV horror, serving as the next evolutionary step beyond VHS collecting, which had sustained the cycle for years. Obscure as SOV horror may be within dominant genre film discussions, its reputation has steadily grown through various paracinematic channels. While a wider range of genre fans were exposed to SOV horror through these new editions, a devoted community of analog media collectors were responsible for the increasing stature of these works.

Analog Media Loyalism

AS THE VIDEO glut reached its peak and distributors were hesitant to purchase subpar SOV products for their shops, the movement was forced further underground. By the early-1990s, SOV filmmakers began to promote their tapes almost exclusively via the pages of fanzines and at various horror conventions around the country. Direct sales and promotion put fans and consumers into direct contact with filmmakers, opening avenues of interaction and sustaining a network

Camp Motion Pictures ad for SOV releases on DVD, **Rue Morgue #64** (2007)

of communication that empowered the underground community. As shooting on video became standard for independent productions in the late-1990s, and earlier films fell deeper into obscurity, the subculture grew and mutated, with fan activities defining the reception of all prior SOV horror. These include collecting out of print and obscure films, producing fanzines and original artwork, hosting and attending genre-oriented conventions, and the redistribution of earlier works to DVD and Blu-ray. The following resources are valuable, much like the earlier fanzines I've consulted, because they originate from within the community in question. I don't aim to pathologize the habits of collectors, as this approach is taken by much of the existing scholarship concerning SOV horror, such as David Church's comment referring to the "ethos of bad faith lurking beneath this esoterically residual commodity fetish." In one sense, Church is referring to the nostalgic sensibility of valorizing antiquated media and entertainment, critiquing the paracinematic embrace of trash as culture at the cost of historical perspective. On the other, this criticism echoes David Sanjek's analysis of the first generation of horror fanzines, derided for their nihilistic, conservative viewpoints and celebrations of films echoing these regressive attitudes.

While VHS tapes were prohibitively expensive in the early days of video stores, as more releases became available and Blockbuster Video extended its monopoly over the rental industry, tapes were devalued. The inability to compete with Blockbuster and other chain video stores led to the widespread closure of independent video shops, who were forced to liquidate their stock at low prices. Fans and collectors seized these opportunities and built their own collections of both obscure and popular films, now redistributed into the hands of their target audience. Collectors searched out remaining video shops, flea markets, and thrift stores in the hopes of acquiring low-priced product and adding to their collections of tapes. As one fanzine article notes, "[there] is nothing quite like strolling through your seemingly everyday flea market or yard sale and happening upon a table chock full of priced-to-go VHS tapes."[1] Largely operating in solitude, or at most among small peer groups, fans in the new millennium took up the task of celebrating forgotten video efforts, prioritizing enthusiasm over rigorous critique.

By the mid-2000s, VHS collecting had become the primary means of preserving SOV horror films. The 2005 home video release of David Cronenberg's **A History of Violence** marked the final commercially-produced VHS tape released to the market for some time.[2] Following this, as DVD ascended to the dominant position in the home media

1 "Rummage," p.27.
2 Rice, p.23.

economy, analog video was considered dead. In the mid-2000s, few SOV features had been released on DVD, a problem that likewise applied to hundreds of other films mainstream, independent, and underground. Acquiring a VHS tape of these films was the only means of viewing them with no expectations of wider release in the future. Several collectors have also made a case for the preservation of the works themselves. In this light, the efforts of collectors are archival, accumulating titles that would otherwise be lost to time, celebrating them in various outlets, and spreading awareness of the wastefulness of technological advancement.

Early celebrations of VHS culture and SOV horror films were purely enthusiastic. An early issue of Josh Schafer's **Lunchmeat** zine proclaims that it "has been utterly and truly invigorating to find out that there are indeed other grossly perfervid VHS heads out there that share our passion for this format and realize just how awesome it really is."[1] Comprised of reviews screened on VHS, as well as articles on collecting habits, pulp magazines, and even horror toys and videogames, the zine offers a cross section of collecting culture. Another early editorial praises the "sense of community [Schafer has] experienced and gained while doing **Lunchmeat**...people do indeed still care about these films and still want to get a look at them even though the rest of the world has either shunned or forgotten them."[2] First published in 2008, **Lunchmeat** offered fans an outlet to read about films that were long neglected in other corners of genre fandom and proved that outdated analog media could still offer jaded viewers pleasures when the current crop of horror cinema failed to do so.

Matt Desiderio of Horror Boobs, a small outfit releasing new and obscure older SOV titles on VHS, began the zine **Blood Video** in 2012. Concerned with more in-depth analysis of VHS culture, particularly films and distributors that had yet to find widespread recognition, the publication also participated in the wider acknowledgment of SOV horror's contributions to cinema history. The first issue's editorial notes that the featured films are all to be screened at New York's Museum of Art and Design. Desiderio argues that himself and his

1 "Earthborns," p.1.

2 Schafer, #3, p.1.

contributors "validate our sick obsession with hunks of tangible media by showing off our knowledge of the under-appreciated all with a wide-eyed attempt to make it seem normal."[1] This self-analysis echoes Church's comments on tape collecting, but highlights the active labor of disseminating information. As much as the subculture is rooted in commodity fetishism, there is a desire to champion the obscure objects and works which have yet to be accorded their proper attention in the eyes of the fans themselves.

By the next issue, he concludes his introduction by noting "it's safe to say VHS is back too...or at least as big as it will probably ever get."[2] In another triumphant editorial, Desiderio writes "I do believe our Cult of Cult Cinema is starting to be examined as an important part of the world of cinema...can you believe that Yale University's Sterling Memorial Library is now acquiring VHS and VHS-related texts to be preserved for academic purposes?."[3] Fan efforts made a notable mark on the culture of film studies, and even if serious analysis of the works in question was slow to follow, the role of the VHS era in American genre film history was no longer overlooked.

Though shorter-lived than either **Lunchmeat** (which is irregularly published to this day) or **Blood Video**, Dan Kinem's **Tape Mold** zine mined more obscure VHS releases for much of its content. An outgrowth of the popular VHShitfest blog, the debut issue's editorial expresses Kinem's growing boredom with the orthodoxy of VHS collecting, proclaiming "I want to be the guy digging around looking for the stuff that no one else is talking about...to talk to the people that you won't see interviewed in any other zines in 2012 and review the movies the majority of the world would have never given a chance."[4] Just as earlier underground fanzines such as **Shock Xpress**, **A Taste of Bile**, and **European Trash Cinema** grew out of a displeasure with the repetitive, one-note coverage in other publications, so too did VHS zines express frustration with the limitations of current fandom. A growing contingent of fans found the repeated canonization of the same few titles and the obsession over expensive tapes to be stifling,

1 Desiderio, #1, p.1.
2 Desiderio, #2, p.1.
3 Desiderio, #4, p.1.
4 Editorial, p.1.

reducing a vibrant subculture to the very caricature that most on the outside presumed it to be.

Kinem, along with his VHShitfest collaborator Levi Peretic, undertook one of the most significant projects of any collector-fans, producing and releasing the 2013 documentary **Adjust Your Tracking; The Untold Story of the VHS Collector**. Featuring the pair's friends, acquaintances, and submitted interviews with other collectors, the documentary traces the growing subculture and details its origins. Less concerned with particular films, the documentary is comprised of solitary interviews and demonstrations of individual collections. Specifically citing Blockbuster Video's ascendancy as "the beginning of the end" for the earlier independent video era, several interviewees detail the beginnings of their collecting habits and emphasize the initial low cost appeal of accumulating obscure films on videotape. Much time is spent on the material properties of VHS itself, as well as the technical attributes of crackling, staticky picture, and bleeding colors evident in many used tapes. This echoes Daniel Herbert's statement that the VHS format itself is responsible for the distinct look of SOV features, which is in turn embraced by fans rather than derided as a deficiency.[1]

The same year also saw the release of Josh Johnson's **Rewind This!**, a documentary analyzing the role of VHS in the home video marketplace. Featuring interviews with several collectors profiled in Kinem and Peretic's film, as well as historical overviews provided by exploitation filmmaker Frank Henenlotter and Something Weird Video's Mike Vraney, among others, the film offers a more detailed look at the VHS revolution. Intended as a historical overview and celebration of the VHS format, **Rewind This!** is even less concerned with examining the contents of the films themselves. As a result, while SOV horror is featured as part of the 1980s video landscape, it is not mentioned as a particularly revelatory component of its timeline.

Adjust Your Tracking cites one recent event as a turning point in VHS collecting and the reception of SOV horror: artist Earl Kess' $660 eBay purchase of an original copy of Chester Turner's **Tales from the Quadead Zone**. An extended portion of the documentary details the origins of the event, from the growing reputation and rarity of

1 Herbert, p.8.

Turner's second film to another collector's two-dollar purchase of the used tape and subsequent decision to place it on the auction site. Kess notes that he wanted the tape badly enough and was able to afford it, while other collectors mention the auction testing their self-imposed limits on spending. Despite the disdain of earlier genre fans and consumers, SOV horror had now found a devoted audience of fans desperate to possess the original objects themselves. This was influenced in no small part by the collections of others, but this moment represents a point where these films were invested with an undeniable (if still subjective) monetary value and afforded a measure of serious respect from their audience.

Expensive in their initial releases, then devalued by technological advances, VHS tapes once again have ascended to the realm of prohibitively priced collectibles. SOV horror titles are particularly appealing to collectors, reflecting the underground's ongoing preoccupation with authenticity and the original object as artifact. As Evan Husney of Severin Films told Herbert about the Intervision VHS re-release of **Sledgehammer**, the format "is where it originated, [and] that is how you're supposed to watch it."[1] In the cases of original first-run releases of these films, however, fans are willing to expend even more capital to obtain these desired items. Where Kess' purchase was once considered an aberration, auctions have continued to increase in price. Copies of Gary Cohen's **Video Violence** have sold for thousands of dollars, with other titles trailing not far behind in cost. While many early SOV releases on disc are currently out of print, these DVD editions are available used for significantly lower prices. The longevity of these films and their growing subjective value have far exceeded any expectations their original releases and obscurity engendered.

Oversights of Fandom

THOUGH ALL THE above fanzines save **Lunchmeat** have ceased publication, SOV horror is regularly celebrated in current zines such as **Dangerous Encounters**, **Skum Kulture**, and others. The internet has

1 Herbert, p.6.

provided the greatest platform for discussion of SOV cinema itself, with numerous sites continuing to unearth and share their impressions of films. **Lunchmeat** now maintains a website which posts regular features, as well as a store promoting its zines, stickers, and limited releases of various video projects. Most notable among these online outlets is **BLEEDING SKULL!**, which has received the highest visibility and success among broader groups of genre fans.

Begun in 2004 by Joseph Ziemba and Dan Budnik as a forum to review and share information on the low-budget horror films the pair enjoyed watching on VHS, the site grew to encompass all manner of cinematic strangeness. 2013 saw the release of the book **BLEEDING SKULL!: A 1980s Trash-Horror Odyssey**, which collected many of the site's reviews as well as newer contributions. Approached in humorous but affectionate reviews that nonetheless accorded deeper respect for especially distinctive films, the book coincided with the release of several titles by Massacre Video and other distributors. These developments reflect a high point in subcultural interest in SOV horror that exceeds the reach of the earlier collector communities.

Following Budnik's departure, Ziemba and contributors Annie Choi and Zack Carlson kept the format of the site much the same, offering reviews while writing on a greater variety of experimental shorts and international releases. 2021's follow-up book, subtitled **A 1990s Trash-Horror Odyssey**, also makes a pronounced effort to recognize the contributions of marginalized groups, highlighting the works of queer, female, and filmmakers of color who had largely been overlooked by other resources on SOV horror. Alongside reviews of films by Todd Cook and the Polonia brothers are films such as Tina Krause's **Limbo**, and gay filmmaker Jason Paul Collum's 1990s works. Several other reviews reflect the importance of these voices, which have been continually lost in the coverage of SOV horror. Utilizing their platform and growing audience, the authors take several opportunities throughout the book to address the oversights of fan communities and provide a space for these works to gain the recognition they were previously denied.

Important as it may be to retrospective appraisals of SOV horror, nostalgia also replicates the oversights and exclusions of marginal communities within this already subterranean field. Just as it capitalized on mainstream influences and trends, SOV horror also mirrored

Ad for James Tucker's **Steps from Hell**, **Film Threat Video Guide #3** (1991)

the dominant American film industry in its lack of representation and opportunities. Turner's two films are the most famous contributions of an African American filmmaker to this period of underground horror cinema. Writing on the revival of his films following their 2013 DVD releases, a New York Times feature cites concerns of "condescending hipster racism" in genre fans' appreciation of the films, recalling earlier paracinematic embraces of blaxploitation cinema. Both Turner and the programmer then remark on the sincerity of fans in attendance, as well as the fairness of Massacre's deal with the director as positive surprises.[1] Despite this, Turner remains the only SOV director of color to be profiled in a mainstream outlet, and his reputation is an anomaly among the underground.

Other filmmakers of color working within the cycle have not received the widespread infamy of Turner's two films and their works have yet to be reissued. Actor James Adam Tucker, a steady presence in Hollywood productions, released his debut SOV feature, **Devil Snow** (aka **Neighbor Hoodz**) in 1991. Citing dissatisfaction with the film's distribution, he embraced a fully independent model of production and distribution for his following features, which also included a shift to

1 Piepenburg.

Super 8 film.[1] Jess Turner, a radio host and Christian speaker, made his SOV debut with **Zombies Invade Pittsburg** (alternately credited 1988 and 1996), a leisurely-paced film noted as being "the only SOV film outside of Chester [Turner's] works that features a predominantly African-American cast."[2] As with many SOV productions, the obscurity of the cycle itself, coupled with independent distribution, prevents their recognition as much as inherent prejudices in fan communities.

The misogyny of countless SOV productions has been detailed in the previous chapter, a troubling trend in dominant cinema that was not counterbalanced by the SOV revolution. Female directors fare little better than artists of color in the celebration of video horror, recalling Clover's insistence on predominantly male audiences for gory genre films. Few women worked within the cycle, and they continue to receive only a small fraction of the adulation bestowed upon the male directors associated with video filmmaking. Betty Stapleford's **The Zombie Army** (1991) was released by Video Outlaw and promoted heavily within the pages of **Alternative Cinema** and **The B's Nest**. Citing the title as "the first—and only—feminist SOV zombie movie," Ziemba praises its inclusion of a female perspective, realized through an army brigade comprised entirely of women who are employed once their male colleagues have failed.[3] Contrasted against the juvenile excesses of many prominent SOV releases, Stapleford's film was recently released to Blu-ray for the first time, reflecting the growing interest in the work of female horror directors.

While it may contain numerous homosexual acts and elements, **Splatter Farm's** representations are far from positive or progressive. As with race and gender, alternative sexualities were not provided with much of a platform in the SOV cycle. Gay author James Robert Baker directed the early SOV thriller **Blonde Death** (1983), later resurrected for a brief VHS/DVD reissue by **BLEEDING SKULL! Video**, reflecting the initial promise of video's freedoms. By the 1990s, however, fewer queer filmmakers received recognition while working with the format; as Joseph Ziemba notes "Jason Paul Collum might have been the only

1 "Horraction," p.21.

2 Ziemba, **1980s**, p.223.

3 Ziemba, **1990s**, p.249.

THE ZOMBIE ARMY
Directed by Betty Stapleford
80 Mins. · Cat. No. 1030 · $19.95
Army Sergeant Saddow has a problem. The Pentagon brass bought a former insane asylum to use as a base for the elite experimental female unit The Lethal Ladies. The problem is that they didn't check the asylum fallout shelter for leftover inmates! Two were left behind when the nuthouse was abandoned. The two freaks wreak havoc on the Army by capturing soldiers and turning them into mindless zombies. Trapped in the tunnels under the old asylum, The Lethal Ladies must invent weapons to destroy the living dead! Watch out, Saddam Hussein...you're no match for Operation "Zombie" Storm and...*The Zombie Army!*

Ad for **The Zombie Army, Alternative Cinema #1** (1994)

openly gay filmmaker making SOV trash-horror films."[1] Other films from this era make regular use of homophobic language as well as reducing homosexuality to the butt of crude jokes. Rather than dismiss this as the outdated expressions of culture at the time of production, works like the second **BLEEDING SKULL!** text recognize these details as some of the many barriers to fully appreciating the SOV cycle as a broader art form.

These are just a sampling of the oversights in representation and diversity in the SOV horror community, serving as a reminder that by and large, "the bread and butter of the modern horror genre [is] white and young," not to mention heterosexual and male.[2] The juvenile culture of fanzines and underground activity identified by David Sanjek in his 1990 essay "Fans' Notes" proves especially true in this regard.[3] While many, myself included, have recognized the egalitarian potential of analog video for independent production, the reality proves far less encouraging. SOV culture deviated from the restrictions of the dominant film industry but was nonetheless emulating it from the beginning. While my own work on this project has sought to provide a

1 Ibid, p.158.
2 Piepenburg.
3 Sanjek, p.154.

space for the broader variety of SOV horror to be critically examined, much work remains for the films that have yet to receive proper recognition even among fans.

SOV, The Poor Image, and The Stakes of Analog Representation

THE OBSCURITY OF many SOV films has contributed to their lack of repute among fans, as many important and interesting titles are simply not available for viewing. Often there's no information beyond reviews in fanzines from the 1990s (themselves now pricy collectibles), or website posts from collectors and fans. In the present moment, the role of the internet in disseminating SOV horror cannot be overlooked. As a result of their limited releases and economic failures, only a small number of fans have access to numerous films released during the height of the SOV cycle. Daniel Herbert notes the redistribution of works undertaken through various re-releases, but also identifies an earlier trend that brought SOV horror into focus for many. While the new releases offer occasionally legitimate means of purchasing obscure films, a previous exchange saw "a flow of cult movies from VHS to YouTube."[1] Videos ripped from tapes and DVDs to video sites, as well digital files on torrenting platforms are common points of entry to the most marginal SOV features.

Herbert identifies the re-releases of films on VHS as reformulating "the cultural meaning of VHS technology by yoking it solely to cult movie texts."[2] While this is especially true of collectors—it isn't mainstream dramas or romance features seeing redistribution on VHS in the present—the dissemination of cult and SOV cinema via digital outlets must be considered a democratization of the works themselves. Often illegal in their uploading, or at least occupying a gray area when rights are uncertain, these videos operate much like earlier video bootlegs did within the underground but are even further removed from networking politics. One need not be connected with

1 Herbert, p.8.

2 Ibid.

the originator of the file or concerned with material for trade, but can instead find films through common search engines. Hito Steyerl notes that bootleg networks kept obscure works alive in the pre-internet era, but argues that in the age of the internet, this process has shifted to digital files, providing access to rare works in greater numbers.[1] The economic aspects of earlier bootlegging and trading activities fall to the wayside when digital copies of SOV works become the primary means of their dissemination.

Defining the concept of The Poor Image, Steyerl argues that these files "are poor because they are not assigned any value within the class society of images—their status as illicit or degraded grants them exemption from its criteria."[2] Already inferior to celluloid in their original forms, SOV films' inherent videobility marks them as lesser objects in any form. Even remastered and restored editions of SOV horror titles cannot escape the aesthetic pugnacity (to use Pinion's phrase) of their medium, rendering them illicit or degraded in whatever manner they appear. Furthermore, where value is dictated by collector communities, the appearance of digital files suggests freedom from the secondhand controls of capital. Due to their often-illegitimate sourcing, these uploads are left even poorer than legitimate copies. In contrast to high priced tapes listed for auction or even trade copies of the same, anyone can download the YouTube videos or torrents of these films, screen them in their home or redistribute them as they see fit. Steyerl claims that poor images are "permeated by the most advanced commodification techniques," digital copies of these titles are now democratized for users, but not without the added cost of making them also "the editors, critics, translators, and (co)-authors" of these works themselves.[3] No longer is the object itself the primary focus, but the films alone can be accessed and celebrated divorced of their packaging and commercial properties. With this, however, comes the loss of context, deeper discourse, and above all responsible handling of the films themselves as they are fed into the void of the internet.

Citing Juan García Espinosa's "For an Imperfect Cinema," Steyerl highlights his discussion of video as an emerging medium, stating that

1 Steyerl, p.36.
2 Ibid, 38.
3 Ibid, p.40.

Espinosa "clearly predicts that the development of video technology will jeopardize the elitist position of traditional filmmakers and enable some sort of mass film production: an art of the people."[1] While this premise reflects my own statements about the potential of home video, it does not carry the same weight in this particular cinematic context. Though decidedly not a political cinema, SOV, when considered as a deviation from the mainstream film industry, made no real threat to dominant cinema in the United States. In fact, as celluloid production becomes less common within the mainstream, video itself is becoming the capitalist standard of film production. Never truly anti-capitalist as it was merely independent, SOV horror defined its opposition in terms of aesthetics. As a result, its confrontational and oppositional nature has rarely been accorded the respect such distinctive movements command. Scores of American independent and underground filmmakers have successfully transitioned to the mainstream cinematic realm, with Sam Raimi of **The Evil Dead** providing one particularly notable example. This early, uncompromising work was distinctive, a vital influence on later SOV horror, proving for some that original works could indeed pave the way to success and recognition. Despite this influence, no SOV directors have transitioned to mainstream notability, limiting even commercially aspiring films from the cycle to subcultural and paracinematic discourse.

Now valued by fans and collectors and held (if not studied) by academic institutions, SOV horror has broken from the underground film world into public awareness. While tape collectors invest the films with much import, articulate analysis of the films themselves has come at a much slower pace. In his discussion of **Blood Cult** and the emergence of video horror, Johnny Walker concludes by arguing that these films are "*worth* preserving after all and that they deserve a place in the history of horror and cult cinema."[2] Walker's primary concern may be with the economic impact of that particular film and SOV horror as a brief filmmaking cycle, but an appreciation of the films as texts is also necessary. As historical artifacts and signifiers of widespread independent film production, SOV horror films are

1 Ibid, p.39.
2 Walker, **Blood Cults**, p.230.

crucial documents. Representing communal production, economic independence, and unfettered creative expression, this cycle of films has proven influential even in spite of its many aesthetic failings. No longer ostracized by genre purists, shot-on-video horror films have slowly returned to the status of popular entertainment, their intended function from the beginning. This growing audience and expanded means of encountering films, while admittedly still marginal, reflects the retrospective impact of these works in the present era.

As diverse as their contents, SOV horror films are a vital counterpoint to discussions of mainstream genre cinema. Unified by their technical properties yet disparate in their approaches and concerns, and without a dominant articulation of their purposes, there is much to still explore with these titles. The films discussed in this work are the among the most notable SOV works released between 1984-1994 and reveal how average fans and consumers-turned artists engaged with their own neuroses and the concerns of their era. These are films unmatched in their depictions of average Americans grappling with everyday anxieties manifested via the supernatural, just as their captures of the mundane, often embarrassing realities of daily life are unlike anything offered in more visible cinema. Regrettably, the more obscure works produced at the end of this period, among the most difficult to locate and without many detailed resources documenting their existence, are some of the most fascinating and personal genre films produced by amateurs. Despite its limitations and oversights, SOV horror cinema is a rich, varied cycle of filmmaking that revels in the unlimited potential of egalitarian film production, demonstrating that capital resources, technical competence, and industrial backing are not endemic to successful artistic expression.

SOURCES

Adjust Your Tracking: The Untold Story of the VHS Collector. Directed by Dan Kinem and Levi Peretic, VHShitfest, 2013.

Albright, Brian. **Regional Horror Films, 1958–1990: A State-by-State Guide with Interviews**. Jefferson, McFarland, 2012.

Anon. (Todd Cook). Classified ad. **Fangoria**, no. 138, Nov. 1994, p. 84. Internet Archive, https://archive.org/details/Fangoria_138_1994_Frankenstein_HQS_c2c. Accessed 1 Jan. 2021.

Aragon, Louis. "On décor." **The Shadow and its Shadow: Surrealist Writings on the Cinema**, edited by Paul Hammond, San Francisco, City Lights, 2000, pp. 50–54.

"Assault Your Senses! The 25 Underground Films You Must See." Edited by David E. Williams and Dominic Griffin, **Film Threat Video Guide**, vol. 2, no. 11, 1994, pp. 38–55.

Aston, James. **Hardcore Horror Cinema in the 21st Century: Production, Marketing and Consumption**. Jefferson, McFarland, 2018.

"Back to the Farm: The Making of **Splatter Farm**." **Special Features**. **Splatter Farm**, Camp Motion Pictures, 2007. DVD.

Barefoot, Guy. **Trash Cinema: The Lure of the Low**. London, Wallflower, 2017.

Bazin, André. "The Ontology of the Photographic Image." **What Is Cinema?**, by André Bazin et al., University of California Press, 2005, pp. 9–16.

—. "The Evolution of the Language of Cinema." **What Is Cinema?**, by André Bazin et al., University of California Press, 2005, pp. 23–40.

Beesley, Professor. "Alien Beasts." Review of **Alien Beasts**, directed by Carl Sukenick. **Alternative Cinema**, no. 11, 1997, pp. 50–51.

Benson-Allott, Caetlin. **Killer Tapes and Shattered Screens: Video Spectatorship from VHS to File Sharing**. Berkeley, University of California, 2013.

Bertrand, Merle. "Alien Beasts." Review of **Alien Beasts**, directed by Carl Sukenick. **Film Threat Video Guide**, no. 7, 1993, p. 15.

Bookwalter, J.R.. **B-Movies in the '90s and Beyond**. 3rd rev. ed., Tempe Press, 2018.

Brakhage, Stan. "In Defense of Amateur." **Essential Brakhage: Selected Writings on Filmmaking**, edited by Bruce R. McPherson, Documentext, 2001, pp. 142–150.

Brown, Thomas. "Center Stage Review: **Ozone**." **Alternative Cinema**, no. 1, Spring 1994, p. 53.

Brown, William. **Non-Cinema: Global Digital Filmmaking and the Multitude**. New York, Bloomsbury Academic, 2018.

Bookwalter, J.R. "Center Stage Review: Zombie Bloodbath 2: Rage of the Undead." **Alternative Cinema**, no.4, Winter 1995, pp.56–57.

Butler, Robert W.. "Blood, beasties and bimbos…" **The Kansas City Star**, Metropolitan ed., sec. Arts, 6 Dec. 1992, p. K10. NewsBank, infoweb.newsbank.com/apps/news/document-view?p=WORLDNEWS&docref=news/0EAF3E8C1FBBCDFD. Accessed 21 June 2021.

—. "Blood on a budget..." **The Kansas City Star**, Metropolitan ed., sec. Star Magazine, 7 Mar. 1993, p. 12. NewsBank, infoweb.newsbank.com/apps/news/document-view?p=WORLDNEWS&docref=news/0EAF3EF210B7F3AA. Accessed 21 June 2021.

—. "Invasion of the incredibly cheap..." **The Kansas City Star**, Metropolitan ed., sec. Arts, 28 June 1992, p. K2. NewsBank, infoweb.newsbank.com/apps/news/document-view?p=WORLDNEWS&docref=news/0EAF3DDF6296307B. Accessed 21 June 2021.

—. "'Zombie Bloodbath...'" **The Kansas City Star**, Metropolitan ed., sec. Arts, 26 Sept. 1993, p. K10. NewsBank, infoweb.newsbank.com/apps/news/document-view?p=WORLDNEWS&docref=news/0EAF3F9D10791FC7. Accessed 21 June 2021.

C., Steve. "Editorial." **In the Flesh**, vol. 1, no. 1, 1991, p. 2.

Church, David. "The Untold Story of the Original, Factory-Produced, Horror/Exploitation VHS Collector." **Flow Journal**, 26 Nov. 2014. https://www.flowjournal.org/2014/11/the-untold-story-of-the-vhs-collecto/. Accessed 4 Oct. 2021.

Clark, David Aaron. "Twisted Issues: The Colorfully Rotting Brain Cells of Charles Pinion." **Film Threat Video Guide**, no.3, Summer 1991, pp. 64–66.

Clover, Carol. **Men, Women, and Chainsaws: Gender in the Modern Horror Film.** Princeton UP, 1992.

Cobb, C.B. "Crippled + Speed Freaks with Guns (1992/1991)." Review of **Crippled** and **Speed Freaks with Guns,** directed by Joe Christ. **Dangerous Encounters**, no. 7, October 2020, p. 6.

—. "Faith in Filth: The SOV of Transgression with Joe Christ." **Dangerous Encounters**, no. 7, October 2020, p. 7.

—. "Toxic Slime Creature (1982)." Review of **The Toxic Slime Creature**, directed by Kenneth Zollo. **Dangerous Encounters**, no. 5, June 2020, p. 17.

Collins, Robert and Sam Loomis. "Heartlands of Darkness." **Independent Video**, no. 7, 1993, pp. 4–7.

Cook, Todd. "Commentary." **Special Features. Demon Dolls**, Screamtime Films, 2013. DVD.

Cook, Todd Jason. "Horrorscope Films." **Independent Video**, no. 9, 1994, p.8.

"Creative Concepts Unlimited." Advertisement. **Independent Video**, no. 7, 1993. p. 30.

Danto, Arthur C. "Art and Disturbation." **The Philosophical Disenfranchisement of Art** by Arthur C. Danto. New York, Columbia UP, 1986. pp.117–133.

Deren, Maya. "Amateur Versus Professional." **A-BitterSweet-Life**, 14 Mar. 2014, a-bittersweet-life.tumblr.com/post/79578599444/amateur-versus-professional-by-maya-deren. Accessed 1 Jan. 2021.

Desiderio, Matt. Editorial. **Blood Video**, no. 1, April 2012. p.1.

—. **Blood Video**, no. 2, April 2013. p.1.

—. Editorial. **Blood Video**, no. 4, April 2015. p.1.

Durant, Jimmy and Lance Randas. "Missouri Invaded by Killer B's." **Alternative Cinema**, no. 1, Spring 1994, pp. 22–26.

Durant, Jimmy. "Video Outlaw News: Todd Sheets on 'Goblin' and 'Prehistoric Bimbos in Armageddon City.'" **The B's Nest**, no. 12, Mar/Apr. 1993, pp. 6–7.

Ebert, Roger. "Friday the 13th, Part 2." Review of **Friday the 13th, Part 2**, directed by Steve Miner. https://

www.rogerebert.com/reviews/friday-the-13th-part-2-1981. Accessed 1 September 2021.

Everleth, Mike. "Charles Pinion Interview: Parts 1-4." **The Underground Film Journal**, 28 Apr. 2014, www.undergroundfilmjournal.com/charles-pinion-interview-part-one/. Accessed 1 Jan. 2021.

Gallagher, Hugh. "Alien Beasts." Review of **Alien Beasts**, directed by Carl Sukenick. **Draculina**, no. 16, 1993, p. 47.

—. "Horraction Distribution: Steps from Hell! Interview with James Tucker." **Draculina**, no. 13, 1992. pp. 21–23.

—. "Todd Sheets." **Draculina**, no. 17, Dec. 1993, pp. 26–31.

Goodsell, Greg. "The Unwatchables." **The Deep Red Horror Handbook**, edited by Chas Balun, Fantaco Enterprises, Inc., 1989, pp. 32–42.

Griffith, Del. "Up for Adoption." **Alternative Cinema**, no.2, Winter 1994, p. 54.

—. "Zombie Bloodbath." Review of **Zombie Bloodbath**, directed by Todd Sheets. **Alternative Cinema**, no. 1, Spring 1994, p. 50.

—. "Taking Sides: Camcorder Movies: Good or Evil?" **Alternative Cinema**, no. 2, Summer 1994, pp.57–58.

Herbert, Daniel. "Nostalgia Merchants: VHS Distribution in the Era of Digital Delivery." **Journal of Film and Video**, vol. 69, no. 2, 2017, pp. 3–19.

Hilderbrand, Lucas. **Inherent Vice: Bootleg Histories of Videotape and Copyright**. Durham, Duke UP, 2009.

Hills, Matt. "Para-Paracinema: the **Friday the 13th** Film Series as Other to Trash and Legitimate Film Cultures." **Sleaze Artists: Cinema at the Margins of Taste, Style and Politics**, edited by Jeffrey Sconce, Durham, Duke University, 2007, pp.219–239.

Hunchback, Mike. "Special Edition: Charles Pinion." **Blood Video**, no. 1, 2016.

Jeriko, Orion (Nick Zedd). "The Cinema of Transgression Manifesto." **The Underground Film Bulletin**, no. 4, 1985. pp. 3–5.

Kerekes, David. "The Small World of the Snuff Fetish Custom Video." **From the Arthouse to the Grindhouse: Highbrow and Lowbrow Transgressions in Cinema's First Century**, edited by Cline, John and Robert G. Weiner, Scarecrow Press, 2010, pp. 205–211.

Kerekes, David and David Slater. **Killing for Culture: An Illustrated History of Death Film from Mondo to Snuff**, Updated ed., Creation, 1995.

Kilgore, Charles. "Amateur Hour." **Ecco**, no. 8, 1989, p. 2.

Kinem, Dan. "Chairman of the Board." **Tape Mold**, no. 3, 2013, pp. 17–22. Internet Archive, https://archive.org/details/Tape_Mold_3. Accessed 1 Jan. 2021.

Kinem, Dan. Editorial. **Tape Mold**, no. 1, 2012, p. 1. Internet Archive, https://archive.org/details/Tape_Mold_1. Accessed 4 Oct. 2021.

Kracauer, Siegfried. "Basic Concepts." **Theory of Film: the Redemption of Physical Reality**, by Siegfried Kracauer, Princeton UP, 1997, pp. 27–40.

Landis, Bill. "Exploitation Cancer." Review of **The Evil Dead**, directed by Sam Raimi. **Sleazoid Express**, vol. 3, no. 2, March 1983, p. 2.

Landis, Bill and Jimmy McDonough. "The Psychedelic Fortune Cookie." Review of **Boardinghouse**, directed by John Wintergate. **Sleazoid Express**, vol. 3, no. 8, pp.2/12.

Landis, Bill and Michelle Clifford. **Sleazoid Express: A Mind-Twisting Tour Through the Grindhouse Cinema of Times Square**. Simon & Schuster, 2002.

Lazarus, David. "Interview: Nathan Schiff." **Draculina**, no. 6, July 1987, pp. 27–32.

Ledbetter, Craig. "Editorial." **European Trash Cinema**, vol. 1, no. 1, 1988, p. 1.

—. "Editorial." **European Trash Cinema**, vol. 2, no.2, 1990, p. 3.

Lobato, Ramón. "Subcinema: Theorizing Marginal Film Distribution." **Limina**, vol. 13, 2007, pp. 113–120.

Lyotard, Jean-François. "Acinema." **Wide Angle**, no. 2, 1978, pp.52–59.

"The Making of Zombie Bloodbath." Special Features. **The Zombie Bloodbath Trilogy**, Camp Motion Pictures, 2007. DVD.

McTavish, Brian. "Todd Sheets 'Zombie' auteur." **The Kansas City Star**, 19 May 2005, p. 3. NewsBank, infoweb.newsbank.com/apps/news/document-view?p=WORLDNEWS&docref=news/10A4210B52C4FDA8. Accessed 21 June 2021.

Mogg, Richard. **Analog Nightmares: The Shot-on-Video Horror Films of 1982–1995**. RickMoe, 2018.

Nirenberg, Michael Lee. "Conversation with Matthew Desiderio (Part One)." **The Huffington Post**, 15 Oct. 2016, www.huffingtonpost.com/entry/conversation-with-matthew-desiderio-part-one_us_58002c57e4b06f314afeb156. Accessed 1 Jan. 2021.

Norman, Spiney. "Ozone." Review of **Ozone**, directed by J.R. Bookwalter. **Film Threat Video Guide**, no. 10, 1994, p. 30.

Ouellette, Laurie. "Camcorder Dos and Don'ts: Popular Discourses on Amateur Video and Participatory Television." **The Velvet Light Trap: A Critical Journal of Film and Television Studies**, no. 36, 1995, pp. 33–44.

Piepenburg, Erik. "Fairy Tale Ending in the Horror Realm." **The New York Times**, 14 Nov. 2013. https://www.nytimes.com/2013/11/17/movies/chester-novell-turner-and-black-devil-doll-are-back.html. Accessed 4 Oct. 2021.

Pinion, Charles. "Pulp Video Manifesto." http://www.charlespinion.com/MOVIES.html. Accessed 21 June 2021.

Polonia, Mark. Letter. **Draculina**, no. 18, Winter 1994, pp. 5–6.

Polonia, Mark and John. "Commentary." **Bonus Material. Splatter Farm**, Camp Motion Pictures, 2007. DVD.

Puchalski, Steven. "Amy Strangled a Small Child." Review of **Amy Strangled a Small Child**, directed by Joe Christ. **Shock Cinema**, no. 14, 1999, p. 40. Internet Archive, https://archive.org/details/ShockCinema141999/page/n41. Accessed 1 Sept. 2021.

—. "Black Devil Doll from Hell." Review of **Black Devil Doll from Hell**, directed by Chester N. Turner. **Shock Cinema**, no. 3, 1991, p. 16. Internet Archive, https://archive.org/details/ShockCinema31991/page/n14. Accessed 1 Jan. 2021.

—. "Tales from the Quadead Zone." Review of **Tales from the Quadead Zone,** directed by Chester N. Turner. **Shock Cinema**, no. 9, 1996, p. 24. Internet Archive, https://archive.org/details/Shock_Cinema_09/page/n24. Accessed 1 Jan. 2021.

Randas, Lance. "Tempe Adds Cinema Home Video Product to Its Line." **The B's Nest**, no. 12, May 1993, pp. 1/8.

Return to the Quadead Zone. Special Features. The Films of Chester Novell Turner, Massacre Video,

2013. DVD.

Rewind This! Directed by Josh Johnson, Imperial PolyFarm Productions, 2013.

Rhodes, John David. **Meshes of the Afternoon**. London: Palgrave Macmillan on behalf of the British Film Institute, 2011.

Rice, Justin. "VHS: The New Vinyl?". **Blood Video**, no. 2, April 2013. p. 22–23.

Sanjek, David. "Fans' Notes: The Horror Film Fanzine." **Literature/ Film Quarterly**, vol. 18, no. 3, 1990. pp. 150–159.

Sargeant, Jack. **Deathtripping: The Extreme Underground**, 3rd revised ed., Soft Skull Press, 2008.

—. **Flesh and Excess: On Underground Film**. Los Angeles, Amok, 2015.

—. "Pulp Videos: The Twisted World of Charles Pinion." **Cinema Contra Cinema**, by Jack Sargeant, Fringecore, 1999, pp. 95–124.

Schafer, Josh. "Greetings, Earthborns!!!" **Lunchmeat**, no. 2, 2008. p. 1. Internet Archive, https://archive.org/details/lunchmeat-02/. Accessed 4 October 2021.

—. "Greetings, Videovores!!" **Lunchmeat**, no. 3, 2009. p. 1. Internet Archive, https://archive.org/details/Lunchmeat_03. Accessed 4 October 2021.

—. "Greetings, Videovores!!" **Lunchmeat**, no. 6, 2011. p. 1. Internet Archive, https://archive.org/details/Lunchmeat_06/. Accessed 4 October 2021.

—. "Rummage, Raid, and Rejoice: The Dubious Art of Collecting and Preserving the VHS Tape." **Lunchmeat**, no. 2, 2008. pp. 27–28. Internet Archive, https://archive.org/details/lunchmeat-02/. Accessed 4 October 2021.

Schrader, Herb. "Black Devil Doll from Hell." Review of **Black Devil Doll from Hell**, directed by Chester N. Turner. **Video Drive-In**, no.8, mid-1980s, p. 2.

Sconce, Jeffrey. "'Trashing' the Academy: Taste, Excess, and an Emerging Politics of Cinematic Style." **Screen**, vol. 36, no. 4, 1995, pp. 371–393.

—. "The Golden Age of Badness." **Continuum**, vol. 36, no. 6, 2019, pp. 666–676.

Shapiro, Tex. "Videos by Joe Christ." Review of **Communion in Room 410** and **I Just Thank God My Thoughts Are Pure!**, directed by Joe Christ. **Film Threat**, no. 16, 1988. p.8

Sheets, Todd. Letter. **Draculina**, no. 18, Winter 1994, p. 5.

—. Letter. **Draculina**, no. 19, Spring 1994, p. 51.

—. "Sheets Happens." Letter. **Alternative Cinema**, no.5, Spring/ Summer 1995, p. 6.

Siskel, Gene. "'Friday the 13th: More bad luck.'" Review of **Friday the 13th**, directed by Sean S. Cunningham. **Chicago Tribune**. http://www.fridaythe13thfranchise.com/2012/06/gene-siskels-original-friday-13th-mini.html. Accessed 1 September 2021.

Sitney, P. Adams. **Visionary Film: The American Avant-Garde 1943–2000**, 3rd ed, Oxford, 2002.

Space Robot Warriors. Advertisement. **Independent Video**, no. 3, Sept. 1992, p. 25.

Steyerl, Hito. "In Defense of the Poor Image." **Wretched of the Screen**, by Hito Steyerl, Sternberg, 2012, pp.31–45.

Sullivan, Rick. **Gore Gazette**, no. 98, 1993.

Szpunar, John. **Xeroxferox: The Wild World of the Horror Film Fanzine**,

Headpress, 2013.

Szurek, Dave. "Carnage." Review of **Carnage,** directed by Andy Milligan. **Sub-Human**, no. 3, Oct./Nov. 1986. pp.11–12.

Tashiro, Charles. "Videophilia: What Happens When You Wait for It on Video." **Film Quarterly**, vol. 45, no.1, 1991, pp.7–17.

Thrower, Stephen. "The Exploitation Independents." **Nightmare USA: the Untold Story of the Exploitation Independents**, by Stephen Thrower, FAB Press Ltd., 2014, pp. 11–48.

Turner, Chester. "Commentary." **Special Features. The Films of Chester Novell Turner**, Massacre Video, 2013. DVD.

Vale, V. "Introduction." **Incredibly Strange Films**, edited and published by V. Vale, Marian Wallace, and Scott Summerville, 2nd ed., RE/Search, 2017, pp. 4–6.

"Videos by Joe Christ." Advertisement. **Film Threat**, no. 15, 1988. p.43.

Wagner, David. "Bloodthirsty Cannibal Demons." Review of **Bloodthirsty Cannibal Demons**, directed by Todd Sheets. **Alternative Cinema**, no. 2, Summer 1994, p.51.

—. "The 10 Least Fave." **Alternative Cinema**, no. 4, Winter 1995, p. 37.

Walker, Johnny. "Blood Cults: Historicizing the North American 'Shot on Video' Horror Movie." **The Routledge Companion to Cult Cinema**, edited by Ernest Mathijs and Jamie Sexton, Abingdon, Routledge, 2020, pp. 223–232.

—. "Traces of Snuff: Black Markets, Fan Subcultures, and Underground Horror in the 1990s." **Snuff: Real Death and Screen Media,** edited by Neil Jackson, et. al., New York, Bloomsbury Academic, 2016, pp. 137–152.

Williams, David E. "Editorial." **Film Threat Video Guide**, no. 1, Winter 1991, p. 5.

—. "Mutant Massacre." Review of **Mutant Massacre**, directed by Carl Sukenick. **Film Threat Video Guide**, no. 3, Summer 1991, p. 21.

Williams, Linda. "Film Bodies: Gender, Genre, and Excess." **Film Quarterly,** vol. 44, no.4, 1991, pp.2–13.

"World Exclusive! Vermilion Eyes." **In the Flesh**, vol. 1, no. 10, 1992, p. 40.

Yates, Rowdy. "Trim Bin: Shameless Plug!." **Film Threat Video Guide**, no. 4, 1992, p. 69.

Young, Clive. **Homemade Hollywood: Fans Behind the Camera**. New York, Continuum, 2008.

Ziemba, Joesph, and Zack Carlson and Annie Choi. **BLEEDING SKULL!: A 1990s Trash-Horror Odyssey**, Fantagraphics, 2021.

Ziemba, Joseph, and Dan Budnik. **BLEEDING SKULL!: a 1980s Trash-Horror Odyssey**. Headpress, 2013.

Ziemba, Joseph. "Alien Beasts (1991)." Review of **Alien Beasts**, directed by Carl Sukenick. **BLEEDING SKULL!**, 24 July 2014, bleedingskull.com/alien-beasts-1991/. Accessed 1 Jan. 2021.

—. "Demon Dolls." Review of **Demon Dolls**, directed by Todd Cook. **BLEEDING SKULL!**, 8 Aug. 2013. Wayback Machine, https://web.archive.org/web/20150730073652/http://bleedingskull.com/demon-dolls-1993/. Accessed 1 Jan. 2021.

—. "Zombies Invade Pittsburg." Review of **Zombies Invade Pittsburg**, directed by Jess Turner. **BLEEDING SKULL!: A 1980s Trash-Horror Odyssey**. Headpress, 2013.

Zimmerman, Patricia. **Reel Families: A Social History of Amateur Film**. Bloomington, Indiana UP, 2005.

INDEX

People

Studios/Distributors

Films

Publications

CPSIA information can be obtained
at www.ICGtesting.com
Printed in the USA
BVHW050806180723
667391BV00002B/3